DEVOLUTION IN THE UNITED KINGDOM

Vernon Bogdanor is Professor of Government at the University of Oxford, and a Fellow and Tutor in Politics at Brasenose College, Oxford. His publications include *The Monarchy and the Constitution* (1995), *Politics and the Constitution: Essays on British Government* (1996), and *Power and the People: A Guide to Constitutional Reform* (1997).

If we can make arrangements under which Ireland, Scotland, Wales, portions of England, can deal with questions of local and special interest to themselves more effi-ciently than Parliament now can, that, I say, will be the attainment of a great national good.

(W. E. Gladstone, Midlothian, 1879)

DEVOLUTION IN THE UNITED KINGDOM

VERNON BOGDANOR

OXFORD
UNIVERSITY PRESS

OXFORD
UNIVERSITY PRESS

Great Clarendon Street, Oxford OX2 6DP

Oxford University Press is a department of the University of Oxford.
It furthers the University's objective of excellence in research, scholarship,
and education by publishing worldwide in

Oxford New York

Athens Auckland Bangkok Bogotá Buenos Aires Cape Town
Chennai Dar es Salaam Delhi Florence Hong Kong Istanbul Karachi
Kolkata Kuala Lumpur Madrid Melbourne Mexico City Mumbai
Nairobi Paris São Paulo Singapore Taipei Tokyo Toronto Warsaw

with associated companies in Berlin Ibadan

Oxford is a registered trade mark of Oxford University Press
in the UK and in certain other countries

Published in the United States
by Oxford University Press Inc., New York

British Library Cataloguing in Publication Data

Data available

Library of Congress Cataloging in Publication Data

Data available
ISBN 0-19-280128-7

1 3 5 7 9 10 8 6 4 2

Typeset in Times
by Cambrian Typesetters, Frimley, Surrey

Printed in Great Britain by
Cox & Wyman Ltd,
Reading, Berkshire

For Judy, Paul, and Adam
with thanks

Preface

In 1979, at the time of the referendums, I published a book entitled *Devolution*. This book is based on that earlier work, but it has been almost completely rewritten. Part of the reason for this is obvious. I have had to take account of the legislation of 1998 which, unlike all previous legislation on Home Rule or devolution, with the partial exceptions of the Government of Ireland Act of 1920, and of devolution in Northern Ireland in the years 1974 and 1982–6, will actually come into effect. The years since 1979, moreover, have spawned a large literature on the history and politics of devolution which I have tried to take into account. In addition, although my basic attitudes towards devolution have not changed, I have altered my mind on some important matters. I now feel that, in *Devolution*, I tended to underestimate the scope and depth of Gladstone's attempted resolution of the Irish problem, the problem of holding together a multinational state, as difficult today as it was in the nineteenth century. In writing *Devolution in the United Kingdom*, I have become aware of how much current approaches to devolution owe to Gladstonian precedents. It is a nice coincidence that the third reading of the Scotland Bill in the House of Commons took place on the centenary of Gladstone's death.

Devolution in the United Kingdom seeks to analyse the political and constitutional aspects of Home Rule and devolution from the time of Gladstone's espousal of Irish Home Rule in 1886 to the present day. I hope that, in doing so, it succeeds in casting some light both on how we are governed, and on how constitutional ideas are affected by political realities.

The book was read in draft by Brigid Hadfield and Kenneth Morgan, to its very great advantage. I am grateful also to the following for reading and commenting on various chapters: Nick Barber, Sir Kenneth Bloomfield, Tony Bradley, James Campbell, Sir John Chilcot, Ian Dewar, Sir Nicholas Fenn, Valerie Flint, Sir John Garlick, Sir Michael Quinlan, John Robertson, Conrad Russell, Kevin Sharpe, Michael Steed, Anthony Teasdale, Richard Tur, Brian Walker, Sir Michael Wheeler-Booth, Lord Windlesham, and Patrick Wormald. I am particularly grateful to Michael Steed and Anthony Teasdale for conversations over many years from which I have learnt much about devolution. I should also like to thank Oonagh Gay and David Heald for helping me in various ways. But these kind friends are not to be implicated in my arguments, still less my errors.

I am deeply indebted to the Principal and Fellows of Brasenose College for providing, over a very long period, so stimulating an intellectual atmosphere. I am fortunate indeed to be a member of such a convivial and lively society.

I am grateful also to George Miller of Oxford University Press for being so patient and helpful a publisher, to Shelley Cox, and to Belinda Baker for her skilful copy-editing.

But my greatest debt is to my wife and to my sons, Paul and Adam, for encouraging me to complete this book and for tolerating my constant absences at the word processor.

This book was completed in September 1998 and takes no account of developments since then.

V.B.

Oxford, 1998

Contents

The Making of the United Kingdom

What know they of England
Who only England know?

(Rudyard Kipling, 'The English Flag')

I

Devolution is the most radical constitutional change this country has seen since the Great Reform Act of 1832. This is because it seeks to reconcile two seemingly conflicting principles, the sovereignty or supremacy of Parliament and the grant of self-government in domestic affairs to Scotland, Wales, and Northern Ireland.

The supremacy of Parliament, our central, perhaps our only constitutional doctrine, is of course primarily a legal principle, but its influence resonates throughout our political system, influencing the thought even of those who would seek to escape from it. If the principle has, as some believe, become a fiction, it is, nevertheless, a fiction which remains highly potent.

The principle implies that power is centralized in one supreme and omnicompetent parliament. Westminster, under the British Constitution, is the sun around which every planet revolves. We do not find it easy to think in terms of a separation of powers, nor to understand government as a series of interdependent layers, each with its own rights and responsibilities. We have remained a highly centralized country, more so even than France, traditionally the paradigm of centralized government, which, since 1982, has adopted a policy of regionalism and decentralization. Britain has been, amongst stable democracies, the largest of the unitary states, apart from Japan; no other democracy seeks to manage the affairs of so large a population through a single parliament. Our conception of parliamentary supremacy, moreover, makes it difficult for us to accommodate ourselves to structures of government, such as that of the European Union, whose raison d'être is that of power-sharing. It will make it difficult also for us to accommodate ourselves to the devolution of power downwards to a parliament in Edinburgh, a national assembly in Cardiff, and an assembly in Belfast. European Union and devolution offer complementary challenges to the profoundly unitary nature of the British state. This unitariness, as expressed in the supremacy of Parliament, has been one of the strongest of the tacit understandings which underpin our Constitution.

Our Constitution rests of course on certain defining features of British society. One authority has referred to:

the overwhelming unitariness of British political culture, especially in the great trunk of England, which works against all forms of territorial politics. This anti-territorial dimension is doubtless partly derived from the extraordinary continuity and stability of the British state. ... Equally, too, the extent of cultural homogenization of British society following two hundred years of industrialization must also be taken into account in identifying the components of the anti-territorial bias. Finally, some recognition would need to be given to the relatively low status of sub-national government, to what one observer has called the centre's 'culture of disdain' for it.[1]

The challenge of altering this culture through devolution was first posed in the late nineteenth century when Irish nationalists began to demand Home Rule, an Irish parliament in Dublin. But Westminster refused to concede Home Rule until it was too late to satisfy Irish nationalists. Nevertheless, the Home Rule controversy, which racked British politics between 1885 and 1921, raised the question, which still remains unresolved, of whether Home Rule or devolution, the concession of a local and subordinate parliament in one part of the United Kingdom, is compatible with the supremacy of Westminster and the maintenance of the United Kingdom. The purpose of this book is to answer these questions. First, however, it is necessary to define what we mean by devolution.

Devolution involves the transfer of powers from a superior to an inferior political authority. More precisely, devolution may be defined as consisting of three elements: *the transfer to a subordinate elected body, on a geographical basis, of functions at present exercised by ministers and Parliament.* These functions may be either legislative, the power to make laws, or executive, the power to make secondary laws—statutory instruments, orders, and the like—within a primary legal framework still determined at Westminster.

Devolution involves the creation of an elected body, subordinate to Parliament. It therefore seeks to preserve intact that central feature of the British Constitution, the supremacy of Parliament. Devolution is to be distinguished from federalism, which would divide, not devolve, supreme power between Westminster and various regional or provincial parliaments. In a federal state, the authority of the central or federal government and the provincial governments is co-ordinate and shared, the respective scope of the federal and provincial governments being defined by an enacted constitution as, for example, in the United States or the Federal Republic of Germany. Devolution, by contrast, does not require the introduction of an enacted constitution.

Admittedly, 'federalism' is a term used rather loosely in current discourse in Britain on constitutional change; and in most of the proposals for a 'federal solution' in Britain, 'federal' is intended to mean not a division of power between Westminster and provincial units of government, but rather a policy of devolution applied to the whole country, and not just to parts of it such as Scotland and Wales. Such a policy in the nineteenth and early twentieth centuries was known as 'Home Rule All Round', and such proposals might now be termed 'federal devolution', to avoid confusion with a strictly federal system of government.

Devolution has profound implications for the way in which we are governed, and for the kind of society in which we are to live. One of the main purposes of what follows is to show how the issue has arisen in British politics, and then to spell out the implications of devolving power from Westminster. But to understand the implications of devolution, we need first to understand how the United Kingdom came about, and how it has been held together.

II

The United Kingdom was formed through the coming-together of four nations, England, Wales, Scotland, and Ireland. Wales, Scotland,

and Ireland were joined to England by very different means. Wales was incorporated into England by two Acts of Parliament, in 1536 and 1543; Scotland was made part of the kingdom by means of a treaty signed between two independent states in 1706, and then ratified by the English and Scottish parliaments, thereby creating, in 1707, the new kingdom of Great Britain; while Ireland was made part of the kingdom through Acts of Union passed by Westminster and Dublin in 1800, following resolutions passed in the British and Irish parliaments. These Acts created the United Kingdom of Great Britain and Ireland. The union with Ireland, however, was the only one that did not succeed, being dissolved in 1921 under the terms of the Anglo-Irish Treaty, which provided for the granting to Ireland of dominion status as the Irish Free State with an independent parliament of her own. The six counties which now comprise Northern Ireland were, however, allowed to exclude themselves from the new Irish Free State, and promptly did so, thus remaining part of the United Kingdom under the 1800 Act of Union. Thus the United Kingdom is no longer that of Great Britain and Ireland, but of Great Britain and Northern Ireland.

The United Kingdom came into existence, not through the growth of a single national or linguistic consciousness, but as the outcome of a series of historical contingencies. It was created by ordinary Acts of Parliament, and not by a constitutional document. The United Kingdom, in the words of Richard Rose, was 'not the product of a compact, drafted and signed by its constituents, as is usually the case in a country with a written constitution. It is an agglomeration created by the expansion and contraction of territorial power in the course of a thousand years.'[2] Union was achieved by placing England, Wales, Scotland, and Ireland under a common and supreme parliament, and by abolishing the parliaments of England, Scotland, and Ireland. It is representation in a common and supreme parliament that has been the crucial feature, the very essence of the process of union. Westminster had begun, however, as the English parliament, and the constitution of the United Kingdom was marked by the dominance of the institutions of the English state, the largest and most powerful of the components of the United Kingdom. Thus the formation of the United Kingdom came about through the expansion of

England which, through a process of conquest, treaty, and negotiation, played by far the major role in the creation of the state.

England itself was formed through the expansion of Wessex, which, during the reign of Alfred the Great between AD 871 and 899, began the absorption of central England. Alfred's grandson Aethelstan, who reigned from 924 to 939, extended control over the whole of England south of the Humber–Mersey line and west of Offa's Dyke. By the middle of the tenth century, the contours of an English state could be seen, although its northern borders were to remain ill defined for many years.

England came to be permanently unified far earlier than any Continental state, and there was already a powerful English consciousness and sense of national identity before the Norman Conquest. The dominance of England meant that notions of Scottishness and Welshness were to be formed in opposition to that of Englishness. The idea of Englishness, however, came to be an integrating one, binding the other parts of the United Kingdom to the centre. Yet the heart of England lay in London and the south-east, and it is there that power was centralized. England came to be ruled by a strong central government which left little room for provincial loyalties, although this was not of course inconsistent with regional diversity and a firmly rooted shire-system of local government which, created in the tenth century, lasted substantially unchanged until local government reorganization in 1974.[3]

It is not possible to give a precise date for the formation of the English state. 'England', Conrad Russell has argued, 'is unique among the states of Western Europe in that it cannot claim a recorded foundation. We can say that England became a state sometime between 899 and 956, but the English omitted to make any record of the fact.'[4] This is of fundamental importance for British constitutional development. The English state has no document recording its foundation, and therefore no source of authority, such as a constitution, capable of limiting its power. The English state never began. Rather, it evolved. Thus it had no place for any fully agreed and defined constitutional principle limiting the supremacy of the king, nor, following the establishment of parliamentary government, of the king in parliament. The principle of supremacy was retained when the

English parliament expanded to include the representatives of Wales, Scotland, and Ireland.

The parliament of the United Kingdom took on the characteristics of the parliament of England; in particular, it was, as the English parliament had been, a supreme parliament. In Britain, as Maitland once argued, we have substituted the authority of Parliament for a theory of the state. In the sixteenth century, Thomas Cromwell sought a strong central administration as a means of extirpating competing powers. In the seventeenth century, Thomas Hobbes lamented the dangers of the absence of a supreme authority. 'If there had not been an opinion received of the greater part of England that these powers were divided, the people had never been divided and fallen into this civil war.'[5] The doctrine of parliamentary supremacy, however, proved inadequate to meet the challenge from the American colonies in the eighteenth century, and from the Irish Home Rulers in the latter part of the nineteenth century. As the twentieth century comes to an end, the doctrine may have become, once again, a threat to the unity of the United Kingdom, rather than a means of holding it together.

In the twelfth century, England began to acquire lands in Wales. During the reign of Edward I between 1272 and 1307, the conquest of Wales was completed, and in 1277 Welsh independence was ended by the Treaty of Aberconwy. In 1284, lands in the north and in the west of Wales were annexed by the Crown, but these were separated from England by quasi-independent buffer lands owned by great feudal families known as the lords marchers.

Royal authority was defined over the whole of Wales in the reign of Henry VIII by two Acts, in 1536 and 1543. The first of these Acts is commonly but misleadingly known as the Act of Union. It was in fact entitled 'An Act for laws and justice to be ministered in Wales in like form as it is in this realm', and claimed that Wales was already part of England, declaring that 'as it rightfully is and ever hath been', Wales was 'a very member and joint of the English realm'. It has been held therefore that this Act confirmed the union with England rather than creating it.[6] The Act of 1536 laid down the general terms of union. It provided for Wales to return Members to Parliament, and in 1542 elections were held in Wales for the House of Commons. Representatives from Wales were thus present in the Commons for the Act of 1543, which was entitled 'An Act for certain ordinances in the King's dominions and principality of Wales'. This Act complemented that of 1536 by laying down the details of union. Its 130 clauses provided for the legal and political assimilation of Wales into England. The Tudors sought to eliminate competing sovereignties and to construct a powerful administrative system with a single system of law in place of the separate jurisdictions of the lords marchers. It was for this reason, and not out of an intent to suppress the Welsh language, that the Tudors insisted that English and not Welsh be the official language of Wales. In 1563, Elizabeth I ordered the translation of the Bible and Prayer Book into Welsh to secure Welsh allegiance to the state Protestant religion, and this exerted a profound impact on Welsh life by ensuring the survival of the language.

Although the Tudors established a strong central administration, they were content for this to remain in the hands of local Welsh élites, and separate Welsh courts were to survive until 1830. It has indeed been the characteristic technique of the state to insist upon political unity but to rely upon local interlocutors and the mechanisms of indirect rule for the administration of the peripheries. This meant, in the case of Wales, that union was not incompatible with the retention of Welsh cultural identity and a sense of Welshness. Moreover, the Tudors themselves were in origin a Welsh dynasty. Thus nationalism, when it arose in Wales at the end of the nineteenth century, was motivated not, as in Ireland, by a desire to break the British connection; nor, as in Scotland, by a desire to refashion government so as to guarantee her distinctive institutions. Welsh nationalism was concerned less with political independence than with the defence and preservation of a culture and way of life which seemed under threat. Thus, since the sixteenth century, the union with Wales has been seen as a success, and in 1775 Burke, in his great speech on conciliation with America, was to invoke its beneficial consequences as an illustration of wise and generous statecraft.[7]

III

Scotland emerged as a kingdom during the ninth and tenth centuries and, unlike Wales or Ireland, was never conquered by

England. The attempts by Edward I, 'the hammer of the Scots', to subjugate the country at the end of the thirteenth century were unsuccessful, and England recognized Scottish independence in the Treaty of Northampton in 1328. During medieval times Scotland became a monarchy uniting together its Celtic and non-Celtic population. The Celts in Scotland, by contrast with their Irish counterparts, were, from early times, treated not as second-class citizens, but as a part of the Scottish nation.

Scotland came to be constitutionally linked to England in 1603 when James VI of Scotland succeeded to the English throne, after the death of Elizabeth I, as James I of England. James called himself 'Emperor of the whole island of Britain', and claimed to govern Scotland from London: 'Here I sit and govern it with my pen—I write and it is done, and by a Clerk of the Council I govern Scotland now—which others could not do by the sword.'[8] The Union of Crowns did not create a new state, nor did it create a new British nation. It was a purely dynastic union. England and Scotland retained their separate laws, and the rules for succession to the throne remained different in the two countries.

A union of this kind could work only so long as the king remained the true source of authority in both kingdoms. By the terms of the Bill of Rights, however, William III became, in 1689, responsible to the English parliament. It was difficult to see how the Union of Crowns could survive a constitutional monarchy. The king could not easily be responsible to two different parliaments following different policies. Because the actions of the king were falling under the control of the English parliament, Scottish independence was becoming illusory. Of William III, it has been said:

The more helpless he found himself to defy the wishes of the wealthier and stronger nation, the more completely was the weaker nation entangled in his claims and dragged with him at the heels of the English Parliament. The growth of parliamentary government in England crushed out all possibility of parliamentary government in Scotland.[9]

The Crown came to be tied to the English parliament by the need for regular, annual meetings of Parliament to grant taxation, an unanticipated result of the war against Louis XIV.

If the Scots were not prepared to be governed by an English ministry, then 'either the monarchies must be separated or the parliaments must unite.'[10] Thus, the Treaty of Union was, in a sense, nothing but a logical corollary of the restoration of constitutional government in England in 1689.

In 1701, by the Act of Settlement, the English parliament unilaterally altered the line of succession to the throne. The Act provided for the throne to pass to the Electress of Hanover and her descendants, on condition that they were Protestant. Scotland, however, threatened not to accept the Hanoverian succession, and England, in retaliation, passed the Aliens Act of 1705, declaring all Scots in England to be aliens and prohibiting Scottish imports of cattle, linen, and coal. The Aliens Act implicitly threatened war with Scotland if she did not make provision for a closer union.

Scotland, however, also had much to gain from union. She would gain access to England's expanding markets and to those of her colonies; and she would be able to avoid the threat of a Stuart and Catholic restoration. Above all, she would ensure peace with her southern neighbour. In the words of Lord Roxburgh, 'if Union fail, War will never be avoided; and for my part the more I think of Union, the more I like it, seeing no security anywhere else.'[11] For the Scots, the loss of their parliament was not quite so high a price to pay for Union as might seem the case today, for until 1690, the Scottish parliament had not assumed the dominant position in Scottish life which the English parliament had long claimed. It was, even after 1690, 'only one of a number of rivals for the exercise of executive, and even of legislative authority';[12] and 'In 1707 ... a free Scottish Parliament was not a time-hallowed institution but a novelty (though highly appreciated) of seventeen years standing.'[13] The kirk lay far more at the centre of Scottish national life than parliament. If, therefore, a settlement with England could preserve the kirk together with other Scottish institutions, then the Scots might be able to co-exist with the English in a unitary state with a common parliament, while at the same time maintaining their national identity.

The precise constitutional status and significance of the Treaty of Union have been a subject of much dispute. Scottish nationalists argue that the Scottish parliament was abolished against the wishes

of the Scottish people, and that the vote for union was secured solely through bribery and the promise of high office in the new state.
Thoroughgoing unionists, on the other hand, claim that the new state
of Great Britain created by the Treaty was to be so firmly unitary that
Scotland's position in it would be no different from that of Cornwall
or Yorkshire.

Both of these two extreme interpretations—the nationalist and the
unionist—serve but to obscure the reality of what happened in 1707.
The nationalist interpretation is not accepted by serious historians,
since it entirely ignores the concrete arguments which persuaded the
Scottish negotiators to accede to Westminster's demand for union;
and yet, contrary to the unionist interpretation, the Scots never
intended Scotland's status to be that of a mere province or region of
England. The Scottish negotiators accepted union not only because
they were political realists, but also because they came to be convinced that even an incorporating union could safeguard Scotland's
vital interests.

There can, admittedly, be no doubt that bribery and the promise
of high office in the new state were important factors in persuading
the Scottish parliament to ratify the Treaty of Union. Indeed, the
Scottish Act of Union was, in the words of one historian, 'probably
the greatest political job of the eighteenth century'.[14] Perhaps, however, in the circumstances of the time, it would have been more surprising if bribery had not been involved; and Scottish acquiescence
to the Treaty is not to be explained by bribery alone. For the Scots
drove a hard bargain. They secured the preservation of the Scottish
legal system, in Articles 18 and 19 of the Treaty. Article 18 guaranteed Scots private law, distinguishing between 'public right', i.e.
public law, which would be regulated by the new parliament of Great
Britain, and 'private right', which was to remain unaltered 'except
for evident utility of the subjects within Scotland'. Article 19 laid
down that the Scottish Court of Session would 'after the Union and
notwithstanding thereof, remain in all time coming within Scotland
as it is now constituted by the Laws of that Kingdom, and with the
same Authority and Privileges as before the Union'. Other Scottish
courts were similarly guaranteed. No Scottish lawsuit was to be tried
before an English judge; and English judges were explicitly debarred

from 'recognising, reviewing, or altering the acts or sentences of the judicature within Scotland, or stopping the execution of the same'. Admission to English markets was of equal importance to the Scots, and the Treaty provided for free trade and a common fiscal system—indeed fourteen of the twenty-five articles of the Treaty deal with economic issues.

Finally, the Scots gained recognition for their state church. The Treaty was accompanied in 1706 by, in England, an Act of Security for Securing the Church of England as by law established; and in Scotland by a Scottish Act of Security, for securing the Protestant Religion and Presbyterian Church Government in Scotland. The Scottish Act provided that this form of church government was to be 'held and observed in all time coming as a fundamental and essential condition of any Treaty of Union to be concluded between the two Kingdoms without any alteration thereof, or derogation thereto in any sort for ever'. This Act has been held to represent 'a real concession by England',[15] and without it the Scots would almost certainly have refused to agree to the Treaty.

It is the first three articles of the Treaty of Union that define its essential purpose. The first declares that there will be union between the two countries for ever, the second that the rule of succession to the throne in Scotland is in future to be the same as in England, and the third that both kingdoms are to be represented by a single parliament. Thus the Treaty created a new state with one parliament, but two systems of law and two established churches.

The Scots agreed to an incorporating union because they believed that it was not incompatible with the preservation of their nationality, but also because there seemed no realistic alternative. One authority on the Treaty has expressed 'regret that the Scots Parliament, largely as a result of its new-found vigour and vitality, had to be abolished, and that the federal solution was not tried.'[16] But the regret is anachronistic. The first federal constitution was not established until 1787, in the United States, eighty years after the Treaty of Union. It is true that some of the Scottish negotiators, and in particular the Scots patriot, Andrew Fletcher of Saltoun, called for a federal solution. But by 'federal', they meant not a division of powers between a federal government, with a common parliament, and provincial units, but something more like a *confederal* arrangement, such as that in existence in the Dutch confederation, the United Provinces, or eighteenth-century Switzerland before she became a federal state in 1848— a league of states without any constitutional provisions for unity of action. By 1707, however, the United Provinces had become weak and had fallen prey to Louis XIV. The constitution, once lauded, was now discredited. A confederation, therefore, an association of two equally sovereign parliaments, would be subject to just those quarrels and disagreements which had bedevilled Anglo-Scottish relations in the period leading up to the Union; and it would have been unacceptable to England.

The Scottish negotiators of union regarded Fletcher's 'federal' proposal as, in the words of Sir John Clerk of Penicuik, 'ridiculous and impracticable' and it seems to have been 'no more than a gesture for the benefit of the Scottish public, something to show that at least an attempt had been made to save their Parliament'. 'Federation', however, was 'not worth the paines . . . and will be a mother of future dangers and discords at some unhappy occasion'.[17] Seton of Pitmedden declared in November 1706 that 'Federal Union . . . may be handsomely fitted to delude unthinking people'.[18]

Fletcher of Saltoun, however, appreciated that a confederation might prove unworkable because of the dominant position of England. Fletcher took the view that a workable confederation required a rough equality between the units composing it. He therefore suggested breaking up both England and Scotland, dividing the two kingdoms into separate regions. Fletcher's proposal would thus have secured the sovereignty, not so much of Scotland, as of regions within Scotland. The new kingdom would have contained a number of regional capitals—London, Bristol, Exeter, York, Norwich, Edinburgh, Stirling, Dublin, Cork, and Londonderry. Fletcher in fact accepted the English argument that a parliament had to be sovereign, and that its powers could not be divided. He sought not to *divide* power, something he believed impossible, but to *distribute* it amongst a number of different sovereign authorities, rather than have it concentrated in just one sovereign parliament of Great Britain.

Fletcher was thus not so much a precursor of Madison, but rather a footnote to the Greeks. Far from looking forward to the United

States of America, he was looking backwards to the city-states of the ancient world; or perhaps he was an early prophet of a Europe of the Regions. But, in the Scotland of the early eighteenth century, his proposals were completely unrealistic.

However, the absence of the federal idea from the Treaty meant that there was a crucial weakness in the settlement from the Scottish point of view; for there was no machinery through which Scottish interests could be defended in the face of a permanent English majority. The Treaty could thus make no political or juridical provision by which Scotland's wishes could be ascertained, other than through her representatives at Westminster. The referendum and the convention were unknown to the constitution at this time, and there was no overall system of public law to which both England and Scotland could appeal. In general, judicial review of legislation had to await the United States Supreme Court decision in *Marbury* v. *Madison* (1803), before being admitted to the armoury of instruments of constitutional protection.

The new state of Great Britain would have a new parliament which, although located in Westminster as the English parliament had been, was, nevertheless, the parliament of a new state. The English parliament was a sovereign parliament, but the Scottish parliament was not. It is by no means clear why the new parliament of Great Britain should have been expected to take on the characteristics of the English parliament, rather than those of the Scottish parliament. Yet, there was little doubt, even amongst the Scottish negotiators of union, that the new parliament would in fact take on the characteristics of the English parliament, and that, in particular, it would be a sovereign parliament. How, then, could the Scots have held with any confidence that the provisions of the Treaty would be respected by a parliament in which Scottish members would be but a small minority? It remains a puzzle that the Scots could believe that words such as 'for ever' and 'in all time' could constrain a sovereign parliament. While, from time to time, Scottish judges and commentators have declared that the Treaty is a form of fundamental law, constraining the British parliament, that argument has never been accepted by the courts. The 1706 Act preserving the Scottish form of church government was in fact amended as early as 1712 in the

Toleration and Patronage Acts whereby Westminster altered the powers of lay patrons within the Scottish church. Westminster could hardly have affirmed its sovereignty more explicitly, but no court suggested that it was acting *ultra vires*. Later, in 1800, the Act of Union with Ireland was to declare that the established position of the Church of Ireland was unalterable, but when Gladstone disestablished this Church in 1869, the courts, in *Ex parte Canon Selwyn* (1872) 36 JP 54, refused to rule that it was unconstitutional. The Union with Ireland Act of 1800 which was also declared to be 'for ever' was in effect repealed by Parliament, except with regard to the six counties of Northern Ireland, in 1921.

The Treaty of Union with Scotland has undergone considerable modification since it was signed. Almost every one of its articles has been amended or repealed, including provisions which were intended to be binding.[19] Yet no court has ever struck down legislation emanating from Westminster on the ground that it breached the Treaty; and, in a Scottish case *Murray* v. *Rogers* 1992 SLT 221, in which defaulting poll-tax payers argued that the Scottish legislation providing for the poll tax was contrary to the Scottish Act of Union, Lord Kirkwood stated that 'there is, so far as I am aware, no machinery whereby the validity of an Act of Parliament can be brought under review by the courts'.[20]

What, then, was the point of phrases such as 'for ever' and 'in all time'? Dicey argued that, although such phrases could not bind, they had a purpose, and that:

the enactment of laws which are described as unchangeable, immutable, or the like, is not necessarily futile . . . A sovereign Parliament . . . although it cannot be logically bound to abstain from changing any given law, may, by the fact that an Act when it was passed had been declared to be unchangeable, receive a warning that it cannot be changed without grave danger to the Constitution of the country.[21]

Thus the bald statement that the Treaty created an incorporating union fails to capture its full flavour. It would be better to say that the state of Great Britain which resulted was not a unitary state, but a union state. The distinction between the two has been drawn in the following way:

The unitary state [is] built up around one unambiguous political centre which enjoys economic dominance and pursues a more or less undeviating policy of administrative standardisation. All areas of the state are treated alike, and all institutions are directly under the control of the centre. The union state [is] not the result of straightforward dynastic conquest. Incorporation of at least parts of its territory . . . [is] through personal dynastic union, for example by treaty, marriage or inheritance. Integration is less than perfect. While administrative standardisation prevails over most of the territory, the consequences of personal union entail survival of pre-union rights and institutional infrastructures which preserve some degree of regional autonomy and serve as agencies of indigenous elite recruitment.[22]

The spirit in which political transactions are carried out can be as important as their outcome. The Treaty had been freely negotiated on a footing of equality, and it had the character of a contract between two equal consenting parties. For nearly 300 years, it seemed to have achieved its purpose of enabling the Scots to reconcile their national identity with membership of a United Kingdom.

Devolution revises the terms of the Treaty of Union. But it does not signify a return to the pre-1707 condition in which Scotland possessed a parliament co-ordinate with that of England. That policy, the policy of re-establishing the Union of the Crowns, is favoured by the Scottish National Party, but it is far from the purpose of the Labour government which has legislated for devolution. Devolution instead provides for a parliament which is constitutionally *subordinate* to Westminster. Devolution seeks to revise the Union, not to destroy it.

IV

From earliest times, Ireland had been culturally unified, but had found it difficult to attain political unity. Following the defeat of the Viking invaders in 1002, Brian Boru became, in effect, king of Ireland, styling himself emperor of the Irish. But when Henry II invaded Ireland in 1169 the kingship rapidly collapsed, and since that time, Ireland has enjoyed political unity only under English rule.

Henry II did not, however, complete the subjugation of Ireland and it was not until 1534 that England assumed direct rule over the country, Henry VIII being accepted in 1541 as 'king of Ireland'. By

the end of the reign of Elizabeth I in 1603, Ireland had become constitutionally subordinate. In the seventeenth century, following the
plantation of Ulster by Protestants, primarily from Scotland, the
Celtic, Catholic population of Ireland came to be treated as second-
class citizens, being excluded from the Irish parliament in 1692 and
disfranchised in 1727. Largely for this reason, the Irish Celts were
never assimilated as the Scottish Celts had been. Moreover, there
were, in Ireland, no dynastic links with the throne as there were in
Wales, through the Tudors, and in Scotland, through the Stuarts. In
Ireland, the king and the English state were associated not with local
aspirations, but with alien Protestant settlers, and the Catholic majority came to develop a separatist ideology.

The Irish parliament, unlike the Scottish, lay at the centre of the
nation's political life; but in Ireland the political nation was the
Protestant nation. Until 1782, the Irish parliament was subordinate to
Westminster. In that year, however, with the repeal of Poynings' Law,
it became a parliament with co-ordinate powers to those of
Westminster, although, like the Scottish parliament but unlike the
British, it had no control over the executive. It was not, moreover, a
representative parliament, since it contained no Catholic members;
indeed, until 1793, no Catholic could vote in Ireland.

This arrangement, of co-ordinate parliaments, proved unsatisfactory to British interests, especially after the rebellion of 1798 which
led the British government to fear that Ireland could become a base
for a hostile landing by the forces of Bonaparte. The government
therefore proposed union with Ireland; and, in 1800, Acts of Union
were passed by Westminster and Dublin following resolutions by the
two parliaments, providing for a permanent union between the two
countries under one parliament. Although, as with Scotland, there is
no doubt that bribery played a role in securing the assent of the Irish
parliament to union, it would, again, be mistaken to ascribe union
solely to corruption. The Irish parliament was moderately responsive
to public opinion in Ireland, and the British government had to modify some of the provisions of union in order to secure its passage
through the Irish parliament.[23]

Yet, in any case, the methods by which union was secured were
not responsible for its failure. The Catholic population of Ireland was

induced to support union by the promise of Catholic emancipation. Indeed, those Irish parliamentarians who opposed union did so precisely because they feared that it would destroy the Protestant ascendancy. But, when Pitt sought to implement his promise, George III vetoed it, arguing that it would be contrary to the coronation oath requiring him to maintain the Protestant religion. Thus, whereas in Scotland, the Scottish Act of Security safeguarded the church of the majority of the Scottish people, in Ireland, by contrast, the Union guaranteed the Anglican church in Ireland, the Church of Ireland, which was the church of a minority. Many Catholics came to believe that their disabilities would be removed only by agitation, and the Catholic cause came to be identified with Irish nationalism. Catholic emancipation indeed was not secured until 1829, after a long struggle led by Daniel O'Connell.

The Union also failed to resolve Ireland's economic and social problems, and indeed, in the view of nationalists, exacerbated them when Britain displayed an indifference amounting to callousness during the great famine of the 1840s. The bulk of the Catholic population, therefore, came to believe that Ireland's problems could be resolved only by separation from Britain; or, if that were not possible, by a revision of the terms of the Union allowing Ireland her own parliament, so that Irishmen could at least be in control of their own domestic affairs. In 1885, in the first general election in which the majority of Irish males could vote, 85 out of the 103 Irish seats were won by nationalists. This was a challenge which Gladstone, as Liberal leader, could not ignore, representing as it did the fixed desire of a nation, constitutionally expressed. In 1886, therefore, Gladstone proposed Home Rule, the restoration of a legislature in Ireland.

Many liberal-minded people, however, took issue with Gladstone's approach. For them, the Union of 1800, by whatever methods it had come about, was the consummation of a long historical process which had united the British Isles under one parliament. To undo this process by conceding Home Rule was, they believed, contrary to the course of British history, and would, in Dicey's words, 'undo the work not only of Pitt, but of Somers, of Henry VII and of Edward I'.[24] Unionists believed that the times were unpropitious for small states.

The future, as the victory of the North in the American civil war and the recent unification of Germany and Italy had shown, lay with large states. Thus the Irish nationalist movement was not to be equated with Continental nationalisms such as those in Germany, Italy, or Poland. For, whereas those movements had created new nations, the Irish nationalists were intent on destroying an already existing nation, the British nation, in the creation of which the Act of 1800 was but the final stage in a long and irreversible process of historical evolution. Opponents of Home Rule thus saw it as a threat to the building of a new homogeneous British national identity. Gladstone and his supporters, by contrast, saw Britain not as the country of a single nation, but as 'a partnership of three kingdoms, a partnership of four nations'.[25] Unity was to be achieved not by absorbing the identity of these different nations into one undifferentiated whole, but by explicitly recognizing that Britain was a multinational state, and devising institutions which allowed the various identities of her component nations to be expressed. The conflict between these two standpoints lies at the heart of the debate on devolution, and it remains unresolved.

Irish Home Rule

The Channel forbids union, the ocean forbids separation.

(Henry Grattan)

I

'The long, vexed, and troubled relations between Great Britain and Ireland', claimed Gladstone in 1886, 'exhibit to us the one and only conspicuous failure of the political genius of our race to confront and master difficulty, and to obtain in a reasonable degree the main ends of civilized life'.[1] Irish Home Rule sought to secure those 'main ends of civilized life' by allowing Ireland to govern herself in her domestic affairs within the framework of the United Kingdom, and it proved the most convulsive issue in British politics between 1886 and 1914.

During this period, three Home Rule Bills were introduced into Parliament. The first, in 1886, was defeated in the Commons by 343 votes to 313, as the result of a split in the ruling Liberal party, 93 Liberals voting against it. The second, in 1893, passed the Commons, but was defeated in the Lords by the overwhelming majority of 419 votes to 41. The third bill, introduced in 1912, was again rejected by the Lords but, under the provisions of the 1911 Parliament Act, limiting the delaying power of the Lords to three sessions, it became law in 1914. With the outbreak of war, however, the Act was suspended, and in fact it never came into effect. Its passage was accompanied by threats of direct action on the part of Ulster Unionists and Conservatives of a kind not seen in British politics since the seventeenth century, threats which led many to believe that Britain was on the verge of civil war in 1914.

Perhaps the best definition of Home Rule was that given by John Redmond, the Irish nationalist leader, in a lecture delivered at Melbourne in 1883. 'What do I mean by Home Rule?' Redmond asked.

I mean by Home Rule the restoration to Ireland of representative government, and I define representative government to mean government with the
constitutionally expressed will of a majority of the people, and carried out
by a ministry constitutionally responsible to those whom they govern. In
other words, I mean that the internal affairs of Ireland shall be regulated by
an Irish Parliament—that all Imperial affairs and all that relates to the
colonies, foreign states and common interests of the Empire, shall continue
to be regulated by the Imperial Parliament [i.e. Westminster], as at present
constituted. The idea at the bottom of this proposal is the desirability of finding some middle course between separation on the one hand and over-cen-
tralisation of government on the other.[2]

Home Rule thus entailed the establishment of a legislature in Dublin
responsible for Ireland's domestic affairs—the term 'parliament' was
deliberately avoided, since that was seen to imply a challenge to
Westminster's sovereignty—with an Irish executive responsible to
that legislature. The sovereignty of Westminster would remain.

The policy of Home Rule, then, was designed to modify, though
not to repeal, the Act of Union of 1800. Under the union, Ireland's
governmental arrangements were distinct from those of other parts of
the kingdom. There remained a separate Irish administration in
Dublin, headed by the Lord Lieutenant, representing the sovereign,
and the Chief Secretary, normally a member of the British Cabinet.
There was a separate Irish Privy Council and a separate judiciary and
law officers. Thus Ireland had an executive and a judiciary of its own
but no legislature of its own, while the Chief Secretary, the political
head of the Irish government would spend around nine months of the
year in Westminster. The constitutional implication of the union
between Ireland and Great Britain had been the legal equality of
Ireland with Great Britain; in practice, however, Ireland was governed under a system which seemed to the majority of her population
to put her in a position of inferiority. For she was ruled not by
Irishmen but by the British. Scotland had been treated as a partner
after the union, but Ireland seemed a dependency.

In 1884, the third Reform Act extended the franchise to the agricultural labourer, giving Ireland for the first time popular if not yet
universal suffrage, and increasing the Irish electorate fivefold. In the
1885 elections, the first held under the new system, eighty-five of

Ireland's 103 MPs were members of the Irish parliamentary party, and committed to Home Rule. In consequence, whether Liberals or Conservatives were in power at Westminster, the Chief Secretary and the Irish administration were bound to be in the hands of a party which enjoyed only minority support in Ireland. Thus, although Ireland was, in Gladstone's words, 'nominally under a free Constitution',3 her representatives would no longer be able to play a part in the government of their country.

When expansion of the franchise was being planned, Gladstone's Home Secretary, Sir William Harcourt, feared that:

there will be declared to the world in larger print what we all know to be the case, that we hold Ireland by *force and by force alone* as in the days of Cromwell, only that we are obliged to hold it by a force ten times larger than he found necessary . . . We have never governed and we never shall govern Ireland by the good will of its people.4

This was because, for all but two years since the first Reform Act of 1832, Ireland had been administered through special coercive legislation which had no counterpart in the rest of Britain. Despite such special legislation, however, agrarian crime had not been rooted out, but had become more habitual. Indeed, Gladstone believed that agrarian crime was 'at times threatening to break up the foundation of social order, and bring us to touch upon a state of things essentially belonging to civil war'. The prevalence of agrarian crime was, however, Gladstone believed, 'not so much the cause as the symptom of a yet more deeply rooted evil, that is to say, a want of sympathy with the criminal law in all that relates to or bears upon the holding of land'.

Repressive legislation had, in Gladstone's view, failed. It was 'morally worn out'. The success of further coercion required 'two essential conditions, and these are the autocracy of Government and the secrecy of public transactions'. Neither of these conditions could be met for long under a liberal political system. Indeed, Gladstone believed that the British public would not admit the case for further coercion until all other alternatives had been exhausted. Coercion, moreover, had been unsuccessful because it bore the character of an imposition by a foreign authority, and 'stamped on the

Executive Government in Ireland' there was 'the aspect of a Government essentially foreign'. The 'inevitable consequence' was 'to produce in Great Britain not only disparaging and hostile judgment but estrangement of feeling from Ireland and thus to widen the breach between the countries'. Government in Ireland, however, could succeed, only if 'as in England the law is felt to be indigenous'.[5]

It was essentially these practical considerations rather than any idealistic view of the rights of small nations which turned Gladstone's mind towards Home Rule. Gladstone followed Burke in opposing 'the opening of abstract questions respecting the indefeasibility of natural rights; questions which are . . . capable of introducing confusion into affairs'.[6] He was concerned less with the supposed right of the Irish to self-government than with the practical question of whether the Irish demand for self-government could be reconciled with the central principle of the British Constitution, the supremacy of Parliament.

That it could be so reconciled flowed, in Gladstone's mind, from three separate considerations. The first was his understanding of the nature of Irish nationalism; the second his belief that the insights of Edmund Burke could be applied to the Irish problem; and the third was the practical experience both of other European countries and of the self-governing colonies, which showed 'that the concession of local self-government is not the way to sap or impair, but the way to strengthen and consolidate unity'.

Irish nationalism was, for Gladstone, not a demand for separation or for independent statehood, but a 'local patriotism . . . The Irishman is more profoundly Irish, but it does not follow that because his local patriotism is keen he is incapable of Imperial patriotism.'[7] Gladstone was accustomed to speak not of Irish nationalism, but of Irish 'nationality', which was similar to Scottish or Welsh nationality. Thus, just as a Scot's loyalty to Scotland was compatible with his loyalty to the United Kingdom as a whole, so also the loyalty of an Irishman to Ireland could be made compatible with loyalty to the United Kingdom. For separate Irish nationality 'does not mean disunion with England. It means closer union with England.'[8] Irish nationality, Gladstone believed, was 'a nationality which has regard to circumstances and traditions . . . a reasonable and reasoning, not . . . a blind and headstrong nationality',9 which 'vents itself in the demand for local autonomy, or separate and complete self-government in Irish, not in Imperial affairs'.10 The sense of Irish nationality could be satisfied, therefore, through a judicious policy of Home Rule, placing Irish government on the firm foundations of consent and representative institutions.

While preparing the first Home Rule Bill, Gladstone studied the writings of Edmund Burke on Ireland, and his speeches on conciliation with America. He found them 'a mine of gold for the political wisdom with which they are charged',11 for Burke, the theorist of responsible government in the colonies, had shown how the imperial connection could accommodate a sense of nationality in the colonial communities.

Burke had noticed that the imperial parliament at Westminster performed two functions; it was not only 'the local legislature of this island', but also possessed an 'imperial character, in which as from the throne of heaven, she superintends all the several legislatures, and guides and controls them all without annihilating any'. These functions were, for Burke, separable, and, in the case of the colonies ought to be separated by devolving to the colonies responsibility for local legislation. Such devolution would prove that the imperial rights of Britain and the privileges of the colonists could be reconciled; they were 'just the most reconcilable things in the world'.12 Imperial supremacy, therefore, and the supremacy of Parliament were not dependent upon the centralization of all local functions in the imperial parliament. What Burke had shown was the possibility of two political communities, the one supreme and the other subordinate, with the subordinate enjoying practical autonomy in its own affairs.

It was not, however, necessary to rely on the beliefs of political philosophers for a solution to the problem of reconciling Irish demands with the supremacy of Parliament and the maintenance of the United Kingdom. Nor was it necessary to look for the solution in terms of abstract principles of government. For other countries had attempted to resolve a similar problem: indeed, Gladstone, citing the union between Sweden and Norway and the dual monarchy of

Austria–Hungary as examples of countries which remained united but with separate legislatures, believed that the 'last half-century [is] rich in lessons', whereby, 'unity not only preserved but strengthened'.[13]

If such a solution had been adopted in these cases, then, *a fortiori*, it would be possible in Britain which had '*greater advantages*'. For 'if two independent and nearly equal States can, by the expedient of autonomy, be made to work as an organic unity, how much slighter must be the strain, where there is no question of constitutional independence, and where in the last resort the superior Parliament retains the power to solve any and every controversy between them in such manner as it may think fit?'[14]

These advantages had been exploited by granting responsible government in the colonies, in Canada and in the Australian and South African states, where the concession of local parliaments had, as Burke would have predicted, served to preserve the imperial connection and to remove grievances. The British North America Act of 1867 establishing the Confederation of Canada yielded, for Gladstone, an example 'not parallel', but 'analogous'.[15] It is strictly and substantially 'analogous', and the great lesson of imperial history was that 'forcing uniformity and centralizing authority have caused severance', while 'local independence and legislative severance' had maintained union.[16]

Gladstone's policy of Home Rule was based, then, upon principles that had already, in his view, been applied in imperial relations; it offered the same remedy as had been successfully adopted in Canada. It was a policy, moreover, which, owing much to Burke, was 'especially founded on history and tradition'; a policy which aimed 'in the main at restoring, not altering the Empire';[17] for it was an undoubted fact that 'the creation of such legislatures had in certain cases been an instrument, not of dismembering, but of consolidating Empire'.[18] Home Rule was, for these reasons, the policy of an enlightened imperialist, and most emphatically not a Little England policy. It was, moreover, a policy which 'Surely . . . has high title to a conservative character', for:

it is a policy which, instead of innovating, restores; which builds upon the ancient foundations of Irish history and tradition; which by making power local, makes it congenial, where hitherto it has been unfamiliar, almost alien;

and strong, where hitherto it has been weak. Let us extricate the question from the low mist of the hour, let us raise the banner clear of the smoke of battle, and we shall see that such a policy is eminently a conservative policy.[19]

It represented conservatism of the kind that Gladstone had noticed in his mentor, Peel, 'the conviction that it is possible to adjust the noble and ancient institutions of this country to the wants and necessities of this unquiet time, without departure from the fundamental principles, not which theory, but which history ascribes to them.'[20]

However, although these principles had already been applied elsewhere, modifications were necessary when applying them to Ireland. Because Ireland was so much nearer Britain than Canada or Australia, an Irish legislature would inevitably lie in a relationship to Westminster which differed from that of a legislature in Canada or New South Wales. Moreover, in view of the danger that would be posed by a hostile Ireland in time of war, Britain would have to retain some powers, such as control of defence, which had been devolved to the self-governing colonies.

There were, therefore, precedents for Home Rule, but they were not exact precedents, and a measure had to be devised which took into account Ireland's specific circumstances. In establishing an Irish legislature, Parliament, moreover, would be assuming obligations of honour not to interfere with its working under normal conditions. Parliament had done something similar when it had promised to respect Scottish legal and ecclesiastical institutions in the Treaty of Union. Gladstone believed that the 'same care should be exercised in constituting such obligation of *honour* as if we gave away *powers*'.[21]

The method of the legislation providing for colonial self-government had been to devolve power on a plenary basis to the colonies. Imperial supremacy was preserved not through the exercise of reserve powers, but by means of the Governor-General's veto, and by the Judicial Committee of the Privy Council, which acted as a final Court of Appeal on the jurisdiction of the colonial government. Gladstone, however, sought to give Ireland self-government only in domestic affairs, reserving imperial matters to Westminster. Home Rule, therefore, involved a contract by means of which the Irish were pledged 'to an express admission of that supremacy by the same vote which accepted Local powers'. Gladstone thus required the Irish 'to accept as a satisfactory charter of Irish liberty a document which contained an express submission to Imperial power and a direct acknowledgment of Imperial unity'.[22] But, in addition to the weapons of veto and reservation of powers, each of the Home Rule Bills added further prohibitions on the exercise of devolved powers, the primary prohibition being on laws interfering with religious equality. In this way, Gladstone sought to undermine the unionist contention that Home Rule was incompatible with parliamentary supremacy. For, if, he argued, devolution had worked in subordinate communities such as the Canadian provinces, communities which had been given wider powers than those to be granted to Ireland, then, *a fortiori*, Home Rule would work in Ireland; for if supremacy was compatible with a weaker degree of subordination, it could more easily be maintained with a greater degree of subordination to Westminster.

The problem remained of defining those imperial rights which would need to be retained at Westminster. There had to be, Gladstone believed, a 'strict and thorough severance of Imperial from Local affairs', with a 'reservation of the first', and 'transference of the second'. And this should be based 'on the principle of Trust—which is adverse to Exceptions'.[23] But, what ought to be the extent of the reserved powers? Here, too, Gladstone looked at the historical precedents. There were indeed two examples of constitutions based on a division of powers which would have naturally presented themselves to him. The first, the Constitution of the United States, was unsuitable for his purposes, because it did not secure sufficient power for the federal government; this had been a prime cause of the American Civil War, which had begun in 1861, just twenty-five years before the first Home Rule Bill was presented to Parliament. But the second example, the division of powers between the federal government in Canada and its constituent provinces, was of far more relevance, since the aim of those who had drawn up the Canadian Constitution, in contrast with that of the United States, had been to maintain the power of the centre at the expense of the provinces.

Gladstone, therefore, decided to reserve to the imperial parliament at Westminster those powers which the British North America

Act of 1867, the Act establishing the Canadian Constitution, had reserved to the Dominion Parliament in Canada. Clause 3 of the 1886 Government of Ireland Bill is in fact taken from clause 90 of the British North America Act, enumerating the reserved powers of the Dominion Parliament. These reserved powers were of four kinds. First, there were matters relating to the Crown and defence; second, foreign and colonial relations; third, 'subjects reserved on practical grounds',24 such as patents, copyright law, and contracts; and finally 'all power of protection and differential duties'.25 Gladstone's original intention had been to allow the Irish legislature the power to vary revenue duties, but he changed his mind on this matter during the preparation of the bill, and, in its final version, all indirect taxation was reserved to Westminster.

The structure of the first Home Rule Bill, presented to Parliament in 1886, formed the basis for all later Home Rule measures. It blended two different constitutional models into a hybrid that was entirely *sui generis*. The idea of a devolution of power to satisfy the principle of nationality was, as we have seen, based on the model of colonial self-government, and especially upon the model of responsible government in Canada. The particular division of powers between Parliament and the Irish legislature, however, was based upon the federal division of powers between the Canadian provinces and the Dominion Parliament.

The complexity of the first Home Rule Bill, however, meant that it was widely misunderstood, both by supporters and by opponents of the measure. John Morley, one of Gladstone's closest colleagues, wrote to him in January 1887 that the object of the first Home Rule Bill had been 'to bestow on the Irish body the functions of provincial legislatures in Canada'.26 Yet the Irish legislature would have enjoyed wider powers than those legislatures, and it would in fact have enjoyed all the powers not specifically reserved to Westminster. In the Canadian provinces, by contrast, the powers of the provinces were specifically enumerated and the Dominion Parliament was given all residuary powers.

The opposite criticism was made by Joseph Chamberlain, a leading Liberal opponent of Home Rule, when he argued that the bill, instead of being based on the federal principle, which, he claimed, he could have supported, was based instead on the relationship of Canada to Britain, a relationship which in his view was fundamentally different from that of Ireland to Britain. But, as we have seen, this criticism was misconceived because the Irish legislature, in contrast to the Dominion Parliament of Canada, was not to have control of taxation, trade, and commerce or military or defence matters. The scope of the powers of the Irish legislature, therefore, lay between those of the Dominion Parliament of Canada, and the powers of the provincial parliaments such as Ontario.

The hybrid nature of Home Rule laid it open to damaging criticisms that might perhaps have been avoided if a clear-cut choice between the two models—the colonial and the federal—had been made. On the other hand, it could plausibly be argued that neither of the two pure models would have been as appropriate to the particular circumstances of Ireland as the Home Rule Bill actually produced by Gladstone.

The central distinction between the two models is clear enough, for the colonial model is marked by two features which distinguish it from the federal model. The first is that the colony had never been represented at Westminster, the second—seemingly a logical corollary—is that the colony was not taxed by Westminster. In a federal relationship, by contrast, the different units continue to be represented in, and contribute their share of taxation to, a federal parliament.

Since, under Home Rule, Ireland would continue to receive the benefits of the reserved services, she would be required to contribute her share of the costs of these services. She would, therefore, unlike the colonies, have to pay what was called an Imperial Contribution, and this was to be a first charge on her expenditure. Thus the colonial solution for Irish finance could not be applied.

On the other hand, Gladstone proposed, in the first Home Rule Bill, that Irish members be removed from Westminster, as in the colonial model. It was at this point that the hybrid scheme of Home Rule began to present difficulties; for Ireland was to be taxed by Westminster, but no longer represented there. Thus, the first Home Rule Bill raised the spectre of taxation without representation, the very constitutional contradiction which had led to the loss of the American colonies.

In considering the reasons for the defeat of Home Rule, it is of course important not to exaggerate the importance of defects in the legislation itself. A full historical account would have to give considerable and perhaps preponderant weight to wider factors, and especially to changes in the intellectual climate at the end of the nineteenth century, as Gladstonian imperialism came to be superseded by a very different sort of imperialism, based on *Realpolitik*; nor should the factor of anti-Irish prejudice be minimized, for there is ample evidence to confirm the view of one commentator that 'what really killed Home Rule . . . was the Anglo-Saxon stereotype of the Irish Celt'.[27]

There is little doubt, however, that all the Home Rule Bills, and the first Home Rule Bill in particular, displayed considerable faults of constitutional logic, faults which may well have played some part in their defeat, and which must also cast some doubt on the contention that Home Rule would have yielded a permanent settlement of the Irish question.

The Home Rule legislation had three central deficiencies. The first was the failure to find a solution to the conundrum of how Ireland was to be represented at Westminster after Home Rule. The second was the failure to divide taxation-powers in a way which would combine equity between the different parts of the United Kingdom with the financial independence of Ireland. The third was the failure to show that the supremacy of Parliament would remain a real supremacy rather than a merely symbolic one.

II

The exclusion of Irish members from Westminster in the first Home Rule Bill was, according to Joseph Chamberlain, 'not a technical point, but the symbol and flag of the controversy'.[28] For Ireland would not long tolerate a situation whereby her foreign and tariff policy were decided at Westminster without Irish representation there. Sooner or later, Ireland would demand control of these functions, and that would imply national independence. Thus taxation without representation would lead, inevitably, to separation, as had been the case with the American colonies.

So Gladstone had to face what in his notes for the second reading speech on the Home Rule Bill in 1886, he called 'the double dilemma'. The first horn of the dilemma was:

Ireland is to have a domestic legislature for Irish affairs.
   Cannot come here for English or Scotch affairs . . . [29]

'The one thing', Gladstone told the House of Commons, 'follows from the other. There cannot be a domestic legislature in Ireland dealing with Irish affairs, and Irish Peers and Representatives sitting in Parliament at Westminster to take part in English and Scotch affairs.'[30]

Could Irish MPs be recalled, then, solely for reserved matters, such as foreign policy and defence? This, the so-called 'in and out' proposal, was ruled out by Gladstone in 1886. He did, however, consider it for the second Home Rule Bill, in 1893, but the final version of the Bill, as presented to Parliament, provided for continued but reduced Irish representation at Westminster. There would, under the final 1893 proposal, have been eighty Irish MPs at Westminster, instead of 103.

In 1886, Gladstone decided against the 'in and out' proposal for two reasons. First he argued that the distinction between imperial and non-imperial affairs, 'cannot be drawn. I believe it passes the wit of man.'[31] Yet, in dividing powers in the Home Rule Bill, Gladstone seems to have made that very distinction. The problem was perhaps rather different: it was that the distinction, once drawn, would not in fact be of much assistance, since any proposal to spend money, whether on English, Scottish, or Welsh matters, or on Irish matters, would compete in terms of priorities with any other proposal. The amount of money which accrued to Ireland would remain dependent upon the amount which English, Scottish, and Welsh MPs decided to spend upon their own priorities. Therefore, the standard of living of the Irish would depend upon decisions made at a forum from which they would have been excluded.

There was, however, a second and even more fundamental objection to the 'in and out' proposal. In his notes, Gladstone wrote that it was 'impossible (because opinion touches responsibility)'.[32] The 'in and out' proposal would bifurcate the government of

Britain since there might be one government with the Irish MPs present—a Liberal-Irish government—on foreign and colonial affairs, and a government of an opposite political colour—a Conservative government—with the Irish absent, for domestic English, Welsh, and Scottish affairs. The 'in and out' proposal would thus undermine the principle of collective responsibility according to which a government must stand or fall as a whole, and therefore command a majority on all the issues that come before Parliament, not just a selection of them.

Gladstone, therefore, came to the conclusion that 'Irish members *cannot ordinarily* sit in the Imperial Parliament'. Moreover, so he believed, 'Painful Parly relations of later years recommend a period of intermission.'[33] Many Liberals were anxious to bring an end to the parliamentary obstruction which Irish MPs had practised since 1880, and ensure that the government in London was no longer dependent on Irish votes. Lord Granville, to be colonial secretary in Gladstone's third government, told Harcourt, who was to become the Chancellor, in December 1885, 'The great bribe to me and I expect to England and Scotland would be to get rid of the Irish MPs here, who are introducing the dry rot into our institutions.'[34] If the Irish were to remain at Westminster, then, John Morley believed, 'there is no power on earth that can prevent the Irish members in such circumstances from being . . . the arbiters and the masters of English policy, of English legislative business and of the rise and fall of British Administration.'[35]

To exclude the Irish from Westminster, however, impaled Gladstone on the other horn of the dilemma:

How then is Ireland to be taxed?[36]

The powers reserved to Westminster under the Home Rule Bill were primarily the Crown and defence, foreign and colonial relations, and indirect taxation. It was the last which caused Gladstone the greatest difficulty.

With regard to the Crown and defence, Gladstone was forced to confess that he did 'not see how to modify the Bill with any advantage'. Concerning foreign and colonial relations, 'the "sentiment" presses for a change. But how could Irish members, unless always here, be enabled to participate in dealing with a class of subjects which are mainly in the hands of private members (at least I should say in proportion of twenty occasions against one) and perfectly uncertain as to the time and method of handling?' To deal with this problem, Gladstone made two suggestions, the first a series of 'regular communications between the British and Irish executives ... Foreign policy is thus managed as between Sweden and Norway'. The second suggestion was the Austro-Hungarian model of a joint delegation or standing committee from the two legislatures, with Ireland being represented 'in some reasonable proportion such as perhaps one third'.[37]

But this still left the difficulty that changes in indirect taxation which would affect Ireland could be made without the participation of the Irish themselves. It could perhaps be argued, as it was by Lord Thring, the parliamentary draftsman, that 'Ireland could not be said to be taxed without representation when her representatives agreed' to the provisions of the Home Rule Bill.[38] Gladstone, however, was willing to go further and to concede that 'When the Government makes a proposal for the alteration or repeal of any tax now levied in Ireland by the authority of Parliament, or for the imposition of any new tax', the Irish members would be granted the right to return. They would also be granted the right to return in the case of any proposed amendment to the Home Rule settlement.

It might seem as if Gladstone had now reached by a rather roundabout route the 'in and out' proposal which he had earlier repudiated as impossible, but in fact his scheme was subtly different. The 'in and out' solution provided that the Irish would remain at Westminster as of right, and with the right, therefore, to participate in parliamentary votes on which issues were to count as reserved and which as transferred. Gladstone's provisions of 1886, however, would make it much more difficult for Irish leverage to be applied to every single reserved issue at Westminster.

There might, Gladstone admitted, be 'some inconvenience in this, as there might be intrigues with the Irish to overthrow a ministry through its Budget'. But this inconvenience would probably not be very great: 'we know the worst of this inconvenience now. Since the Act of Union, I think that only two Ministries (one of them already in a minority) have been overthrown, i.e. driven out, on Budgets. These cases were in 1852 and 1885.'39 Further, it could be argued that on what Gladstone called a 'question of class', the Irish members might be just as divided as the English, Scottish, and Welsh, and that 'on any question of national interests, . . . they would still require over 260 British MPs to win a majority'. Moreover, 'It would not seem very unjust that they should gain their point when Ireland was unanimous on a matter primarily affecting her or was supported by more than 5/12 of the British representatives.'40

In this way, Gladstone sought to escape from his 'double dilemma'. But he did so only at the cost of bringing over the members of the Irish legislature to Westminster on what the jurist Anson called 'a sort of imperial or financial excursion'.41 A solution of this kind would have required a good deal of tolerance and mutual forbearance if it were to be made to work.

The alternative to exclusion or to the 'in and out' solution, and one which was adopted in the 1893 bill and the 1912 bill, was to allow the Irish to continue to attend at Westminster, and to be able to vote on all matters, but in reduced numbers. Indeed, Gladstone was to come to the conclusion, after 1886, that such retention was necessary as an outward and visible sign of the supremacy of Parliament. Retention, however, raised the objection that Irish members would be voting on English, Scottish, and Welsh domestic affairs, although English, Scottish, and Welsh MPs would have no say in the domestic affairs of Ireland. Moreover, to reduce the number of Irish MPs at Westminster was of little help in terms of constitutional logic, since, as Harcourt pointed out to Gladstone in 1889, 'though it may lessen the *amount* it does not really touch the *principle* of the objection. When parties are pretty equally divided fifty Irish votes may be as decisive as 100 . . . and when you have once conceded the objection to Irish interference you don't get rid of it any more than the young woman did of the baby by saying it's such a little one.'42

Retention of the Irish MPs would also deprive Britain of one of the principal advantages which she hoped to gain from Home Rule, the opportunity to devote more parliamentary time to the discussion of English, Scottish, and Welsh affairs, and the removal of the Irish question from Westminster. In fact, Irish MPs might have proved just as unreasonable, from the point of view of the English, in a post-Home Rule Westminster, as they had been in the early 1880s. For they might well have come to see themselves as agents or delegates of the Irish legislature. Thus Irish issues would have to be fought out first in Dublin, and then once again at Westminster.

It is hardly surprising, then, that Gladstone told Parnell, the Irish leader, in 1889, that 'the real difficulty' still lay 'in determining the particular form in which an Irish representation may have to be retained at Westminster'.[43] For each of the answers to the problem of Irish representation—exclusion, 'in and out', and retention with reduced representation—suffered from crucial weaknesses in constitutional logic. These weaknesses were unavoidable in principle, resulting as they did from the attempt to devolve power to one part of the kingdom, while retaining a fundamentally unitary constitution elsewhere. Thus, the failure to find a solution to the problem of how Ireland was to be represented at Westminster after Home Rule was logically unavoidable. This does not, however, mean that a solution to the problem was not *practically* possible; for the success of a constitutional arrangement does not depend only, or even perhaps mainly, upon its logical coherence. What it does mean, however, is that the Gladstonian settlement had within it the seeds of friction.

Gladstone had been grappling, with great intensity, with a fundamental problem that was to resurface in the 1970s, when British governments came once again to propose asymmetrical devolution, this time for Scotland and Wales. The problem of parliamentary representation for an area with legislative devolution was to prove as insoluble in the 1970s as it had been for Gladstone. It was resurrected by Tam Dalyell, MP for West Lothian, as the West Lothian Question. Dalyell asked why it was that, after legislative devolution to Scotland, Scottish MPs would be able to vote on English domestic matters such as education and health in West Bromwich, while English and Welsh MPs would no longer be able to vote on education and health in West Lothian. Gladstone had struggled to find an answer to a question which, as he came to realize, had no answer. Tam Dalyell, ninety years later, sought to embarrass supporters of devolution by demanding an answer to the same question. The key issue is whether the logical impossibility of finding an answer of itself condemns asymmetrical Home Rule or devolution. To that issue we shall return in Chapters 7 and 8.

III

The attempt to discover workable and fair financial arrangements for Ireland led to difficulties as serious as those involved in resolving the problem of representation.

Gladstone laid down as one of the conditions of a good plan of Home Rule that there be a fair and equitable division of the financial burden. But what was Ireland's fair contribution to total British revenue, and how was it to be assessed? All three Home Rule Bills proposed a payment from Ireland to the British exchequer in the form of an 'Imperial Contribution' to cover the cost of Ireland's share of reserved services. It was vital, therefore, to form some estimate of what the value of this share might be.

Unfortunately, however, there seemed to be no objective method of determining the correct amount, and the Irish were disposed to argue that the sums being required of them by the Exchequer were excessive. The Irish argument was that the Imperial Contribution should 'be measured by the only genuine test—how much can Ireland spare?'44 This meant that the Imperial Contribution should be not a first charge, as Gladstone proposed, but a residual, to be paid after Ireland's local needs had been met. The trouble was, however, that the Irish legislature would, understandably, seek to use its financial resources for the purposes of economic development, rather than paying what it might regard as tribute to Britain. Thus, as a residual element, the Imperial Contribution would sink to nothing.

Some members of the Irish parliamentary party went even further, suggesting that Ireland be granted special consideration on account of alleged over-taxation in the past. One MP, Tim Healy, suggested that Britain should make reparation for her past ill-treatment of Ireland by not seeking an Imperial Contribution at all, a proposal which the *Economist* on 7 January 1893, dubbed 'an impudent request'.

These problems of relative taxable capacity and historical obligation were, in the words of a government committee on Irish finance, chaired by Sir Henry Primrose in 1912, almost certainly 'insoluble, not in the sense that no answer to them is possible, but because so many plausible answers are possible that the number of solutions threatens to equal the number of solvers'.[45] Nevertheless, the need for Ireland to pay the Imperial Contribution as a first charge meant that Irish revenue would probably be insufficient to meet her basic requirements; and as Healy said, again in *The Economist* of 7 January 1893, if the Irish legislature began by saying, 'We will have to impose a new tax', then, 'he would say that the members of that Parliament would deserve to be hissed out of the country.'

Gladstone was by temperament on the side of financial retrenchment. For him, one of the advantages of Home Rule was that it would stimulate economies in public expenditure. He would have agreed with the comments made by his former secretary, Sir Edward Hamilton, in 1893, that, after Home Rule, 'Great Britain being rid of an expensive partner will be no longer subject to the constantly growing demands of Ireland on the common purse'.[46] Gladstone was ill disposed to any request from the Irish for additional revenue to improve the condition of the education system in Ireland or the Irish railways. 'If the Irishmen don't like my proposals,' he told Hamilton in 1893, 'they must lump it.' It is hardly surprising that Hamilton wrote of Home Rule in his diary as 'the dissolution of a partnership in which the partner with no capital and most spendthrift habits was leaving the firm'.[47]

In addition, however, it was not clear how the taxing power should be divided so as to reconcile Irish autonomy with the freedom of the Chancellor of the Exchequer in London to manage Britain's financial affairs. Three-quarters of the Irish revenue was derived from customs and excise duties. Some Irish nationalists believed that a tariff policy would be necessary to stimulate economic development in Ireland. Britain, however, was a Free Trade country, and on ideological as well as material grounds would hardly be willing to countenance a protectionist Irish legislature which might use its power to impose tariffs against Britain or to make commercial treaties with foreign countries.

Surprisingly perhaps, Gladstone, in 1886, was at first perfectly prepared to devolve the power to vary customs and excise to the Irish legislature. But his Cabinet overruled him. 'I feel confident', Gladstone's

Home Secretary, Hugh Childers, argued, 'that English and Scottish public opinion will never tolerate any plan which gives to an Irish Legislature power to impose Customs duties, to make Ireland a "Foreign country" and trade with Ireland "Foreign trade" '.[48] Thus, in all three Home Rule Bills, customs and excise duties were retained by Westminster.

This meant, however, that the Irish legislature had control of just one-quarter of total Irish revenue. Of this quarter, one-quarter came from the Post Office, and it was difficult to alter postal rates to any significant extent; of the remainder, roughly half was derived from income tax. While it might be possible to raise income tax in Britain, one could not easily do it in Ireland without, as Healy put it, being 'hissed out of the country'. Thus the system of finance proposed seemed devised for English and not for Irish conditions.

The financial arrangements attached to Home Rule would have imposed strict limitations upon the extent of the autonomy which Ireland would enjoy. Moreover, on both of the contentious issues bedevilling the financial relationship—the value of the Imperial Contribution and the division of the taxing power—Gladstone and the Liberal Party found themselves at odds with their Irish allies.

As with the issue of parliamentary representation, Gladstone strove hard to overcome the financial difficulties. In the 1886 bill, he sought to circumvent the problem of ascertaining Ireland's true revenue with all the ammunition for discord which that search involved. Instead, he proposed that Ireland pay a fixed proportion of a specific sum as the Imperial Contribution. This was assessed, in clause 15 of the Government of Ireland Bill, as one-fifteenth of total imperial expenditure, that is, expenditure on the reserved services, and was to be a first charge on the Irish Exchequer. All other revenue collected in Ireland was to be the property of the Irish Exchequer. Moreover, the sum of one-fifteenth of total imperial expenditure in 1886 was to remain fixed for thirty years—it was not to alter with variations in British revenue, and it could be changed only by agreement between London and Dublin. This would ensure that it could not be altered to Ireland's disadvantage by the Westminster Parliament in which the Irish would no longer be represented, and would, it was hoped, provide Ireland with a surplus on her domestic account of £404,000, sufficient to allow her to begin self-government with a margin for domestic expenditure.

Parnell, however, regarded a surplus of this size as inadequate, believing that at least £1¼ m was necessary. More importantly, however, the 1886 arrangement would have meant that the Chancellor of the Exchequer in London could make no change in indirect taxation without disrupting Irish financial arrangements. For, if the Chancellor in his budget raised customs duties, Ireland would enjoy a windfall benefit, while if he lowered duties, she would suffer an unexpected loss.

If the Chancellor reduced duties, Irish revenue would fall but she would still have to meet a fixed Imperial Contribution. The Irish administration, therefore, would either have to reduce its spending, or budget for a sharp rise in Irish direct taxation which, it will be remembered, constituted less than one-quarter of Ireland's total revenue. Some idea of the magnitude of the sums involved can be gained by considering that it would have required a 40 per cent rise in Irish direct taxation to compensate for the repeal of the tea duties.

To Ireland, therefore, it would seem as if Britain was compelling the payment of a tribute through the Imperial Contribution while at the same time disrupting Ireland's budget through her fiscal policy. Britain and Ireland would be 'brought into direct hostile collision. The rich English [*sic*] government appears in the light of an imperious creditor, the Irish government stands in the position of a poverty-stricken debtor.'[49]

If, on the other hand, Britain were to raise customs duties, Ireland would gain a windfall benefit. Were she to lower direct taxation in compensation, this would have socially regressive consequences, since the poor would be paying higher taxes on consumption goods, while the rich would be relieved of part of their burden of income tax. Ireland would, therefore, have forced upon her a change in her financial arrangements which she might not want, and, moreover, 'a ratio between direct and indirect taxation which might be both financially unsound and socially harmful'.[50] Direct taxation, which appeared to be under Irish control, would not in fact be so, because it would vary inversely with variations in indirect taxation, determined by decisions made in London. Thus the Irish government would be dependent upon a British budget which could at any moment upset all its calculations of revenue.

Nor would the British budget be in a healthier situation. Suppose that an increase in the cost of imperial services meant that Britain required additional revenue. If this revenue were to be obtained through increasing direct taxation, Ireland would be making no contribution towards it. The Irish might well not respond to a patriotic appeal from the British government to raise direct taxation given, as Harcourt rather delicately put it, 'the ethical and patriotic temperament of the men with whom we have to deal'.[51] Therefore, to ensure that Ireland made a proportionate contribution to any increase in revenue, Britain would have to raise her customs duties, a difficult option for a Liberal and Free Trade government to accept.

The financial scheme of 1886, therefore, might well not have worked successfully. The finances of Britain and Ireland would have become hopelessly intertwined. The arrangements would both have restricted the freedom of the Chancellor of the Exchequer, and eroded the financial autonomy of the Irish legislature almost to non-existence.

Such a dilemma was inevitable in any financial scheme unless it either gave to Ireland control of customs—something ruled out in 1886—or, alternatively, credited Britain with Irish customs duties, treating a proportion of the sum raised through customs as the Imperial Contribution. This second solution was adopted in 1893, when it was proposed that one-third of Irish customs and excise be credited to Britain, leaving Ireland with a surplus of £½m. This proposal enjoyed the considerable advantage of being easy to comprehend, and it meant that a proportion of customs duties, attribution of which it was difficult to assign precisely, would be retained as British taxes. For these reasons, the proposal appeared to the Primrose Committee on Irish finance, in 1912, as the best available, since 'it would have provided a clear-cut line of demarcation between Imperial and Irish finance', and it did not require any reference to the insoluble problems of relative taxable capacity or historic obligation.[52]

Unfortunately, this scheme too had its defects, for it made the size of the Imperial Contribution entirely dependent upon the fiscal policy of the British government. Under a Free Trade Chancellor, such as Harcourt, Ireland would enjoy an uncovenanted gain. Harcourt's aim was a 'free breakfast table', a reduction of the duty on commodities such as tea, and a recouping of the revenue through death duties. Ireland would then obtain the entire benefit of the reduction of the tea duty while contributing nothing via death duties, since direct taxes had been devolved, towards increased taxation in the rest of the country. The Irish would thus enjoy cheaper tea at the expense of the British taxpayer. It is little wonder that Harcourt told Gladstone: 'I plainly foresee that either the Budget will kill the Irish finance, or the Irish finance will kill the Budget'.[53] Here too the policy of the Irish administration would depend upon the vagaries of the British budget, which could at any moment upset its calculations of revenue. It would, however, be futile to speculate on how this problem might have been resolved, since the scheme had to be withdrawn, after 'an enormous error' was discovered 'in the computation of the Excise revenue due to Ireland and Great Britain respectively'.[54] The effect of this error was to reduce the Irish surplus from £½ m. to £140,000, a sum insufficient for Ireland's domestic expenditure. The scheme was dropped in committee in 1893.

The government's response was to establish an advisory commission under Hugh Childers, which reported that Ireland's taxable capacity was only one-twentieth of Britain's and that an Imperial Contribution could not be fixed, but would have to be variable, and imposed only after Irish local needs had been satisfied. The implication of the Childers report was that the scheme of 1886 and the original scheme of 1893, both of which required a fixed Imperial Contribution, would not have been workable. The new scheme was, however, open to the objection that it required an objective estimate of Ireland's true revenue, a problem which, as we have seen, was likely to prove insoluble.

By the time of the third Home Rule Bill in 1912, the introduction of measures of state welfare, such as old-age pensions in 1908 and the National Insurance Act of 1911, was placing considerable strains upon the Irish domestic accounts, which were now in deficit. This deficit could be expected to increase with the further development of the welfare state. Had Ireland been an independent country, compelled to finance her expenditure from her own revenue, she would not have been able to afford old-age pensions at the British level.

If the Irish account were in deficit, then, so it would seem, there could be no question of requiring an Imperial Contribution from her. Under the 1912 bill, the British taxpayer would find it necessary to subsidize Irish domestic services, as well as the Irish Imperial Contribution, her share of the reserved services, for some years to come. Otherwise, the first act of an Irish legislature would have had to be a drastic increase in direct taxation. The 1912 bill, however, had it been implemented, might have caused, 'a material change in the attitude of the British taxpayer towards the question'.[55] For the British taxpayer might find it anomalous that Ireland would enjoy self-government within the United Kingdom at his expense. In those circumstances, how could Ireland enjoy autonomy when her domestic account was in deficit?

The Irish nationalists did not accept any of the Liberal financial proposals as a final settlement. In 1886, Parnell declared that he would strongly oppose the financial clauses in committee, while in 1893, Redmond declared on the third reading of the Home Rule Bill:

I maintain that no man in his senses can any longer regard it either as a full, a final or a satisfactory settlement of the Irish nationalist question. . . . With regard to the financial part of the bill, if in every other detail the Bill were satisfactory, that part of the Bill is so grave and faulty that it would be impossible for me to allow the third reading to go without uttering a protest and making it clear that my vote cannot be held as approving that part of the scheme. It is not merely that Nationalists regard the financial clauses as ungenerous . . . it is the practical ground that they believe it to be impossible to govern Ireland successfully under these financial clauses.[56]

The 1893 bill, Redmond declared, was a 'toad, ugly and venomous, yet wearing a precious jewel in its head'.[57] The Irish nationalists also condemned the financial clauses of the 1912 bill, and refused to accept them as a final settlement.

Liberal statesmen did not succeed in discovering a financial settlement which could both underwrite Irish autonomy and avoid conflict between the two legislatures. What militated against such a solution was, as we have seen, the peculiar structure of the Irish economy, in particular her dependence upon customs and excise duties for the bulk of her income. This meant that probably the only way to give Ireland financial autonomy was to give her control of customs, as Gladstone had originally proposed. But, as we have seen, such a proposal was unacceptable to the Liberal Cabinet, and probably to Liberal MPs and Liberals in the country as well. Moreover, an Ireland with control of customs, able to impose a protective tariff on British goods, and to sign commercial treaties with other countries, would have been well on the way to a break with Britain. From this point of view, Home Rule, rather than binding Ireland more closely within the United Kingdom, as Gladstone hoped, would have put her on the slippery slope to separatism.

IV

For Home Rulers and unionists alike, the supremacy of Parliament was the keystone of the constitution, the cement which held the country together. There was, however, considerable ambiguity in what the doctrine entailed. It might, at that time, have meant the exercise of real political authority which Parliament enjoyed in relation to the United Kingdom; or it might have meant the more nominal, although not wholly nominal, supremacy that Parliament enjoyed over the self-governing colonies such as Canada.

This ambiguity reflected the different interpretations of Home Rule offered by British Liberals and Irish nationalists. For the Irish nationalists, the supremacy which Westminster should enjoy over Ireland after Home Rule should be a dormant supremacy, very like that which Parliament exercised over Canada. Were it to be a real supremacy, implying the regular intervention of Westminster in Ireland's affairs, that, in the eyes of Irish nationalists, would diminish Irish autonomy to zero.

Liberals, however, did not intend to allow the Irish so great a degree of autonomy. That, indeed, is why the Home Rule Bills reserved certain matters to Westminster and required of Ireland an Imperial Contribution. Nevertheless, once an Irish legislature sat in Dublin, Britain would be under a moral, although not a legal, obligation not to legislate for Ireland in her domestic affairs. For as long as Home Rule worked normally, the Irish parliament would, in Irish domestic affairs, be in practical terms a co-ordinate and not a subordinate body.

Even in an emergency, however, difficulties would arise if Westminster sought to exercise its supremacy. It would not be easy for Parliament to use its veto, for it might prove impossible to secure an Irish administration, resting on a majority in the legislature, except one which insisted on ignoring the veto. The difficulty was that use of the veto would depend in effect upon the consent of the Irish administration. This was a problem which, as we shall see, the British government was to face when it tried to overrule a friendly administration in Belfast, in 1922 (see pp. 74–5). How much more difficult it would have been with an unfriendly administration in Dublin. It was for this reason that a Conservative opponent of Home Rule, Sir Michael Hicks-Beach, argued of the 1893 bill that 'the safeguards in the bill are absolutely unreal. There is not one of them that is not at the complete mercy of the very persons against whom they are devised.'[58] After Home Rule, there would be only two ways in which the British government would be able to secure compliance with its wishes from an Irish government—agreement and force. Agreement, although more necessary after Home Rule, would, however, become more difficult, since the Irish legislature could legitimately claim to represent the Irish nation. Nothing would mobilize that nation more effectively than a British demand which the Irish legislature was determined to resist. It was for this reason that the Primrose Committee declared that 'there is no means, short of the employment of force in the last resort, by which an independent legislature or executive can be compelled to do something positive against its will'.[59] It was, then, not clear how the British government could in practice make the supremacy of Parliament effective once the judiciary and the police were in Irish hands.

Self-government had worked in the colonies, which were generally content with their constitutions; peopled mainly with settlers of British descent, they were in no sense hostile to Britain. Moreover, they knew that if they genuinely sought separation, it would not be refused. With the Irish, by contrast, these conditions did not apply. They were by no means content with the limited degree of autonomy which Home Rule offered them; they sought revision of the financial clauses; and they might well seek to use their political leverage to extract further concessions. The Irish, therefore, were in a stronger position than the colonists to enforce their demands, but Westminster was far less likely to countenance separation.

V

The seemingly insuperable difficulties involved in any scheme of Irish Home Rule led some politicians and opinion-formers to argue that only a 'federal solution' could reconcile the demands of Irish nationalists with the requirements of parliamentary supremacy. The term 'federal' was, however, used with considerable imprecision. It was not intended to imply a juridical division of sovereignty on the model of the American Constitution. Rather, it implied a policy of general devolution or 'Home-Rule-All-Round', by which Scotland and Wales, as well as Ireland, together with either England or the English regions, would be given legislatures of their own. The supremacy of Parliament would be retained, since each of these legislatures would be subordinate to Westminster. Federalism was, admittedly, a misnomer, declared Philip Kerr in August 1910, 'But it is a good fighting word to begin with. Devolution has noisome associations. Home Rule all round, worse. Federalism has been a success everywhere and people will therefore not be inclined to fight shy of the word.'[60]

A federal solution in this sense seemed to offer answers to the three constitutional problems which bedevilled Home Rule. The creation of subordinate legislatures in England, Scotland, and Wales would resolve the problem of representation, since Westminster would become a federal parliament, and the Irish would be represented in it on precisely the same terms as the other nationalities in the United Kingdom. Thus federalism would provide for the equal treatment of the different portions of the United Kingdom. Federalism might also help to secure a more equitable division of revenues between the various parts of the state, since each of the legislatures would enjoy the same taxing powers.

Above all, however, federalism could preserve the unity of the kingdom and ward off separatism, since it would give to Ireland nothing which was not also to be given to other parts of the United Kingdom. Speaking in the House of Commons debate on devolution in 1919, the geographer Halford Mackinder claimed that Joseph Chamberlain, in putting forward the federal idea,

saw that there was safety in numbers. In the number of subordinate Parliaments there is safety, for the majority of subordinate Parliaments will be able to exercise restraint on the recalcitrant Parliament that would cut itself adrift or otherwise misbehave.[61]

Moreover, federalism held out the possibility of resolving the Ulster problem, if it led to the creation of a separate legislature for that province. Under those circumstances, Home Rule would confirm Ulster's membership of the United Kingdom instead of undermining it. By 1919, Sir Edward Carson, leader of the Ulster Unionists, was thus able to declare, 'I do not believe that devolution is a step towards separation. Indeed, I am not sure that devolution, if properly carried out, may not lead to closer union'.[62]

Federalism had been proposed by the former Liberal Prime Minister, Earl Russell, in 1872, as a means of relieving parliamentary congestion. Also in the 1870s, the leader of the Irish parliamentary party, Isaac Butt, advocated it as a solution to the Irish question. Later, leading Liberals such as Lloyd George and Churchill came to espouse it, and the second draft of the 1912 Home Rule Bill included a scheme proposed by Lloyd George for Grand Committees in England, Scotland, and Wales, with wide legislative powers of the same scope as those to be offered to Ireland. The title of the bill was to be Government of Ireland and House of Commons (Devolution of Business) Bill. This scheme was dropped from the final draft of the bill, but all the same, in introducing it, Asquith declared that it was 'the first step and only the first step in a larger and more comprehensive policy'.[63]

Federalism was attractive not only to Liberals, as a means of meeting the claims of the Scots and the Welsh, but also to unionists who, if they could not avoid Home Rule, were determined to ensure that it should not lead to separatism. Disraeli in 1880 was, apparently, 'prepared to consider some sort of federal constitution for Ireland'.[64] Joseph Chamberlain argued in his second reading speech on the 1886 Home Rule Bill that the solution should be found 'in the direction of federalism' as an alternative to Home Rule. For, under federalism, Ireland might 'really remain an integral portion of the Empire. The action of such a scheme is centripetal and not centrifugal, and it is in the direction of federation that the Democratic movement has made most advances in the present century'.[65] However, on other occasions, Chamberlain declared that federalism would involve a massive and unwanted constitutional upheaval, and so it may be that his espousal of federalism was merely tactical. In the years before the First World War, however, Chamberlain's son, Austen, came to be attracted by the federal solution and sought to convert other unionists to it; and he was supported by imperialists of the Round Table school who believed that a federal United Kingdom could be a preliminary to a federation of the self-governing colonies of the Empire—an imperial federation.

Yet the federalist solution remained a constitutionalist's creation. It never became part of the practical agenda of politics. 'The question', declared Gladstone in 1886, 'seems to imply that the wants and wishes of England, Scotland, Wales and Ireland are the same. I have no evidence before me which would lead me to assume that this is the case.'[66] The most obvious objection to federalism was that it gave to England a constitution which she did not want in order to retain Ireland within the United Kingdom. Lord Curzon told the War Cabinet in July 1918 that 'he was not prepared to pull up the British Constitution by the roots in order to get Ireland out of her difficulties'.[67]

There was no popular pressure in England for a federal solution involving the creation of an English legislature. 'After all,' argued Lloyd George, when the federal option was put to him after the First World War, 'here is a population of 34,000,000 out of 45,000,000, and unless you have got a substantial majority of the English representatives in favour of it, it is idle to attempt it.'[68]

Moreover, there was considerable doubt whether a federal constitution would actually succeed in placating the Irish nationalists. Neither Parnell nor Redmond showed much sympathy with federalism, which they saw as an attempt to deny the urgency of the Irish problem by linking it to the far less urgent problems of nationalism in Scotland and Wales. In 1886, Parnell sought, for the Irish legislature, the power to tax imports, declaring that 'An Irish custom-house is really of more importance to Ireland than an Irish parliament.'[69] Such a demand was hardly compatible with a federal constitution. The Irish nationalists were, in any case, not prepared to wait while governments drew up large and complex schemes of federalism. They demanded Home Rule as the solution to what they saw as an immediate and pressing problem.

A federal constitution would require from the Irish at least as much loyalty to the imperial parliament as a policy of Irish Home Rule. For, as Dicey put it,

A Federal Government is, of all constitutions, the most artificial. If such a government is to be worked with anything like success, there must exist among the citizens of the confederacy a spirit of genuine loyalty to the Union. The 'Unitarian' feeling of the people must distinctly predominate over the sentiment in favour of 'state rights'.[70]

England, however, the largest state in the Union, did not seek 'state rights', while Ireland was not particularly enamoured of union. Under these circumstances, federalism would increase, not reduce, the possibilities of conflict between Britain and Ireland.

For Ireland, moreover, the federal parliament might well appear as the English parliament writ large, since England would enjoy such a powerful preponderance within it. In addition, a federal arrangement would allow Irish MPs to employ the same tactics of obstruction that they had used in the 1880–5 parliament, and government could easily become paralysed as a result. 'A sick man fears to lose a limb', Dicey declared. 'He will not be greatly consoled by the assurance that his arm may be retained at the risk of his suffering general paralysis.'[71]

The federal solution thus suffered from the double drawback that the Home Rulers thought it a diversion, while most unionists believed that it would weaken the government of the United Kingdom without resolving the Irish problem. Moreover, although Carson made favourable noises, many Ulster Unionists were suspicious of a federal system based on the principle of nationality, for they came to regard themselves neither as part of the Irish nation, nor as a separate nation of their own. Instead, they saw themselves as an integral part of the

United Kingdom, like Yorkshire or Sussex. Therefore, the only type of federalism which they would countenance would have to be based on regions, not on nations. Yet the Irish nationalists did not regard Ireland as a region, and a regional form of government would not, they believed, satisfy the national aspirations of the Irish people; and the English were not prepared to restore the heptarchy solely to help resolve the Irish problem.

These difficulties were graphically illustrated when, after the First World War, in 1919, a conference on devolution was established, with thirty-two members, sixteen from each House, under the chairmanship of the Speaker of the Commons, James Lowther. The task of this conference was not to consider whether devolution was desirable, but rather to propose a practical scheme. The war and the immediate post-war years saw numerous grandiose schemes for social and economic reconstruction, and the first Speaker's Conference of 1917 had achieved agreement between the parties on universal male suffrage and female suffrage. Federalists, therefore, hoped that a second Speaker's Conference, on devolution, could achieve similar agreement under the auspices of a coalition government under which party divisions seemed, for a time, in abeyance. Unfortunately for the Conference, however, Lloyd George decided, during the course of its sittings, to deal separately with Ireland, and a Government of Ireland Bill was introduced into Parliament. The Conference, therefore, decided to exclude Ireland from further consideration, and nationalist Ireland was not represented on it. But, in any case, Ireland outside Ulster had moved well beyond devolution, and the Sinn Féin landslide in the 1918 general election presaged a more violent phase in Ireland's struggle for independence.

The Conference did indeed reach agreement on four of the crucial matters which it had to consider: the division of powers; the division of financial powers; the territorial organization of the judiciary; and the areas in which subordinate legislatures should be set up. The Conference decided that the principle of nationality should be fundamental, and that, therefore, England ought not to be divided, although the Ulster members continued to argue for a divided England so that they could more easily press for a divided Ireland.

The Conference failed, however, to agree on whether the subordinate legislatures should be directly elected. Murray Macdonald, a federalist MP, argued for direct election, but the Speaker felt that this proposal was unrealistic.

The more I considered the proposal of one supreme and four independent legislatures, the less I liked it. The confusions which might arise, the multiplicity of elections, the novelty of five (possibly even more) Prime Ministers and Cabinets of probably divergent political views, the enormous expense of building four new sets of Parliamentary buildings and Government offices and providing all the paraphernalia of administration, frightened my economical soul.[72]

Moreover, the Speaker felt that the Conference 'was hardly numerous or representative enough to be qualified to undertake the very serious task of drawing up what might in effect be a new Constitution for the component parts of Great Britain'.[73] One of the members of the Conference, Lord Gladstone, son of the former Prime Minister, was more forthright in declaring 'the personnel of the Conference with few exceptions' to be 'incompetent'.[74] Lowther, therefore, proposed, as an alternative to direct election, a system of national Grand Councils, composed of the MPs of England, Scotland, and Wales. These Grand Councils would be an extension of the idea embodied in the proposal for a Scottish Grand Committee, first established in 1894, that bills affecting the different nations comprising the United Kingdom should originate and have their legislative stages in their respective national parliamentary committees. Perhaps these committees might sit not only in London, but also in Edinburgh and Cardiff. A scheme of this kind could perhaps evolve into the larger scheme of directly elected bodies should the demand arise. It could be supported therefore by federalists as a transitional device. The trouble was, however, that the Speaker's scheme would make no contribution to the relief of parliamentary congestion, which was one of the main motives behind the federalist movement.

Each of the two schemes—Murray Macdonald's and the Speaker's—had the support of thirteen members of the Conference. Five members supported both schemes, the Speaker's scheme on an interim basis, and the Murray Macdonald scheme as the desirable terminus. Faced with this deadlock, it is hardly surprising that the deliberations of the Conference were stillborn. 'It may be said', reported the Speaker ruefully to the Prime Minister, 'that the Conference has been more successful in bringing into the open, than in solving, the doubts and difficulties that surround the task of recasting the British Constitution with the aid of imperfect analogies supplied by other countries, which under totally dissimilar conditions have adopted federal principles of government for the purpose of uniting previously separate states.'[75]

In any case, the mood of the country was hardly sympathetic to a grand reconstruction of the Constitution, and the government had no mandate for so radical a change. As Lord Birkenhead, the Lord Chancellor, had said of the federalists, 'It is now actually proposed that an immense revolution of the Constitution of these Islands is to be carried through after a General Election at which it is not possible to pretend even that one constituency voted with this question before them. To attempt to do so would, in my humble judgement be a national scandal.'[76] When Lloyd George's government decided to deal separately with the Irish question, the political dynamic which might have led to federalism disappeared entirely. 'The discussions', declared Lowther in his memoirs, 'had been of great interest, as they often raised recondite and sometimes difficult questions of Constitutional lore and law, but all along I felt that the driving force of necessity which had been so active a factor in the Electoral Reform Conference was absent.'[77]

Lord Salisbury was perhaps being too dismissive when he replied in 1889 to a correspondent who was urging the federal solution upon him: 'As to Home Rule in your sense—which is Federation—I do not see in it any elements of practicability. Nations do not change their political nature like that except through blood.'[78] Federalism might have been made acceptable to the electorate if it had been presented as a remedy for deeply felt and immediate grievances. In the absence of that, however, it was bound to appear as remote and impractical.

VI

Liberal statesmen did not succeed in reconciling Ireland to membership of the United Kingdom by their policy of Home Rule. Gladstone had believed that Irish nationality was a purely local patriotism, like that of Scotland and Wales, and therefore perfectly compatible with the British connection. Had that been the case, then the consensus and goodwill needed to work Home Rule might well have been present. But, if Irish nationality was rather different from Scottish and Welsh nationality, if it was instead a nationalism fuelled by 'a thirst for revenge . . . that hatred, that undying hatred for what they could not but regard as the cause and symbol of their misfortunes—English rule in Ireland',[79] then the attempt to corral it through Home Rule was doomed to failure. It was, to change the metaphor, an attempt to mix oil and water.

The truth is that the Liberals no less than the Conservatives, were unionist, in that they sought to find a method by which Ireland could be kept within the Union. They differed from their opponents not on the necessity of maintaining the Union, but on the subsidiary issue of whether the existing relationship of Ireland within the Union was a tolerable one.

Yet any scheme of Home Rule which a Liberal government proposed, or which the British people could be persuaded to accept, was bound to fall short of what Irish nationalists demanded, even if only in symbolic terms—and of course symbolic issues are often of the utmost importance in relationships between governments. For any scheme of Home Rule was bound to display and indeed make explicit Ireland's practical subordination to the United Kingdom, a subordination from which Irish nationalists wished to escape. The real issue at the heart of the Home Rule controversy was perhaps not so much the conflict between Home Rulers and unionists, but whether any relationship could be devised which retained Ireland within the Union as a subordinate community and yet which the Irish could be persuaded to accept; the resolution of this issue would depend on whether the fundamental attitude of the Irish people to Britain was one of hostility or friendship. For Home Rule, or devolution, 'suggests only a means whereby better government may be secured within a single State. Its value disappears once the unity of the State is questioned'.[80]

However, even if it is accepted that Home Rule would not have satisfied Irish aspirations, the argument does not end there. For after all, if the Home Rulers did not succeed, nor did the unionists. 'All resistance to this measure', Gladstone declared in April 1886, 'is a contribution to the cause of separatism, and those who offer it are not Unionists but Separatists.'[81] The unionists did not achieve their aim of maintaining the Union, which was dissolved by force between the years 1918 and 1921, in an atmosphere of mistrust and hostility which was to poison relations between Britain and Ireland for many years.

Unionism had comprised two elements. The first, that represented by the Conservatives and by the Whig leader Lord Hartington, had declared that any form of Home Rule was a threat to national unity. This element believed that a self-governing Ireland could not remain part of the United Kingdom, unless the United Kingdom were to be transformed into a federation, which was hardly possible. Otherwise, Home Rule was inherently separatist.

Home Rule, however, might not have been defeated if the opposition to it had been constitutionalist alone. In 1886, as in the 1970s, devolution was defeated because opponents from the Right received additional support from defections on the Left. In 1886, the second element in unionism was a radical unionism, led by Joseph Chamberlain, and it depended for its vitality less upon constitutional propositions than upon the view that the problems of Ireland were not at bottom constitutional at all, but fundamentally social and economic in nature. For Chamberlain, the difficulties faced by the Irish peasant were no different in kind from those faced by the Scottish crofter, the Welsh peasant, or the English agricultural labourer. The answer to these problems was not to dilute the forces of radicalism by establishing separate legislatures, but to mobilize them so that a strong radical government could be formed at Westminster to make a serious attack on economic and social grievances. A similar answer was given by many on the Labour Left in the 1970s when devolution once more came to the fore. MPs such as Eric Heffer and Neil Kinnock were to declare that the problems of the Scottish working class and the problems of the Welsh working class were similar to those of the English working class, and were to be resolved not by devolution, but through the installation of a strong socialist government at Westminster. That argument is less an argument about *sovereignty* than about *power*. On both occasions, in 1886 and in the 1970s, the Left chronically underestimated the force of nationalism, treating it as a surrogate for something else, which it was not.

Gladstone, speaking just before the defeat of Home Rule in the Commons in 1886, asked MPs to 'think, I beseech you, think well, think wisely, think not for the moment, but for the years to come before you reject this Bill.'[82] In rejecting Home Rule, the unionists did not settle the question. They had to face the problem of how Ireland was to be governed in the face of the near-unanimous demand of her representatives, outside Ulster, for Home Rule. It was a problem they were unable to resolve.

The Irish parliamentary leaders were ambiguous, perhaps deliberately so, as to whether they would have accepted Home Rule as a final settlement. 'We cannot, under the British Constitution,' declared Parnell at Cork in 1885, 'ask for more than the restitution of Grattan's Parliament. But no man has the right to fix the boundary to the march of a nation. No man has a right to say to his country, "Thus far shalt thou go and no further", and we have never attempted to fix a *ne plus ultra* to the progress of Ireland's nationhood and we never shall.'[83]

Gladstone sought, through Home Rule, to create a 'Union of Hearts' with Ireland, to reconcile her to the British connection. Home Rule, he told Queen Victoria, was 'a proposal eminently Conservative in the highest sense of the term, as tending to the union of the three countries . . . and to the stability of the Imperial throne and institutions'.[84] It is impossible to tell whether Gladstone would have succeeded in his aim. Even if he had been unsuccessful, however, and Home Rule had proved to be a step on the slippery slope to independence, this would have occurred in a far happier atmosphere than in fact it did. From 1886, right up to the Second World War, Ireland, whether part of the United Kingdom or independent, was to prove a perpetual irritant. 'What fools we were', George V told Ramsay MacDonald in 1930, 'not to have accepted Gladstone's Home Rule Bill. The Empire would not have had the Irish Free State giving us so much trouble and pulling us to pieces.'[85]

The apparent triumph of the Irish nationalists in 1921, however, turned out to be as illusory as that of the unionists in 1886. The 1921 settlement had the effect of entrenching the partition of the island, but the greater the distance between Britain and Ireland, the more difficult it became to resolve the position of the Catholic minority in Northern Ireland, since the Protestant majority feared that the Catholics, by seeking to join with the rest of Ireland, were displaying a lack of loyalty to the United Kingdom. The manifold links between Britain and Ireland and their common interest in finding a stable constitutional settlement in Northern Ireland could not be contained within a formal framework of total separation, which, theoretically at least, made Britain and Ireland as foreign to one another as Poland and Chile. In 1998, the Belfast Agreement provided for the establishment of a British–Irish Council, at which the British and Irish governments, together with the devolved governments in Britain, could meet, agree to delegate functions, and decide also on common policies. In the long road towards the Belfast Agreement, both the British and Irish governments had painfully rediscovered the essential truth of the Gladstonian proposition that neither separation nor partition could yield a solution to the Irish problem. A permanent solution, it became apparent, could be achieved only through a process which both recognized and yet also transcended nationalism, through institutions which expressed not only the separate national identities of the various parts of Britain and Ireland, but also the fundamental unity of these islands.

Northern Ireland

If we believe that the sovereign national state is the best form that national sentiment can take and the almost unavoidable form of human government in the modern world, there is probably no lasting acceptable framework of government for Northern Ireland.

(Bernard Crick)

I

Northern Ireland is the only part of the United Kingdom with practical experience of devolution. For just over fifty years—from 1921, when the Northern Ireland Parliament was opened by George V, to 1972, when it was prorogued by the British government, prior to abolition in 1973—six of the nine counties of Ulster enjoyed Home Rule, the form of government which Ulster had taken the lead in resisting since 1886. Any study of devolution in Britain must, therefore, take account of the experience of Northern Ireland in operating devolved institutions.

There are, however, two interconnected factors which limit the value of Northern Ireland as a case-study of devolution. The first is that her parliament was not established, as devolved legislatures generally are, to meet a nationalist or separatist threat. Indeed, a separate parliament was not sought by the Ulster Unionists at all, but was pressed upon them by the British government as a means of ending British rule in Ireland and so resolving the Irish problem. The Ulster Unionists accepted a parliament, not because they sought separation, but for the opposite reason, to ensure that Northern Ireland remained part of the United Kingdom. The circumstances surrounding the birth of the Northern Ireland Parliament conditioned the whole experience of devolution in the province.

The second factor which makes the experience of Northern Ireland atypical of devolution is the community problem, which is not replicated anywhere else in Britain—the antagonism between the unionist community, primarily Protestant, which seeks to maintain the link with Britain, and the nationalist community, primarily Catholic, which seeks union with the rest of Ireland. An analysis of devolution in Northern Ireland must ask whether Home Rule exacerbated the community problem and whether alternative political arrangements might have helped lessen the antagonism which erupted into open violence in 1968 and led to the suspension of devolution in the province.

The community conflict in Northern Ireland has deep historical roots. There was, from earliest times, a significant Scottish presence in Ireland, the Scots referring to themselves as 'the Britons in Ireland'.[1] But the Reformation was firmly resisted by the vast majority of the Irish population, who retained their Catholic religion. In the early seventeenth century, however, the Protestant presence was massively reinforced by the 'Plantation', the colonization of Ulster with immigrants primarily from Scotland but also from England, whose ascendancy was assured after the Battle of the Boyne in 1690. Since that time, the Protestants have tended to regard the Catholics as both disloyal to the Crown and as a threat to religious freedom. Ulster, moreover, developed along different lines from the rest of Ireland, being more orientated towards industry than agriculture and with a different system of land tenure. Already, by the 1830s, Ulster seemed to be separate from the rest of Ireland, and a Protestant preserve.[2]

The rise of Irish nationalism and the growth of a modern sense of Irish identity from the end of the eighteenth century exacerbated the differences between Protestants and Catholics. For, although a number of the leaders of the Irish nationalist movement—Wolfe Tone and Parnell, for example—were Protestant, nevertheless Irish nationalism came to be identified with the Catholic majority. In 1886, the vast majority of Protestants opposed Home Rule and demanded continuation of the union with Britain, so that the terms Protestant and unionist came to be almost interchangeable. It is indeed this superimposition of a nationalist conflict upon a religious one which largely explains the persistence and depth of the Irish problem. There is an unresolved conflict of national identities within a context of incompatible national claims. As a conquered country, Ireland generated a nationalism which sought independence from Britain. As a 'planted' country, Ireland generated a distinct community which sought to retain the link with Britain.

In 1886, the Protestants were a scattered minority in Ireland as a whole, but a concentrated majority in the north-east. They constituted majorities in four counties of the province of Ulster—Antrim, Armagh, Down, and Londonderry; nearly 50 per cent of the population in two other counties in the province—Fermanagh and Tyrone; and a significant minority in the other three counties—Cavan, Donegal, and Monaghan—which are now part of the Irish Republic. In 1886, Joseph Chamberlain declared that Ireland: 'is not a homogeneous community . . . it consists of two nations . . . it is a nation which comprises two races and two religions.'[3]

There is an inconsistency in this claim, which suggests on the one hand that the Protestants were a separate nation, and on the other that Ireland was one nation, but a divided one. In fact, the Ulster Unionists rejected Home Rule not because they wished to claim an alternative nationhood of their own, but because they wished to remain part of the British nation. It is therefore misleading to regard the conflict in Ireland as one between two nations. For the Ulster Unionists did not see themselves as a separate nation, and saw no reason why their Irishness should conflict with their membership of the United Kingdom. What the Unionists sought was, in the words of Ulster's Solemn League and Covenant of 1912, to preserve 'for ourselves and our children our cherished position of equal citizenship in the United Kingdom'. The fact that Ulster Unionists sought nothing more than 'equal citizenship' made it difficult for Britain to ignore their claims. For they were not seeking, as the Irish nationalists were, privileges denied to others, such as a separate parliament. All they desired was to retain a position which was under threat from those who, so they believed, sought to undermine, if not break completely, the link with Britain. Thus Ulster Unionism was not an assertion of a separate Ulster nationhood, but a reaction against the claim made by Irish nationalists that the assertion of Irish nationhood was separatist in nature. There is therefore no symmetry between Irish nationalism and Ulster unionism. The one is a claim based on nationality, the other a claim based on citizenship.

The partition of Ireland had first been suggested by Macaulay in

response to O'Connell's campaign for repeal of the Union. 'If a rooted difference in religion, and the existence of the worst consequences of that difference would justify the separation of the English
[*sic*] and Irish legislatures, the same difference and still more, the
same baleful consequences, would warrant the separation of
Protestant Ulster from Catholic Munster'.[4] When Gladstone introduced his first Home Rule Bill, however, he made no provision for
special treatment for Ulster, whose Protestant population he saw as
part of a minority in Ireland, rather than as a majority in the north-
east part of the island. It seems, however, from the diary of Lewis
Harcourt, the son of Gladstone's Chancellor of the Exchequer, that
Gladstone might, in fact, have been 'prepared to except Ulster from
the Act as a compromise'.[5] There was, perhaps, no inherent reason
why he might not have considered special arrangements for Ulster.
At that time, however, Ulster made no such claim. Ulster Unionists,
together with their counterparts in the rest of Ireland and in Britain,
were confident that they could defeat Home Rule for the whole of
Ireland. Therefore there was no reason for them to consider exclusion.

By the time of the third Home Rule Bill in 1912, it was becoming
apparent that special consideration would have to be given to Ulster.
In the first reading debate on the 1912 bill, Sir Edward Carson, the
leader of the Irish unionists, claimed that the argument for self-determination used by the Irish nationalists could also be used by the
Ulster Unionists, and that every argument for giving Home Rule to
Ireland, was also an argument for giving Home Rule to the north-
eastern part of Ulster. But the central aim of Irish unionists, in both
north and south, was still to kill Home Rule, rather than to establish
a separate Ulster. For this purpose, the 'Orange card', first used by
Lord Randolph Churchill in 1886, was an indispensable weapon. 'If
Ulster succeeds,' Carson had claimed in 1911, 'Home Rule is dead.'[6]
At that time it was widely believed that an independent Ireland,
which unionists regarded as the inevitable consequence of Home
Rule, would not be viable without the industrial wealth and strength
of Belfast and its environs. This assumption was shared by the vast
majority of Home Rulers, who agreed with the Irish nationalist view
that Ireland was a single political unit. One could no more divide

Ireland, Asquith told the House of Commons in June 1912, than one could divide England or Scotland.7

The Ulster Covenant of 1912 pledged its signatories to use 'all means which may be found necessary to defeat the present conspiracy to set up a Home Rule Parliament in Ireland'. The unionists could not, however, prevent Home Rule in any part of Ireland except the north-east. What they proposed, once Home Rule was passed, was to refuse to accept the authority of a Dublin parliament, and to take over for themselves the responsibility for government in that part of Ireland which they could effectively control. Thus, the Northern unionists 'would vote against Home Rule for Ireland to the end of time, but they would only *fight* for the exclusion of Ulster'.8 In that fight, moreover, they would enjoy considerable support from British public opinion, which could not understand why a loyal part of the kingdom should be extruded from it; and, after the Curragh incident of 1914, it seemed that leading army officers would not be a party to forcing Ulster to accept the jurisdiction of a Home Rule parliament in Dublin. Thus, if the Liberals wished to avoid civil war, special arrangements would have to be made for Ulster. That seemed to mean the exclusion of Ulster from Home Rule, and therefore the partition of Ireland, a position which Ulster Unionists and British Conservatives were willing to accept as a second-best if they could not prevent Home Rule. The original unionist position had been that the whole Irish nation was part of the larger British state. When that position became untenable, unionists retreated to a fall-back position, insisting that Ulster had the right to opt out of the proposed new Irish state.

The partition of Ireland had indeed been discussed in Cabinet in February 1912 before the third Home Rule Bill was introduced into the Commons. It was advocated by Lloyd George and Churchill, but the government decided to wait upon events. Partition was first proposed in Parliament by T. Agar-Robartes, a Liberal back-bencher, in an amendment to the third Home Rule Bill in 1912. Arguing that 'I have never heard that orange bitters will mix with Irish whisky',9 Agar-Robartes proposed the exclusion of the four counties with Protestant majorities. His amendment was defeated by sixty-one votes, but two Cabinet ministers, Lloyd George and Churchill, absented themselves on the vote. That was not the end of proposals for partition, however. In January 1913, Carson proposed a 'clean cut' exclusion of the nine Ulster counties, and in March 1914, Asquith, as Prime Minister, proposed an amending bill according to which, on a basis of county option, any county could opt out of Home Rule for six years. Carson, however, rejected what he called 'sentence of death with a stay of execution for six years',[10] and the bill was amended by the Lords to nine-county exclusion on a permanent basis. This in turn was unacceptable to the Liberals and Irish nationalists. At the Buckingham Palace Conference, held in July 1914, the exclusion of six counties was suggested for the first time, but the Conference ended in deadlock, and the issue remained unresolved when Britain declared war on Germany in August 1914.

The third Home Rule Bill finally received the Royal Assent in September 1914, some six weeks after the outbreak of war. It was, however, put on the statute book together with a Suspensory Act providing that it would not come into effect until the end of the war; and Asquith promised that it would not be allowed to come into force until special provision had been made for Ulster. The size of the area to be excluded remained, however, to be settled, as did the question of whether exclusion was to be temporary or permanent.

In 1916, Lloyd George proposed to Irish nationalists and unionists that a six-county area be excluded. Both nationalists and unionists accepted this but could not agree on whether exclusion should be temporary or permanent. Six-county exclusion was also proposed at the ill-fated Irish Convention of 1918. The presumption was, however, that the excluded area would continue to be governed directly from Westminster, rather than be provided with a parliament of its own.

By 1918, Lloyd George faced a 'situation in regard to Ireland' which was 'governed by two fundamental facts: the first that the Home Rule Act of 1914 is upon the statute book; the second that in accordance with the pledge which has been given by me in the past, and indeed by all Party leaders, I can support no settlement which would involve the forcible coercion of Ulster.'[11] Home Rule for Ireland combined with exclusion seemed the only policy that was compatible with these 'two fundamental facts'.

Partition, however, did not necessarily imply that the excluded area should have its own parliament. The unionists, indeed, did not seek a parliament of their own. Their main aim had been, as we have seen, to resist Home Rule for the whole of Ireland. Failing that, they demanded the exclusion of the Protestant areas from the jurisdiction of the Home Rule parliament. The excluded areas should, they believed, be ruled from Westminster, just as the rest of Britain was ruled from Westminster. Consequently, proposals for exclusion from 1912 onwards had provided, not for a Northern Ireland Parliament, but for direct rule from Westminster.

In 1919, Sir Edward Carson told the House of Commons that:

Ulster has never asked for a separate Parliament. Ulster's claim has always been of this simple character: 'We have thrived under the Union; we are in sympathy with you, we are part of yourselves. We are prepared to make any sacrifice that you make, and are prepared to bear any burden that is equally put upon us with the other parts of the United Kingdom. In these circumstances keep us with you.' They have never made any other demand than that, and ... I appeal to the Government ... to keep Ulster in this united Parliament. I cannot understand why we should ask them to take a Parliament which they have never demanded, and which they do not want.[12]

The Ulster Unionist Council, when presented with the proposal in the Government of Ircland Bill for a parliament for Northern Ireland, rejected it. In March 1920, it passed a resolution declaring that:

Inasmuch as the new Bill is based on the principle of Home Rule and would deprive us of our equal citizenship in the Parliament of the United Kingdom, this Council cannot recommend the Parliamentary representatives of Ulster to accept any responsibility for it.[13]

When, however, in 1919–20, a Cabinet committee came to draw up proposals for exclusion, it decided to require Northern Ireland to accept a parliament. Its reason for doing so was that:

the policy of exclusion is open to one general objection of the most serious kind. It involves the retention of British rule in some part of Ireland. There is good reason to doubt whether it would ever be possible to convince Irishmen themselves or Dominion or American opinion that Great Britain was sincere in its policy of Home Rule unless it withdrew its control from the domestic affairs of Ireland altogether. British rule in the domestic affairs of Ireland has been the root of the Home Rule movement from start to finish. If it is retained anywhere in Ireland the opponents of Great Britain will be able to say either that Great Britain is ruling nationalist majorities against her will, or that it is giving active support to Ulster in its refusal to unite with the rest of Ireland.

A separate parliament for Northern Ireland, however, 'gets rid of the taproot of the Irish difficulty by providing for the complete withdrawal of British rule from the whole island. It thus meets the fundamental demand of the overwhelming majority of Irishmen ever since the days of O'Connell'. Moreover, it would 'enormously minimise the partition issue. The division of Ireland becomes a far less serious matter if Home Rule is established for both parts of Ireland than if the excluded part is retained as part of Great Britain. No nationalists would then be retained under British rule'.[14]

Partition was intended to be temporary. In November 1921, Lloyd George wrote to Sir James Craig, the first Prime Minister of Northern Ireland, that dominion status for the North was impossible since it:

would stereotype a frontier based neither upon natural features nor broad geographical considerations by giving it the character of an international boundary. Partition on these lines the majority of the Irish people will never accept, nor could we conscientiously attempt to enforce it. It would be fatal to that purpose of a lasting settlement on which these negotiations from the very outset have been steadily directed.[15]

The 1920 Act provided for machinery to terminate partition, in the form of a Council of Ireland, to be composed of an equal number of representatives from each of the two parliaments in Ireland. This Council was to have power 'by mutual agreement and joint action to terminate partition and to set up one Parliament and one Government for the whole of Ireland'. The unification of Ireland could thus in theory be achieved by mutual agreement, without further reference to Westminster. In the words of Walter Long, chairman of the Cabinet Committee which drew up the Government of Ireland Bill, the bill would provide for:

one Parliament for the three Southern provinces and a second parliament for Ulster, together with a Council of Ireland composed of members of the two

Irish Parliaments to discharge certain immediate functions, but mainly to promote as rapidly as possibly and *without further reference to the Imperial Parliament* the Union of the whole of Ireland under a single legislature'.[16]

Establishing a parliament in Northern Ireland was thus defended on the ground that it would make the eventual unification of Ireland easier to attain. Macpherson, the Chief Secretary for Ireland, told the Commons during the second reading of the Government of Ireland Bill: 'The division of Ireland, I need hardly tell the House, is distasteful to the Government, just as it is distasteful to all Irishmen . . . All of us are aware that the division may be temporary only.'[17]

The conclusion of a Cabinet meeting on 10 December 1919 at which the bill was discussed was the strikingly Gladstonian one that 'a united Ireland with a separate Parliament of its own, bound by the closest ties with Great Britain' was 'the ultimate aim'.[18] Lloyd George himself 'developed the parallel of S. E. Wales which when he began his public life was out of sympathy with Welsh aspirations but which had been won over largely by a policy of persuasion and Cardiff today was the home of several of the chief national institutions.' Moreover, every dominion except New Zealand had begun with partition. In particular, Natal had, in 1910, taken up Ulster's attitude and refused to join the Union of South Africa, but had come in at the last moment.[19]

The fallacy behind this viewpoint was well exposed by the Foreign Secretary, Arthur Balfour:

The doctrine assumed throughout the Committee's Report, and more than once explicitly proclaimed, is that Ireland, *all* Ireland, has a separate national existence, and should naturally and properly be organised as a single undivided unit. The Committee admits, of course, that, so long as Ulster remains the Ulster we know, such an ideal cannot be realised. Hence their very artificial scheme of two Home Rule Parliaments and an Irish Council. But they regard this division of Ireland as a misfortune; and evidently think it rather perverse of Ulster to throw obstacles in the way of complete unification. In their recommendations they carry this view to such length that while, on the one hand, they make it as easy as possible for Ulster to join itself with the rest of Ireland . . . on the other hand they give it no power whatever to remain what it is, and as I think, it ought to be,—an integral part of the United Kingdom. This they call . . . 'respecting the principle of self-determination . . . [20]

In practice, the parity between Northern and Southern Ireland in the Council of Ireland gave the North a veto on Irish unity. Yet, even if Ireland remained divided, the British government would still have washed its hands of the Irish problem. British politics would henceforth, it was hoped, be free of Irish quarrels. Violence and conflict on the island of Ireland would have to be resolved by those who lived there. This perhaps cynical prognostication turned out to be true for nearly fifty years, until in 1969, the civil rights movement and the eruption of sectarian conflict in Northern Ireland forced the incursion of British troops into the province.

Thus the fourth Home Rule Bill, which became the Government of Ireland Act of 1920, proposed that two Home Rule parliaments be established in Ireland, one in Dublin and one in Belfast. This Act, which institutionalized partition in Ireland, was passed without any representatives of the majority in Ireland being present. For Sinn Féin, which won seventy-two of the 103 Irish seats in the general election of 1918, had refused to take its seats at Westminster. It is difficult to believe that the outcome would have been as adverse to Irish nationalist interests if the Sinn Féin MPs had not boycotted Parliament.

The absence of Sinn Féin, however, and the decision to establish a parliament in Northern Ireland, gave the unionists a crucial veto on the size of the excluded area. The British government, until shortly before the Government of Ireland Bill was introduced, favoured nine-county exclusion. In the nine counties, the Protestants, enjoying only a narrow majority overall, would, it was thought, be more likely to treat the Catholics fairly; and, moreover, with a small change in the demographic balance between Protestants and Catholics, the excluded area could be expected to vote to join the Dublin Parliament. But, precisely because of the narrow demographic balance, the Ulster Unionists had come to be suspicious of this proposal. Captain Charles Craig, an Ulster Unionist MP and brother of the first Northern Ireland Prime Minister, Sir James Craig, told the House of Commons in March 1920 that the counties of Cavan, Donegal, and Monaghan contained 70,000 unionists and 260,000 'Sinn Féiners and Nationalists', and would thus reduce 'our majority to such a level that no sane man would undertake to carry on a Parliament with it'.[21] The Ulster

Unionists were determined to be responsible only for an area which they could firmly control, and they therefore insisted on six-county exclusion. The decision to establish a parliament for the six counties was therefore not based on any considered view of good government in Ireland, but was rather the by-product of an attempt by the British government to extricate itself completely from Irish affairs.

The Lloyd George government made three crucial decisions in the years 1919–20: that Ireland was to be partitioned, that the excluded area was to comprise six counties rather than nine, and that the excluded area should have its own parliament. The second and third decisions were dependent upon each other, but they were by no means necessary consequences of the first, which was perhaps inevitable. Partition, it may be argued, was in accordance with the realities of Ulster Unionist opposition to Home Rule, and flowed from the principle of self-determination. But the application of this principle was made subject to two important qualifications. The first was that self-determination would be applied to the six counties as a single unit, and not on a county basis, which would have meant that Fermanagh and Tyrone, with their small Catholic majorities, would have joined the Irish Free State. 'In order to persuade Ulster to come in,' Lloyd George told Sinn Féin, 'there is an advantage in her having a Catholic population.'[22] With Irish unity as the aim, as Lloyd George put it to his Cabinet on 10 November 1921, the 'position of Tyrone and Fermanagh [is] not so important'.[23] The border so created had little logic, for it partitioned Ulster as well as Northern Ireland. It might well not have been chosen had the Lloyd George government believed that it would be permanent.

The second qualification was that the excluded area was not allowed to decide that it did not want a parliament of its own, but would continue to be ruled directly from Westminster. The Ulster Unionists were thus granted the right to self-determination, but, as Balfour had pointed out, not the right to remain an integral part of the United Kingdom, with direct rule from Westminster. The decision to partition Ireland on the basis of six counties and the decision to give the six counties a parliament were, however, in no way a necessary consequence of the decision to partition Ireland. The three decisions together did much to determine the unhappy future of the excluded area.

The Government of Ireland Act was intended to apply to the whole of Ireland. It came into effect, however, only in one part of Ireland, the North. Elsewhere, Sinn Féin demanded not Home Rule, but independence, which was in effect secured by the Anglo-Irish Treaty of 1921. Ireland was to become a self-governing dominion within the British Empire, to be called the Irish Free State. Northern Ireland, however, comprising the six counties, was given the option of seceding from the Free State, and retaining her own Home Rule legislature subordinate to Westminster, an option which she immediately took. The Council of Ireland never came into operation, and its powers in relation to Northern Ireland were transferred to the government of Northern Ireland in 1925. Home Rule for Northern Ireland remained as the relic of a failed attempt to resolve the Irish problem.

The rejection of Home Rule by Ireland outside the six counties was, by 1920, predictable. The long title of the 1920 Government of Ireland Act stated, ironically, that it was an Act 'for the better government of Ireland'; yet, as Asquith wrote in his memoirs, Northern Ireland was to be given a parliament it did not want, and which, arguably, would not provide better government for the province, while the rest of Ireland was to be given a parliament it would not accept.[24] The Act was, it has been said, an Act to govern Ireland with the dissent of the governed. Lord Robert Cecil told the House of Commons in 1920:

we shall have this astounding position, that the only form of Home Rule which will exist in Ireland will be that which exists in Ulster. . . . Home Rule is to be established effectively only in that part of Ireland which hates and loathes the whole idea of Home Rule and where they are only accepting this, as I understand it, through fear of having something worse . . . No one wants Home Rule there, and there is no reason for it.[25]

Carson's case against creating a separate Northern Ireland Parliament had been prescient. He feared that it would isolate Northern Ireland from the mainstream of British politics, and that it would identify unionism, which, for him, meant equal citizenship in the United Kingdom, with sectarianism and Protestant supremacism. He declared in the Commons:

We have never asked to govern any Catholic . . . We are perfectly satisfied that all of them, Protestant and Catholic, should be governed from this Parliament, and we have always said that it was the fact that this Parliament [i.e. Westminster] was aloof entirely from these racial distinctions and religious distinctions which was the strongest foundation for the government of Ulster. Therefore, not only have we never asked to get an opportunity of dealing in a hostile way with the minority, but we have sought from beginning to end of this controversy to be left alone, and to go on hand in hand with Great Britain as one nation with Great Britain.

. . . She [Ulster] has always made the simple appeal to you to leave her alone and to treat her as you treat your own people and she would be perfectly satisfied. And I am bound to say that this breaking up and the giving to Ulster a Parliament may lead to many unforeseen consequences. . . .

. . . Therefore I say try to look ahead, and looking ahead, I believe the policy which we have urged from the beginning of retaining Ulster as she is now as part of the United Kingdom, and treating the people of Ulster exactly as you treat the people of Great Britain, is the truest and surest policy for His Majesty's Government to pursue.[26]

Northern Ireland, in the words of her first Prime Minister, Sir James Craig, accepted 'as a *final settlement* and supreme sacrifice in the interests of peace' a separate parliament, 'although not asked for by her representatives'(my emphasis).[27] Once, however, the Northern Ireland Parliament had been established, the Ulster Unionists began to appreciate its advantages. In 1936, the Ulster Unionist Council declared that:

Had we refused to accept a Parliament for Northern Ireland and remained at Westminster there can be little doubt but that now we would be either inside the Free State or fighting desperately against incorporation. Northern Ireland without a Parliament of her own would be a standing temptation to certain British politicians to make another bid for a final settlement with Irish Republicans.[28]

Northern Ireland returned but a small number of MPs to Westminster. Under direct rule, it would be easy for her to be outvoted and handed over to Dublin against her wishes. During the debates on the 1920 bill, Captain Charles Craig explained what advantages Northern Ireland could expect from a parliament of her own:

we feel that an Ulster without a parliament of her own would not be in nearly as strong a position as one in which a parliament had been set up . . . We
believe that so long as we were without a parliament of our own constant
attacks would be made . . . to draw us into a Dublin parliament . . . We
believe that if either of these parties [Labour or the Liberals] or the two in
combination, were once more in power our chances of remaining a part of
the United Kingdom would be very small indeed.[29]

With a parliament in Northern Ireland, however, it would be difficult
for any Westminster government to hand over Northern Ireland to her
enemies without her consent. This would institutionalize Ulster's
veto and so the Northern Ireland Parliament could prove the means
by which her continued membership of the United Kingdom would
be assured. The parliament would be a bulwark against secession.

After Ireland became a Republic in 1949, the position of Northern
Ireland was formalized in section 1(2) of the Ireland Act of 1949,
which declared that neither Northern Ireland nor any part if it would
cease to be a part of the United Kingdom without the consent of the
Northern Ireland Parliament.

So it was that by accepting a separate parliament, Northern Ireland
ensured that she could determine her own future, even in the face of
a hostile majority at Westminster. So also was vindicated the claim,
first made by Lord Randolph Churchill and Joseph Chamberlain in
1886, that Ireland was not a political unity. By a striking paradox, it
was that part of Ireland which most strenuously resisted Home Rule
that came to accept and indeed to welcome it.

The circumstances attending the birth of Northern Ireland offered
a strong inducement to the success of devolution, since failure might
mean not independence but absorption into the hated Irish Free State.
The Northern Ireland government could not, therefore, use the threat
of nationalism or secession in order to get its own way with London.
The British government, for its part, came to feel a moral obligation
to ensure that citizens of the United Kingdom living in Northern
Ireland enjoyed a similar standard of living to that enjoyed by those
living elsewhere in the country, although, unfortunately, there was no
similar commitment to ensure that standards of civil rights should be
the same as those in different parts of the country. The British government was willing to contribute the financial resources needed to

make devolution succeed. Precisely because the pressures which led to devolution in Northern Ireland were not, as is usually the case, centrifugal, but centripetal, there was a strong incentive, both in Belfast and in Westminster, to minimize conflict and to make devolution work. In other circumstances, devolved administrations would be unlikely to be so passive *vis-à-vis* the centre as Northern Ireland was. Moreover, owing to the centrality of community conflict in the province, Northern Ireland became a one-party state. The Unionists were a permanent majority party, and none of the nationalist or anti-partitionist parties had any hope of displacing them. This was bound to affect the working of devolved government. An administration which faces the continual threat of replacement by a lively opposition acts very differently from one which knows that, whatever it does, it can never be defeated. For these reasons, Northern Ireland can be said to have 'evaded rather than refuted the Unionist thesis that Home Rule is impracticable'. For 'That thesis rested on the natural assumption that a regional legislature would insist on making full use of its powers.'[30]

II

The 1921 Treaty between the British government and the provisional government of Ireland, which led to the setting-up of the Irish Free State, was embodied in legislation in Westminster in the Irish Free State (Agreement) Act of 1922. This Act amended the Act of Union by excluding the twenty-six counties of the Irish Free State from its jurisdiction. When Northern Ireland exercised her right not to join the Free State, she retained her position under the Act of Union of 1800. Northern Ireland's status as part of the United Kingdom derived from the creation of the United Kingdom in 1801, but it was the 1920 Government of Ireland Act which became the Constitution of Northern Ireland.

The Act laid down the division of legislative and financial powers between Westminster and Belfast and provided for machinery by which Belfast could be prevented from acting in breach of the Constitution. Section 1 of the Act set up a parliament which reproduced, so far as was possible, Westminster in Belfast, and consisted of the king—represented until 1922 by the Lord Lieutenant, and after that by the Governor—and two legislative chambers. Section 4 of the Act conferred on the parliament a general grant of legislative power to make laws for the 'peace, order and good government' of the inhabitants of Northern Ireland. This general grant of power was, however, made subject to certain specific limitations. Section 4(1), paragraphs 1–14, enumerated excepted matters on which it was necessary to secure uniformity throughout the United Kingdom. Responsibility for these excepted matters would remain with Westminster; they included the Crown, the Navy, Army, and Air Force, relations with foreign countries, and external trade. Because she enjoyed, unlike any other part of the United Kingdom, a separate parliament, it was provided that Northern Ireland be under-represented in proportion to population, and she was allocated just thirteen seats (reduced to twelve after the university seat at Queen's, Belfast, was abolished in 1948) instead of the seventeen to which she was entitled on a population basis. These MPs tended to see themselves as representatives of the Northern Ireland Parliament, however, rather than of their constituencies; and on the whole the ablest unionists in Northern Ireland tended to gravitate to the Northern Ireland Parliament, where they could expect to obtain ministerial office, rather than Westminster. All this had the effect of increasing the isolation of Northern Ireland from the rest of the United Kingdom.

Because the number of MPs returned from Northern Ireland was so small, devolution did not in practice raise the problems of representation with which Gladstone had grappled. It was perhaps fortunate that, during the period from 1921 to 1972, there was no occasion on which a Conservative government was elected to power in London with a majority of less than thirteen. In May 1965, however, Harold Wilson found himself leading a Labour government with a majority of only two. In a debate on steel nationalization, he warned the MPs from Northern Ireland, all of whom sat on the Conservative benches:

I am sure the House will agree that there is an apparent lack of logic, for example, about steel, when Northern Ireland members can, and presumably will, swell the Tory ranks tonight, when we have no power to vote on questions about steel in Northern Ireland because of the fact that the Stormont Parliament has concurrent jurisdiction in these matters.

Wilson asked the House of Commons 'to look at the question of why he [the leader of the Conservative Party] gets the support of his honourable Friends beside him—for example, on matters affecting housing discrimination in London—when we English, Scottish and Welsh Members cannot express our views about housing conditions in Belfast.'

I would hope that Northern Ireland Members, who are here, and who are welcomed here, for the duties they have to perform on behalf of the United Kingdom in many matters affecting Northern Ireland, would consider their position in matters where we have no equivalent right in Northern Ireland . . . It is certainly the case that Northern Ireland Members have great duties to perform here in the sense of foreign affairs, defence, and matters affecting Northern Ireland, involving taxation and expenditure. What was not envisaged, I am sure, in 1920 was that those who came here, with that responsibility for representing Northern Ireland interests, should just become hacks supporting the English Tory Party.[31]

Section 5(1) of the Act, like the First Amendment in the United States, sought to entrench religious freedom by prohibiting laws interfering with religious equality; while section 8(6) extended this prohibition to the executive acts of government. Sections 21 and 22 reserved to Westminster the power to levy certain taxes, including income tax, surtax, customs and excise duties on goods manufactured or produced, business profits tax, and any general taxes on capital. The transferred taxes, to be under the authority of the Northern Ireland Parliament were, by contrast, of minor significance, the most important of them being the motor vehicle licence tax. Section 25 of the Act gave the Northern Ireland Parliament the power to grant Northern Ireland taxpayers a rebate on income tax or surtax; but, for reasons that will be explained, this power was never used.

The Act also provided for machinery by which the validity of Northern Ireland legislation could be tested and the supremacy of Westminster enforced. Sections 49 and 50 allowed for appeal to the Northern Irish courts, with a right of ultimate appeal to the House of Lords, while section 51 provided for a reference to the Judicial

Committee of the Privy Council on constitutional matters. These sections provided for statutes of the Northern Ireland Parliament being declared *ultra vires* by the courts, a conception which was regarded by one authority as 'novel in our constitutional law',[32] since it allowed the courts to declare Acts of Parliament, albeit acts of a subordinate parliament, invalid.

Section 12 of the Government of Ireland Act required the Lord Lieutenant, and later the Governor, to withhold assent to legislation of the Northern Ireland Parliament when so instructed by the king, acting of course on the advice of his United Kingdom government. Section 6 prevented the Northern Ireland Parliament from amending or altering the Act; and finally section 75 of the Act, with great emphasis, reiterated that the parliament of Northern Ireland was subordinate, through the declaration that:

Notwithstanding the establishment of the Parliament of Northern Ireland . . . or anything contained in this Act, the supreme authority of the Parliament of the United Kingdom shall remain unaffected and undiminished over all persons, matters and things in Northern Ireland and every part thereof.

Because Westminster remained supreme, it retained the right to legislate for Northern Ireland even within the transferred sphere, if it so wished. The constitution was thus a rigid one from the point of view of Northern Ireland, imposing seemingly powerful constraints upon the Northern Ireland Parliament, but a flexible one from the point of view of Westminster.

Precisely because sections 6 (providing that in cases of conflict between Northern Ireland and Westminster, Westminster would prevail), 12, and 75 preserved Westminster's supremacy, Northern Ireland lay in a subordinate, rather than in a federal, relationship with Westminster. In practice, however, Northern Ireland came to enjoy a degree of autonomy more appropriate to that of a provincial unit in a federal system. This was so for two reasons.

The first was that, by convention, Westminster did not attempt to legislate on matters for which responsibility had been transferred. Sir Ivor Jennings, indeed, argued in successive editions of his book *The Law and the Constitution*, that it would have been 'unconstitutional' so to legislate.[33] Moreover, in 1923, the Speaker of the House of

Commons ruled that parliamentary questions could not be asked on matters for which responsibility had been transferred to Northern Ireland, since no British minister could be held responsible for transferred matters. The Speaker's ruling was as follows:

the fact that Northern Ireland sends Members to this House does not affect this question. With regard to those subjects which have been delegated to the Government of Northern Ireland, questions must be asked of Ministers in Northern Ireland, and not in this House.[34]

This ruling had the effect of stultifying discussions of alleged injustices in Northern Ireland. In 1965, when a back-bench MP sought to raise the issue of the property-vote in local government elections in Northern Ireland, the Deputy Speaker ruled him out of order, saying, 'We are now going into the details of local government in Northern Ireland, which is a matter for Northern Ireland ... he must show what the House of Commons can do about it and what some responsible Minister can do about it.'[35]

In July 1964, Henry Brooke, the Home Secretary, went so far as to suggest that alleged religious discrimination in Northern Ireland could not be debated at Westminster, since 'the reserve powers in the Government of Ireland Act do not enable the United Kingdom Government to intervene in matters which under Section 4 are the *sole* responsibility of the Northern Ireland Parliament and Government'(my emphasis).[36] This was a curious argument since, the Northern Ireland Parliament being a subordinate body, there were, as emphasized by section 75, *no* issues that were the *sole* responsibility of the Northern Ireland Parliament or government. In 1965, however, the Deputy Speaker seemed to endorse Brooke's argument, by claiming that it was out of order for the Commons to discuss religious discrimination in Northern Ireland: 'discrimination in housing in Northern Ireland is not a matter for the United Kingdom Government; it is a matter for the Northern Ireland Government ... Any question of religious discrimination in Northern Ireland is not a matter for the United Kingdom Government ... Boundaries for local government and Parliament in Ireland are matters for Stormont'.[37] One result of this, according to an MP who became chairman of the Campaign for Democracy in Ulster, was that it proved impossible 'to

penetrate the blank wall of incomprehension and ignorance about
Ulster. Members who knew about Saigon or Salisbury seemed to
know nothing of Stormont.'[38] It was not until 1967 that Roy Jenkins,
as Home Secretary, put forward a new doctrine that, while 'successive Governments had refused to take steps which would inevitably
cut away the authority of the Northern Ireland Government', nevertheless the British government had to work towards 'common standards of political tolerance and non-discrimination on both sides of
the Irish Sea'.[39]

The second reason why Westminster's supremacy proved to be
more theoretical than real was that the constitutional safeguards
embodied in sections 5(1), 8(6), and 12 proved ineffective. Neither
section 5 nor section 8 was ever invoked to deal with allegations of
discrimination against the Catholic minority.[40] Section 51 appeared
to give the Judicial Committee of the Privy Council power to rule on
whether the executive, as well as the legislative, acts of the Northern
Ireland government were within its lawful authority, but it was used
only once. The failure to use the courts was in part due to a feeling
on the part of the Catholic minority that the courts were a part of the
unionist establishment, and would not deliver a verdict hostile to the
instincts of that establishment. It was alleged in 1973 that of the
twenty High Court judges appointed in Northern Ireland since the
Northern Ireland courts were established, fifteen 'have been openly
associated with the Unionist Party', while in the late 1960s, two out
of five County Court judges were former Unionist MPs, and another
was the son of a Unionist MP.[41] Moreover, the property qualification
for jurors seemed biased against the Catholic community. It is a chas-
tening reminder of the ineffectiveness of what has been called 'an
embryonic form of a legally enforceable Bill of Rights', that the only
area of the United Kingdom where there were constitutionally
entrenched safeguards against religious discrimination was also the
only area in which discrimination was prevalent and unchecked.

Section 12 was invoked just once, by the Lord Lieutenant in 1922,
when the Northern Ireland government proposed to abolish proportional representation in local government elections, which had been
prescribed for all local authorities in Ireland by a Westminster Act of
1919 so as to ensure fair representation for minorities. Proportional

representation in local government had yielded nationalist majorities in the counties of Fermanagh and Tyrone. These county councils, together with other nationalist-controlled local authorities, had proceeded to vote to join the Irish Free State. [42] The bill to abolish proportional representation in local elections lay within the competence of the Northern Ireland Parliament, but assent was, nevertheless, withheld for two months at the request of the British government. The Prime Minister of the provisional government of the Irish Free State, W. T. Cosgrave, told the British government that the bill was a breach of the spirit of the Anglo-Irish Treaty of 1921; and the British government did not dissent from this view. Sir James Craig, however, the Prime Minister of Northern Ireland, argued that 'The Bill was clearly within the powers of the Northern Parliament, and either they must make some patched-up arrangement or his Government must resign.'[43] Faced with this threat, the British government was forced to give way, and Winston Churchill, the Colonial Secretary, wrote to Cosgrave, 'I have come, though most unwillingly, to the conclusion that the Local Government (N.I.) Bill could not be vetoed . . . I have never concealed from Sir James Craig my opinion that the measure was inopportune.'[44] The British government considered reserving legislation on only one other occasion, in 1925, when the Governor was worried lest a provision in the Education Act (Northern Ireland) concerning religious instruction in state schools violated section 5 of the 1920 Act. He wrote to the Home Secretary proposing to reserve the legislation. The Home Secretary replied that, but for the impending dissolution of the Northern Ireland Parliament, he would have advised the king to instruct the Governor to reserve the bill so as to consider its constitutionality. [45]

On no occasion until 1969 did Westminster legislate for Northern Ireland within the sphere of transferred matters against the wishes of the Northern Ireland government. Westminster did, however, apparently threaten to intervene on a number of occasions. One example occurred in 1965 when the Northern Ireland Parliament seemed unwilling to introduce capital gains and corporation taxes, which had been introduced in the rest of the United Kingdom through the budget, into the province. On this occasion the Northern Ireland Minister of Finance advised the Northern Ireland House of Commons: 'we must pass this measure in this Parliament, or have it forced upon us at Westminster.'[46]

Nevertheless, the broad picture, after the failed attempt to reserve legislation in 1922, was one of non-interference.

Reintroduction of the first-past-the-post system in local government was followed by the rearrangement of local government boundaries in the interests of the unionists. The consequence was that despite Catholic majorities in Fermanagh, Tyrone, and Londonderry city, their local councils came to enjoy unionist majorities. In 1969, the Cameron Commission was appointed by the government of Northern Ireland to analyse the causes of the disorders that had arisen in the province. It concluded that amongst the causes were:

(1) a rising sense of continuing injustice and grievance among large sections of the Catholic population in Northern Ireland, in particular in Londonderry and Dungannon, in respect of . . . unfair methods of allocation of houses . . . misuse in certain cases of discretionary powers of allocation of houses in order to perpetuate Unionist control of the local authority . . .
(2) Complaints, now well documented in fact, of discrimination in the making of local government appointments, at all levels but especially in senior posts, to the prejudice of non-Unionists and especially Catholic members of the community, in some Unionist controlled authorities . . .
(3) Complaints, again well documented, in some cases of deliberate manipulation of local government electoral boundaries and in others a refusal to apply for their necessary extension, in order to achieve and maintain Unionist control of local authorities and so to deny to Catholics influence in local government proportionate to their numbers.[47]

These evils were made possible by devolution and by Westminster's failure to scrutinize what was happening in the province. Under direct rule, by contrast, Westminster would have had clear and unequivocal responsibility for the electoral system for local government. Even if Westminster had decided to restore the first-past-the-post system for local government elections, it would have been more likely to have ensured that ward boundaries were drawn fairly and the rights of minorities respected.

The failure of the British government to overrule Craig on the abolition of proportional representation in local government elections doubtless encouraged him, in 1929, to abolish proportional representation for elections to the Northern Ireland Parliament itself, something which had been provided for in the 1920 Government of Ireland Act. The Northern Ireland Labour Party sent a delegation of MPs in 1928 to protest to the British government at this proposed measure. The Home Secretary, Joynson-Hicks, reported the protest to Sir James Craig:

I told them, of course, that this was a matter for the Ulster Parliament, and not for myself, but that I should feel in duty bound to tell you of the Deputation. I don't know whether you would care at any time to discuss the matter with me; of course I am always at your disposal. But beyond that I 'know my place' and don't propose to interfere.[48]

Craig's aim in abolishing proportional representation was not the crude one of increasing unionist representation at the expense of the nationalists. Indeed, first past the post did not greatly increase the number of unionists nor decrease the total number of anti-partitionists in the Northern Ireland House of Commons. Craig sought, rather, to prevent any fragmentation of the unionists which would, he believed, weaken Northern Ireland's leverage *vis-à-vis* Westminster. It was, moreover, in Craig's interests that the main opponent of the unionists should be the nationalists, rather than a non-sectarian Labour Party, campaigning on economic and social issues. For Craig and the unionists, proportional representation, by fragmenting unionist strength, had proved a distraction from the constitutional issue. There was, in Craig's view, room for only two parties in Northern Ireland, a unionist party and a Republican party, and the unionists would of course always constitute the majority. His aim, he told the Northern Ireland House of Commons in 1927, was 'to get in this House, and what I believe we will get very much better in this House under the old-fashioned plain and simple system, . . . men who are for the Union on the one hand or who are against it and want to go into a Dublin Parliament on the other.'[49]

The abolition of proportional representation for elections to Stormont consolidated unionist strength, leading to the disappearance of Independent unionist members, and it also strengthened various anti-partitionist parties at the expense of the Northern Ireland Labour

Party, which might have succeeded in polarizing Northern Irish politics around issues of social and economic policy rather than the border. It served to reinforce the siege mentality of the unionists, of which it was itself an expression.

Under proportional representation, the Catholic minority had secured representation in every part of the province. With the introduction of first past the post, however, election results came to be a foregone conclusion, depending as they did upon the sectarian composition of the constituency, and there was a considerable increase in the number of uncontested seats, from none in the Northern Ireland Parliament elections of 1923, to eight in 1925, twenty-two in 1929 and an average of twenty in the post-war years. The abolition of proportional representation led, therefore, to 'the stagnation of political life in Northern Ireland'.[50] It put an end also to a brief period of hope in the politics of the province, which had occurred in the aftermath of the 1925 election, when the leader of the nationalist minority in Northern Ireland, Joe Devlin, took his seat in the Parliament and declared that he and his party were willing to act as a constructive opposition and work its institutions. In the debate on the address in 1926, Devlin went so far as to declare that:

We are all Ulstermen and proud to be Ulstermen. [*Hon. Members*: Hear, Hear]. We want to further the welfare of our Province. We are all Irishmen and want to see North and South working harmoniously together. The causes that divided them have largely disappeared. We rejoice at that, because we do not believe that unity can ever spring out of conflict.

This interlude of 'voluntary consociationalism' was, however, ended by the abolition of proportional representation in 1929, which was interpreted by the minority as a symbol of unionist triumphalism.[51] It was an action which 'revealed a complete lack of sympathy with the minority outlook. At the worst, it was a party manoeuvre; at the best a psychological mistake.'[52] It meant that every issue would be forced into the mould of the community conflict. As Joe Devlin told the Northern Ireland House of Commons in October 1927 in the debate on the abolition of proportional representation:

when there are too many workers out of employment and you come along to this House and say 'What are you doing for the unemployed', the reply will be 'We are doing what we can for the unemployed, but if you listen to this man it may be that the Pope will be again supreme in Ulster.'[53]

It is just possible that the retention of proportional representation could have prevented the congealing of Northern Ireland politics into a sectarian mode and assisted in the formation of a more inclusive state in which the Catholic minority would have gained legitimacy. In 1934, Devlin told the House of Commons of Northern Ireland:

You had opponents willing to serve. We did not seek office. We sought service. We were willing to help. But you rejected all friendly offers ... You went on the old political lines, fostering hatreds, keeping one third of the population as if they were pariahs in the community.[54]

Further alienation of the Catholic minority occurred with the passage of the Civil Authorities (Special Powers) Act of 1922, which remained in existence until the Northern Ireland Parliament was suspended in 1972. This gave the executive wide powers to frame regulations to provide, *inter alia*, for detention and internment. Admittedly, these powers were little used, once devolved government had been firmly established in the province. Nevertheless, not enough was done to assuage the fears of the minority that special powers were in fact being used to buttress unionist rule, and the Cameron Committee reported that the Act had led to 'widespread resentment among Catholics in particular'.[55]

Westminster, then, proved unwilling to assert its supremacy over Northern Ireland until its problems spilled over into violent protest in 1968. Through the years of devolved government, Westminster devoted on average two hours a year to Northern Ireland.[56] This lack of attention corresponded with ignorance in Great Britain about the province. A commercial survey conducted in 1957 by a Northern Ireland firm in England showed that 45 per cent of the population did not know what Ulster was, while 56 per cent were unaware that it had its own government. Many thought that it was 'part of Eire', of Scotland, or a British colony or independent state.[57] When James Callaghan arrived at the Home Office in 1967, he was offered, in his first full day as Home Secretary, a briefing which included nothing on Northern Ireland.[58] From 1968, however, the British government pressed reforms upon Stormont. Captain O'Neill, Prime Minister of

Northern Ireland between 1963 and 1969, in a radio broadcast in December 1968, warned the people of Northern Ireland that 'Mr Wilson made it absolutely clear to us that if we did not face up to our problems the Westminster Parliament might well decide to act over our heads'.59 In August 1969, the Downing Street Declaration was issued, stating that:

The Northern Ireland Government have reaffirmed their intention to take into the fullest account at all times the views of Her Majesty's Government in the United Kingdom, especially in relation to matters affecting the status of citizens of that part of the United Kingdom and their equal rights and protection under the law.

This was the first time that the Northern Ireland government had acknowledged that it must take account of the views of the British government on matters of civil rights.

Westminster, then, was able to bring its supremacy into play only under pathological conditions when the normal working of devolution had been disrupted by sectarian protest. It did not use its powers before that, in the years between 1921 and 1968, to secure the civil rights of the population of part of the United Kingdom. What James Callaghan called the 'supreme authority to withdraw such power as it had delegated' was a very different thing from the 'unaffected and undiminished supremacy over all persons, matters and things' of section 75 of the Government of Ireland Act. In practice, then, the system of government in Northern Ireland between 1921 and 1968, although not, of course, the legal relationship, may be classified as quasi-federal. For the relationship was much more like that characteristic of a federal state, in which power is divided, rather than devolution, where power is delegated. Indeed, the canons of constitutional interpretation adopted by the courts when dealing with the legislative competence of the parliament of Northern Ireland came to be very similar to those applied in federal systems.

The British government found it difficult to ensure that common standards of civil rights were observed in Northern Ireland. After 1968, the government could threaten action on the basis of section 75, but if that failed, the only weapon left was a threat to repeal the Act or to prorogue Stormont, a step finally taken by the Heath government in 1972.

Thus, the political consequence of the establishment of a separate parliament in Northern Ireland was to sever the six counties from common United Kingdom principles of equity and fairness, and to take away from the Catholic minority in Northern Ireland the redress which they could have expected from Parliament at Westminster.

The constitutional problems faced by Westminster proved very different from what had been expected in 1920. The 1920 Act had been drafted in the expectation that the main problems would arise over the division of legislative powers and the attempt of *Southern* Ireland to circumvent it. Northern Ireland, however, sought not to circumvent the Constitution, but to use it so as to secure unionist supremacy, a supremacy which was in effect a challenge to the supremacy of Westminster. Successive British governments before 1968 proved unwilling to meet that challenge. Indeed, the violent history of Northern Ireland since 1968 is in part a consequence of the failure of British governments to take more effective action in the field of civil rights in the years before 1968.

III

It was paradoxical that Northern Ireland enjoyed a great deal of autonomy in the area of civil liberties and electoral matters, where a common United Kingdom policy would seem to have been justifiable, while enjoying little autonomy in the development of public services—an advantage which devolution is supposed to confer. This failure arose not, however, because the British government intervened in Northern Ireland's affairs, but because Northern Ireland lacked sufficient financial independence to pursue an autonomous policy.

The framers of the 1920 Act aimed to render the two parts of Ireland distinct and self-sufficient fiscal units. They believed that this could be achieved by providing Ireland with her own revenue, and requiring her to use that revenue to pay for transferred services. The taxing power would be divided between reserved and transferred taxes, but Ireland would not be expected to pay for transferred services entirely through transferred taxation.

The British government was determined, however, that Ireland, despite being fiscally distinct and self-sufficient, should not enjoy autonomy at Britain's expense: she would be required to pay an Imperial Contribution. Because, by 1920, the imposition of war taxation had led to a surplus from 1915–16, the Imperial Contribution could be a first charge on the Northern Ireland Exchequer, as Gladstone had intended in his own Home Rule legislation. The size of the Imperial Contribution was to be determined by a Joint Exchequer Board, composed of members drawn equally from the Treasury in London and the Ministry of Finance in Belfast.

The 1920 Act was, however, framed, as we have seen, primarily with Southern Ireland in mind, and the British government sought to retain as many taxes as possible so as to ensure that Southern Ireland could not evade her Imperial Contribution. Transferred taxation, therefore, included only minor taxes, the most important of which were the motor-vehicle licensing tax, entertainment duties, and stamp duties; these were responsible for at most 20 per cent of total taxation in Northern Ireland, and often a much smaller proportion. Thus, raising transferred taxation would yield comparatively little extra revenue, since these taxes produced so small a proportion of Northern Ireland's total revenue. The power to offer income-tax rebates or rebates on surtax was never used. The reason for this was that, since tax relief could not be given at the expense of the Imperial Contribution, the rebates would have meant cuts in public services. Otherwise, major taxes, which included income tax, surtax, customs and excise, and profits tax, remained with Westminster. Thus Northern Ireland would not be able to finance her transferred services entirely from transferred taxation, but would have to rely on a portion of reserved taxation as well. This meant that some estimate would have to be made of the share of total UK taxation which was properly attributable to Northern Ireland as her share of reserved revenue. Northern Ireland was thus to find herself in the anomalous position of being treated as a separate financial region from the point of view of expenditure, in that revenue attributable to Northern Ireland could not be spent in any other part of the United Kingdom, but as a part of the United Kingdom from the point of view of taxation.

From the beginning, however, these arrangements proved unworkable. Northern Ireland found it impossible to finance, from her revenue, a level of services equal to that in the rest of the United Kingdom. In the first financial year of devolution, 1921–2, Northern Ireland was unable to make her accounts balance, and in June 1922, Sir Robert Horne, the British Chancellor of the Exchequer, complained that 'We have already gone far beyond what was contemplated in the Act'.[60] The position worsened with the depression of the 1920s, when revenue fell so far that it reached just one-half of the anticipated level, while expenses proved far greater than foreseen, because of the costs of paying benefit to the large number of unemployed, and of policing the province against the IRA.

If the Imperial Contribution were to remain a first charge upon the revenue of Northern Ireland, the standard of public services there would be very low. Yet the citizens of Northern Ireland were paying the same rate of income tax, surtax, and so on as citizens in the rest of the United Kingdom. Surely they were entitled to the same level of services, especially as they had accepted devolution not because they wanted it, but because it had been pressed upon them by the British government. Had Northern Ireland remained under direct rule, there would have been no doubt that she would have been entitled to the same standard of social services as the rest of the United Kingdom. 'It would be a very sad day for us', Sir James Craig declared, 'if at any time it became known that it is better to live in Norfolk, or Suffolk, or Essex, or in any other county in England, than in the Province of Ulster.'[61] One way of dealing with this problem would have been to increase the share of her revenue which Northern Ireland could finance out of her own resources, by transferring further taxes from Westminster to Northern Ireland. This, however, would have meant that Northern Ireland taxpayers would have to pay higher rates of tax than everyone else in the United Kingdom in order to enjoy a similar standard of service. So, after 'long and irritating controversies', between the Northern Ireland Ministry of Finance and the Treasury, a Northern Ireland Special Arbitration Committee was set up under Lord Colwyn.[62] In its second report in 1925, the Colwyn Committee proposed a drastic modification to the initial financial settlement. It argued that *per capita* spending on services in Northern Ireland ought to increase at the same rate as *per capita* expenditure on services in the rest of the United Kingdom, and the sum required to secure such a rate of increase should constitute Northern Ireland's necessary expenditure. The Imperial Contribution should not be paid until this necessary expenditure had been financed. Thus, the Imperial Contribution would become not a first charge upon Northern Ireland's Exchequer, but a residual. The Colwyn Committee offered to Northern Ireland a guarantee that, if her level of transferred taxation were equal to that in the rest of the United Kingdom, her services would be improved at the same rate as services in the rest of the United Kingdom. A consequence, however, was that Northern Ireland lost much of the limited fiscal autonomy that the Act of 1920 had given her. For, were she to raise the rate of her transferred taxes, she would not be able to secure a level of service beyond her necessary expenditure, but would simply pay the additional amount in the form of a higher Imperial Contribution.

The Colwyn formula did not, however, imply that public services in Northern Ireland would be of the same standard as those in the rest of the UK, since Northern Ireland had a disproportionate number of claimants on her public services. To help meet the cost of payments for unemployment insurance, the Colwyn formula was supplemented by an Unemployment Insurance Agreement in 1926. This Agreement provided that if in any year the payment by the Northern Ireland Exchequer to the Unemployment Fund per head of population exceeded the corresponding payment by the UK government to the fund in Great Britain, then the UK government would meet three-quarters of the difference; and it was the first of a series of agreements through which funds were transferred from the United Kingdom Exchequer to Northern Ireland for specific purposes, thus further subverting the financial arrangements embodied in the 1920 Act.

However, neither the Colwyn formula nor the Unemployment Insurance Agreement resolved the financial problems facing Northern Ireland. By 1931, she was receiving far more under the Unemployment Insurance Agreement than she was paying through the Imperial Contribution, which had dwindled almost to nothing. The prospect arose of the Imperial Contribution becoming a negative amount, i.e. of Northern Ireland being unable to finance even her transferred services to an acceptable level from her revenue. In 1932, therefore, the Colwyn formula was abandoned.

It was becoming clear that Northern Ireland could not hope to finance herself as a self-sufficient revenue unit so as to provide services at a level equivalent to those in the rest of the United Kingdom. This difficulty had not been foreseen in 1920 when the Northern Ireland budget showed a surplus, in a year of limited government and high employment. But 1920 was to prove a highly untypical year. It was becoming obvious by the 1930s that the UK government would have to offer much more help to Northern Ireland.

In 1938, therefore, Sir John Simon, the Chancellor of the Exchequer, laid down the principle of parity, which was to govern future financial relations between the UK and Northern Ireland. This principle provided that, in the event of 'a deficit on the Northern Ireland Budget which was not the result of a standard of social expenditure higher than that of Great Britain nor the result of a standard of taxation lower than that of Great Britain', the UK government would 'make good this deficit in such a way as to ensure that Northern Ireland should be in a financial position to continue to enjoy the same social services and have the same standards as Britain'.[63] This meant, of course, that Northern Ireland's very limited degree of fiscal autonomy was now completely eliminated, since if she lowered taxes, parity would be lost, while if she cut public expenditure, Northern Ireland taxpayers, paying at the same rate as taxpayers in the rest of the United Kingdom, would simply receive worse services.

The parity principle was supplemented in 1942 by another principle, the principle of 'leeway'. Sir Kingsley Wood, the Chancellor of the Exchequer, told the Prime Minister of Northern Ireland in September:

I recognise that in certain spheres Northern Ireland has considerable leeway to make up in order to attain equality of standard with the United Kingdom, and you can confidently rely on the Treasury always considering such a case sympathetically, as indeed the principle of parity requires us to do.[64]

This principle committed the British government to additional expenditure in Northern Ireland to make up the leeway in housing, schools, and hospitals, as well as additional expenditure to offset Northern Ireland's economic disadvantage. In addition, there were further agreements by which the UK government assisted Northern Ireland with the cost of specific services such as, in 1948, national insurance, national assistance, family allowances, pensions, and the health service; in 1966, the regional employment premium; and finally in 1971, supplementary benefits and the new family income supplement.

By this time of course the financial settlement of 1920 had been transformed beyond recognition. The finances of Northern Ireland were now to be determined not by her revenue, but by her needs. The financial arrangements which had begun by being revenue-based, had now become expenditure-based. The sample budget for Northern Ireland for the last year before direct rule, shown in Table 3.1, makes it clear that the Imperial Contribution had become a mere book-keeping item.

The crucial element in the Northern Ireland budget had now become the determination of the size of the funds which were to be transferred to her Exchequer from London. This was, from 1938, to be determined by the parity principle. But what precisely did parity mean? 'It is tempting to conclude', the Royal Commission on the Constitution declared in 1973, 'that "parity" was simply what could be secured by negotiation.'[65]

The central consequence of parity was that the Northern Ireland budget in effect needed to be approved in advance by London. From 1946, the amount to be transferred to Northern Ireland was decided by negotiations between the Northern Ireland Ministry of Finance and the Treasury. London did not, however, give to Northern Ireland a block grant to spend as she pleased. Instead, the principle of parity involved highly detailed scrutiny so as to ensure that it was not being used by Northern Ireland to secure for herself a higher level of service than that to which she was entitled. Moreover, policies with substantial spending implications required Treasury approval.

In theory, disputes about the parity principle could have led to serious conflict between London and Belfast. 'To a large extent,' Terence O'Neill wrote, 'Northern Ireland's income rested on attributions of revenue. How, for instance, does one accurately assess Northern Ireland's fair share of Tobacco Revenue? The answer is that

Table 3.1 Northern Ireland budget, 1971–2

		£m
Revenue		
Share of UK reserved taxes		269
Less: Imperial Contribution	1	
Cost of reserved services in Northern Ireland	4	
		5
Residuary share of reserved taxes		264
Revenue from transferred taxes		45
Total revenue accruing to Northern Ireland under the Government of Ireland Act, 1920		309
Receipts from the United Kingdom Government		
Health Service Agreement	20	
Social Services payments	37	
Remoteness grant payable under the Agriculture Act, 1957	2	
Additional selective employment premiums payable under Finance Act, 1967	11	
		70
Other revenue (mainly interest from local authorities)		39
TOTAL		418

In addition, Northern Ireland received £30m from the United Kingdom Government to pay for agricultural subsidies in Northern Ireland, and £15m for the Northern Ireland National Insurance Fund. The total amount she received from the United Kingdom Govern-ment was therefore £70m—the sum transferred for specific services— + £30m + 15m = £115m, as well as the true value of the Imperial Contribution. Expenditure, in the form of the cost of Northern Ireland services, was £418m.

Source: Report of the Royal Commission on the Constitution, Cmnd. 5460, 1973, para. 1295.

if you put your case well and establish a good rapport you will get a generous attribution.'[66] That more conflict did not occur was not solely because the system was, as the Royal Commission on the

Constitution thought, 'a monument to British pragmatism',[67] but because London and Belfast were predisposed from the start to achieve agreement. That might not have been the case had the Treasury been negotiating with an Irish nationalist administration in Dublin or a Scottish administration in Edinburgh.

Even so, there were serious weaknesses in the financial arrangements from the standpoints of both efficiency and democracy. The authors of the 1920 Act had sought to establish a system which would enable the Northern Ireland Minister of Finance to predict his revenue in advance, so that he could plan a realistic spending programme. Yet, because the transferred taxes were so meagre, he was in practice dependent upon the decisions of the Chancellor of the Exchequer with regard to reserved taxation. This made it difficult for the Northern Ireland Minister of Finance to plan expenditure in advance. 'Our problem', Sir Cecil Bateman, the Permanent Head of the Department of the Prime Minister of Northern Ireland, and of the Northern Ireland Finance Department, told the Royal Commission on the Constitution in 1971, 'is that ... we find it very difficult to plan our expenditure a long time in advance because we are at the mercy of the economic policy of the United Kingdom. The Chancellor may change taxation, which could drastically reduce our revenue.'[68]

The Northern Ireland government was, then, in practice accountable for its financial decisions not to its own electors, but to the Treasury in London. The Northern Ireland budget was decided each year in private negotiations between Belfast and London, negotiations from which the Northern Ireland parliament and people were excluded. In the words of one commentator:

Parliament has effectively ceded power to the executive; the outcome is that neither Parliament exercises sufficient scrutiny over the financial relations between the two governments. Westminster exercises no oversight on the Treasury's role in the negotiations to fix each year's Ulster budget; the Ulster Parliament, faced in recent years with generosity from the Treasury, is glad to take what it can get without stirring up questions of principle.[69]

The result was that 'financial questions of great public interest and importance were shrouded in secrecy ... it is apparently taken for granted that the public have no right to know, except in purely general terms, how Ulster's revenue and permissible expenditure are fixed'. In 1968, when the British Cabinet was approving a subsidy to Short's of Belfast, Richard Crossman asked:

'May I be told what is the exact financial arrangement?' Nobody could say. Neither Jack Diamond [the Chief Secretary of the Treasury] nor the Chancellor knew the formula according to which the Northern Ireland Government gets its money. In all these years it has never been revealed to the politicians and I am longing to see whether now we shall get to the bottom of this very large, expensive secret.[70]

Thus, the financial arrangements between London and Belfast came to violate the canons both of efficiency and of democracy. They violated also a fundamental principle of good government, that the spending power and the taxing power ought, so far as possible, to be in the same hands, for, since spending is generally popular and taxation unpopular, it is only right that government should have to balance expenditure and taxation at the margin. The Northern Ireland government, however, while responsible for around 90 per cent of public expenditure in Northern Ireland, enjoyed transferred revenue which, by 1972, amounted to just 15 per cent of total Northern Ireland revenue. So nine-tenths of Northern Ireland's expenditure was decided in Northern Ireland, while seventeen-twentieths of her revenue came from London. The settlement with Northern Ireland thus came to dissociate the spending power, which remained with Belfast, from the taxing power, which lay primarily in London. Parity had stabilized the financial position of Northern Ireland, but at the cost of drastically undermining her financial autonomy and destroying the connection between expenditure and revenue.

IV

What scope then was left for autonomy in Northern Ireland? Parity did not entirely inhibit the development of different policies, for not all legislation is concerned with finance. On matters of mores, Northern Ireland took her own path, declining to follow the rest of the United

Kingdom in modifying her divorce, abortion, or homosexuality laws in the 1960s. She also declined to abolish capital punishment when Westminster did so in 1965, and decided not to adopt the Industrial Relations Act of 1971.

The Northern Ireland government produced, for the Royal Commission on the Constitution, figures showing the proportion of her legislation and statutory orders determined by the parity requirement. It turned out to be surprisingly small (Table 3.2).

Table 3.2 Proportion of legislation and statutory orders determined by parity requirement

Acts of Parliament	1965	1966	1967	1968	1969
A. Parity legislation	6	13	5	3	9
B. Legislation falling between categories A and C	8	11	15	14	12
C. Legislation peculiar to Northern Ireland	8	17	16	14	15
Technical Acts	3	3	4	3	3
TOTALS	25	44	40	34	39
Statutory Rules and Orders					
A	65	88	92	70	85
B	110	98	109	94	138
C	102	124	143	115	129
Miscellaneous	12	9	5	5	9
TOTALS	289	319	349	284	361

The Northern Ireland government added the comment:

It is estimated that, if legislation is divided into two categories only—parity and non-parity matters—about two-thirds of both administrative and legislative time is spent on purely Northern Ireland matters. This is, however, a rough estimate only and the proportions vary from department to department; in the Ministry of Heath and Social Security, for example, the proportion of time spent on parity matters would be much higher.[71]

This comment draws attention to the fact that devolution made much less sense in health and social security than in other areas of government. The framers of the 1920 Act did not consider how the development of the Welfare State might affect devolution, and where the proportion of time spent on parity matters was very high, as in health and social security, it might have been better if responsibility for the service had been retained in London. Where there was little scope for divergence of policy, devolution seemed not to make much sense. Even in these areas, however, there were some successes. A Tuberculosis Authority was set up which 'worked so vigorously as to undermine its own existence', while in mental health, Northern Ireland's 'post-war legislation leapt at a bound from darkness into light'.[72] In other areas, so it was said, 'The task which faces the Parliamentary Draftsman is to polish the jewel of parity and to put it in an appropriate Northern Ireland setting.'[73]

In agriculture and industrial development, where the problems faced by Northern Ireland were quite different from those experienced in the rest of the United Kingdom, the advantages of devolved government were manifest. The administration of both agriculture and industrial policy underwent an evolution characteristic of that in many federal states in which powers, once divided, come to be shared between the provincial unit and the centre.

Under the 1920 Act, agriculture was a transferred subject, except with regard to exports; yet Northern Ireland could not sustain from her own resources the UK system of agricultural support. The Northern Ireland Ministry of Agriculture acted as an agent for the Ministry of Agriculture, Fisheries and Food in London, so that the agricultural support system could be uniform throughout the United Kingdom. Joint action was taken on agricultural marketing also.

Other aspects of agricultural development, however, remained the responsibility of the Northern Ireland government. This gave Northern Ireland greater freedom of variation and adaptation than Scotland, which had only administrative devolution: where legislation was required, the Northern Ireland government could pass it rapidly, whereas, in the case of Scotland, it could often take two or three years before time could be found in the crowded Westminster timetable. Northern Ireland faced particular problems in agriculture because of the high proportion of her produce which was sent across the Irish Sea. For produce from Northern Ireland to be genuinely competitive, it would need a guarantee of quality. The government of Northern Ireland took early steps to regulate the quality of eggs, by introducing a system of compulsory grading in 1924, and then extending it to other products such as fruit, potatoes, dairy produce, and meat. A system of this kind was not introduced into the rest of the United Kingdom until some years afterwards, and when it was brought in elsewhere, the grading was entirely voluntary. Legislation of this kind, therefore, would probably not have been introduced had there not been a local parliament in Northern Ireland. Giving evidence to the Royal Commission on the Constitution, the Assistant Secretary to the Northern Ireland Ministry of Agriculture was able to speak of the quality-conscious produce of Northern Ireland and to claim that 'we have led the field in this respect'.[74]

In industrial policy also, power came to be shared between London and Belfast. After 1945, London gradually came to assume responsibility for regional policy, seeking, through the use of industrial development certificates, to hold the balance between the depressed regions of the United Kingdom. Moreover, Northern Ireland was bound to be affected by the macro-economic policies followed by the British government.

Northern Ireland, however, remained responsible for industrial development and regional planning, and the record of her government on aid to industry was, on the whole, imaginative. Indeed, the Northern Ireland government can claim to have been a pioneer of regional policy, and many of the measures adopted by Northern Ireland in the immediate post-war years were later to be used in the rest of the United Kingdom by the 1964 Labour government.

Northern Ireland confronted a similar problem to that faced by other depressed areas in the United Kingdom—an outdated industrial structure and heavy regional unemployment. She also faced the extra problem of a cost disadvantage, since her goods had to be transported across the Irish Sea. The government of Northern Ireland established a generous system of capital grants to industry, and pioneered the building of factories for rent or sale. The government also offered grants towards the operating costs of factories situated in areas of particularly high unemployment. To deal with the differential in transport costs, the government provided a cost subsidy on fuels and used the powers to vary road taxes to assist industry by reducing the cost of the licence for heavy vehicles.[75] Northern Ireland opened an industrial development office in the United States two years before the United Kingdom did so.

The government of Northern Ireland also adopted a manpower policy geared to the special requirements of the province, pioneering a manpower survey to identify the particular needs of industry and to develop training facilities in accordance with these needs. The government encouraged the diversification of industry, building upon the particular skills of the labour force. In textiles, for example, the government succeeded in attracting synthetic textile firms to help replace declining textile industries. Its success in this area can be quantified. Between the years 1961 and 1967, the value of the net output of 'miscellaneous textiles'—a category which includes synthetic textiles—increased almost sevenfold from £4m to £27m—and the share of 'miscellaneous textiles' in Northern Ireland's total output of textiles increased from 14 per cent to 47 per cent.[76]

These developments probably owed most to the 'immense intangible advantage of regional government—accessibility of the decision-makers and consequent speed of decision. Red tape tends to be a result of sheer scale.'[77] The Ombudsman for Northern Ireland declared that the standard of administrative performance in Northern Ireland ministries 'compares well with my experience of government departments in the United Kingdom', and that 'The individual citizen frequently gets a better service from a Northern Ireland ministry than he would get from a United Kingdom department in similar circumstances, owing to the easier access to central government that is both feasible and customary in a territory the size of Northern Ireland.'[78]

When the Royal Commission on the Constitution held its hearings in Northern Ireland, the following exchange took place:

Sir Geoffrey Crowther: I have been told that when a member of the public has a grievance or a matter on which he seeks information, his natural and more usual course in Northern Ireland would be to walk into the appropriate Ministry and ask the question himself rather than use the channel of the Parliamentary question: is that so?

Sir Cecil Bateman: Yes, that is correct.[79]

The Royal Commission on the Constitution summed up this advantage of devolution in the following way:

Even the most severe critic of home rule amongst our witnesses . . . considered the devolution of administrative and executive powers to have been an outstanding success. [One witness] argued . . . a dissatisfied farmer anywhere within its boundaries ought to be able (and is able) to travel by public transport to the administrative capital, horse-whip the responsible official and get home again (in time to milk the cow).[80]

The close relationship which the administration was able to build with individual firms was also of great importance in economic policy. In its evidence to the Royal Commission of the Constitution, the Northern Ireland Council of the CBI argued: 'that such steps as have been taken are greater than would have been the case had we depended solely on the activities of a central legislature. The problems of Northern Ireland are pertinent, real and close to an indigenous government, but would be less urgent and pressing if merely those of one of a number of similar areas.' The Council was 'convinced that the existence of the Parliament at Stormont has been, over the years, a major factor in the economic development of the Province'.[81]

Even more striking was the evidence of the Northern Ireland Labour Party, since it was politically opposed to the Unionist administration. The party nevertheless admitted that 'the machinery of regional autonomy, even under a Unionist Government, can be a means of readjusting of regional differences . . . The result . . . has been a better economic performance than the other regions of the United Kingdom which had basically similar economic problems— remoteness, and decline of the major traditional industries.'[82] The party presented the index of the growth of personal incomes in different regions of the UK to prove its point (Table 3.3).

Table 3.3 Index of growth of personal incomes in different regions of the United Kingdom

	1964–5 (1954–5: 100)
Northern Region	174
North West	182
South West	204
Wales	188
Scotland	182
Northern Ireland	204
UK as a whole	194

Of course, these gains might not have been as great if other parts of the United Kingdom had enjoyed devolved government. 'Young man, you must never again make a suggestion like that,' Terence O'Neill was told when he advocated devolution for Scotland, 'we do not want any more provincial calves pulling at the one cow.'[83]

A corollary to the intimacy of regional administration in Northern Ireland, however, was the weaker role of local government in the province. Since Northern Ireland covered a relatively small geographical area, ministers were not compelled to delegate to the same extent as ministers in Whitehall departments. Services such as fire and the police, which in the rest of the United Kingdom were the responsibility of local authorities, were in Northern Ireland the responsibility of the government. Given that the British government was committed to parity in the provision of public services in Northern Ireland, it was of course to the advantage of Northern Ireland ratepayers to be able to transfer responsibility for these services to the British taxpayer. Moreover, the Northern Ireland government took powers in housing and education from local government, which had proved itself weak and unimaginative in these areas.

The poor house-building record in Northern Ireland between the wars led to the creation of the Northern Ireland Housing Trust in 1945 to supplement the efforts of local authorities. This body gained 'a world-wide reputation for the provision of well-planned and competently administered housing estates', and Northern Ireland was the only part of the United Kingdom to enjoy subsidies for private house-building.[84] The Housing Trust, however, was, inevitably, a step towards housing being located entirely with the regional government rather than with local authorities, and in October 1969, the governments of the United Kingdom and Northern Ireland issued a joint communiqué declaring that they had 'reluctantly decided that local authorities are not geared—and cannot be geared—to handle such a task and that the best hope of success lies in the creation of a single-purpose, efficient and streamlined central housing authority . . . to tackle this most urgent problem.'[85]

In some areas of education, too, powers which in the rest of the United Kingdom were exercised by local authorities gravitated to the centre. The salaries of teachers in schools and colleges of further education under the control of the local education authority were, except for those in voluntary grammar schools, paid centrally. The Exchequer, however, limited its liability under this head, and a levy was exacted from local authorities to contribute towards the cost. There was little scope for practical initiative on the part of local education authorities, and, moreover, some of them displayed sectarian attitudes, seeking to discover the denomination of candidates applying for teaching posts, and so arousing the suspicion that Catholic candidates were discriminated against in appointments to maintained schools. There was, therefore, a strong case for a central education authority in Northern Ireland.[86]

Local authorities in Northern Ireland were weakened still further by the restrictive financial arrangements established by the government of the province. The share of local authority finance falling on the Exchequer was greater in Northern Ireland than in the rest of the United Kingdom and it was met to a greater extent than in other parts of the country from percentage or specific grants, rather than the block grant introduced in England in 1958. This led inevitably to close scrutiny of local-authority projects. Moreover, since local authorities had to contribute to the cost of the fire service and the police force, which were run from Belfast, and also to pay the education levy, there came to be a disconnection between local expenditure and local taxation. Devolution in Northern Ireland thus led to a restriction of local autonomy. The dispersal of power from London to Belfast was accompanied by a centralization of power within Northern Ireland itself.

V

The communal disturbances which broke out in Northern Ireland in 1968 brought the problems of Northern Ireland to the attention of ministers and MPs in London and put the relationship between Westminster and Belfast under serious strain. British ministers and Members of Parliament demanded the application of British standards of citizenship in Northern Ireland and pressed ministers in the province to implement reforms rapidly. Behind the formal machinery of devolution, the British government increasingly came to assume control of Northern Ireland's affairs. Joint working parties of officials were established in which London was dominant, and an official from the Foreign Office was attached to the Northern Ireland Cabinet Office, to sit in a room next to the Prime Minister of Northern Ireland, and to 'explain British policy . . . and warn [the Northern Ireland Prime Minister] where he was likely to get into difficulties with us'.[87] In 1972, Westminster demanded the transfer of powers over law and order from Stormont to London, a proposal which was unacceptable to the unionists. The government accordingly prorogued the Northern Ireland Parliament in the Northern Ireland (Temporary Provisions) Act, 1972, and abolished it the year afterwards in the Northern Ireland Constitution Act of 1973.

Between 1972 and 1998, with the exception of the five months between January and May 1974, Northern Ireland was governed under a system of direct rule.[88] The functions of the government of Northern Ireland were taken over by the Northern Ireland Office, headed by the Secretary of State for Northern Ireland, a senior minister in the British Cabinet, who was assisted by various junior ministers. While Acts of Parliament could be enacted for or extended to Northern Ireland, the

Northern Ireland Act of 1974 provided for power to undertake primary legislation for Northern Ireland by means of Orders in Council, subject to resolutions of both Houses of Parliament.

In compensation for the abolition of the Northern Ireland Parliament, the under-representation of Northern Ireland in Westminster was ended, and the number of Northern Ireland MPs was increased, following the report of a Speaker's Conference in 1978,[89] from twelve to seventeen in 1979, and eighteen in 1997. In 1975, a standing committee for Northern Ireland was established in the House of Commons and in 1994 it was renamed the Northern Ireland Grand Committee. It comprises all the MPs from Northern Ireland constituencies and not more than twenty-five other MPs, and now enjoys deliberative and scrutiny powers over proposals for draft Orders in Council; also in 1994, a select committee, the Northern Ireland Committee, was established.

Following the suspension of the Northern Ireland Parliament, it was necessary to replace the guarantee in the Ireland Act of 1949 which provided that neither Northern Ireland nor any part of it would cease to be a part of the United Kingdom without the consent of the Northern Ireland Parliament. Accordingly, section 1 of the Northern Ireland Constitution Act of 1973 provided that neither Northern Ireland nor any part of it would cease to be a part of the United Kingdom 'without the consent of the majority of the people of Northern Ireland voting in a poll'. The consent principle was reiterated in the Belfast Agreement of 1998. Provision was made in 1973 for polls to be held at intervals of not less than ten years to ascertain the views of the population of the province. A poll was accordingly held in March 1973, but its value was considerably lessened by the decision of the nationalist parties to advise their supporters to boycott it. On a 58.1 per cent turnout, 591,820 (98.9 per cent of those voting) supported Northern Ireland remaining part of the United Kingdom, while just 6,463 (1.1 per cent of those voting) supported Northern Ireland being joined with the Republic of Ireland. No further polls have been held.

Direct rule has been regarded by British governments, whether Labour or Conservative, as a temporary expedient rather than a permanent method of rule, for it is subject to considerable weaknesses from the point of view of democratic accountability. Laws, which in other parts of the United Kingdom are made by primary legislation, by Acts of Parliament, are, in Northern Ireland, made largely by Orders in Council. During the period of direct rule, between 1972 and 1997, there were thirty-three Acts passed applying wholly or mainly to Northern Ireland, but 557 Orders in Council. These Orders are not, and cannot be, effectively scrutinized by Parliament. Unlike bills, they cannot be amended, but must be either approved or rejected. They are in fact generally considered late at night, and often approved with little debate, for MPs, other than those representing Northern Ireland constituencies, cannot be expected to be familiar with the details and implications of proposals contained in draft Orders. In consequence, there has been less parliamentary control of Northern Ireland legislation than there has of legislation for the rest of the United Kingdom.

'Scrutiny of Northern Ireland at Westminster was lamentable,' James Prior, a former Northern Ireland Secretary, has written; 'the usual ration, year-in, year-out, was monthly forty-five minute question time on the floor of the Commons, a few poorly attended debates usually held late at night, and the occasional statement to the House following some particularly awful atrocity'.[90]

This lack of accountability was exacerbated by the fact that local authorities in Northern Ireland have far more limited powers than in Britain, the bulk of local powers being located in non-elected and nominated boards such as the Housing Executive and the Education and Library Boards.

However, the most serious defect of direct rule as it operated since 1972 was that, as James Prior said when Secretary of State, it gave the political parties in Northern Ireland 'all the advantages of political activity with none of the disadvantages of responsibility'.[91] Direct rule left a political vacuum in Northern Ireland which extremists were able to fill more easily than responsible political leaders, who found it difficult to display the concrete advantages of moderation in the absence of a political forum. In particular, Sinn Féin, the extreme wing of the nationalist movement, was able to portray the problems of Northern Ireland as a conflict between an indigenous nationalist movement in Northern Ireland and a colonial government in London, thus obscuring the reality of conflicting identities and allegiances inside the province.

Direct rule, then, was intended as a temporary expedient. It could have been replaced either by devolution or by full integration of Northern Ireland within the United Kingdom. Direct rule, it should be noted, is the opposite of integration in that it implicitly recognizes the distinctiveness of a particular area of the country. No one claims, for example, that Scotland or Yorkshire is under direct rule. The option of integration, on the other hand, proposes that Northern Ireland be governed, if not like Yorkshire, then like Scotland. It has at times been advocated by a number of commentators, primarily Conservative or unionist. The main purpose of integration would be to submerge the Northern Ireland conflict in United Kingdom-wide issues, to replace communal conflict with conflict over socio-economic issues more familiar to those living in other parts of the United Kingdom. There are, after all, tensions between Protestants and Catholics in Liverpool and in Glasgow, but these have not led to disturbances and terrorism of the kind that has disfigured Northern Ireland since 1968.

No British government, however, has been prepared to espouse integration, and for very good reasons. A significant difficulty is that the party system in Northern Ireland is now so very different from that in the rest of the United Kingdom. While in the 1920s, integration might well have been successful in assimilating the party system in Northern Ireland to that in the rest of the United Kingdom, by the 1970s, communal divisions had become so congealed that this was no longer possible. Indeed, no United Kingdom party has been able to win a Westminster seat in Northern Ireland. The Labour Party has never contested an election in Northern Ireland, nor does it accept membership from those living in the province. It rejected the approach of the Northern Ireland Labour Party for affiliation both in 1924 and in 1970, treating the NILP not as an affiliated party but as a 'fraternal' one, like, for example, the French or German Socialist parties. The Conservatives maintained, until 1974, a formal relationship with the Ulster Unionists, whose MPs sat and voted with Conservative MPs in the House of Commons. But the Conservatives did not, until 1989, contest elections in Northern Ireland, nor set up constituency associations in the province, nor accept membership applications from those residing in Northern Ireland. Since 1989, they have indeed formed constituency associations in the province and contested elections there, but they have secured only a derisory vote. The Liberals fought very occasional elections in Northern Ireland from the 1950s, but their Gladstonian tradition deprived them of Protestant votes, while the nationalist parties were more successful in winning the anti-partitionist vote. The Liberal Democrats do not contest elections in Northern Ireland so as to avoid splitting the vote with their sister party in the Liberal International, the non-sectarian Alliance Party of Northern Ireland.

None of the major British parties, then, offer a serious electoral alternative in Northern Ireland. Conversely, none of the Northern Ireland parties represented at Westminster compete in Great Britain. This has the consequence that, because the government of the United Kingdom is formed by British parties, the Secretary of State for Northern Ireland can never be a representative of the area for which he is responsible. This is in contrast to the Secretaries of State for Scotland and Wales who generally represent Scottish or Welsh constituencies, and political parties which enjoy electoral support in Scotland and Wales. The parties which represent Northern Ireland, by contrast, have no representation at all in the government of the United Kingdom and the Secretary of State for Northern Ireland is electorally disconnected from the province. He or she represents MPs from any part of the country excepting only Northern Ireland. James Prior felt, as Northern Ireland Secretary, 'as though I was a foreigner in another land',[92] while Tom King declared that 'The longer I have had the wide powers that a Secretary of State exercises, the more it has convinced me that people in the province and elected representatives in the province should take a greater share of those powers and responsibilities.'[93] Under direct rule, Northern Ireland came to assume the aspect of a dependency incapable of self-government.

The voter in Northern Ireland has been unable to play a direct role in choosing the government of the United Kingdom. The communal conflict in the province means that Westminster elections in Northern Ireland are not about whether the Conservatives, Labour, or the

Liberal Democrats should form the government, but rather about the balance of representation between and within essentially communal parties.

The main objection, however, to integration now is that it would make the prospect of agreement between the two communities more remote, since it would take away from the people of Northern Ireland responsibility for their own affairs. By preserving the political vacuum left by direct rule, integration would thereby prolong its most serious defect. Moreover, integration would be seen by the nationalist community in Northern Ireland as a sign that the aspirations of the unionists were being preferred to their own, that the British identity of the unionists was being given a privileged status as compared with the Irish identity of the nationalists. 'I rejected integration', James Prior wrote, 'because it would have made a bad situation worse. It offered as a permanent solution an approach favoured by only a minority of the Unionists—one section of the Official Unionists. It would have made the position of moderate democratic Nationalists impossible, and played into the hands of the terrorists. It would have scuppered any hope of institutional co-operation with Dublin.'94

Successive governments have insisted, however, that any new system of devolution must, unlike the parliament which existed from 1921 to 1972, be such as to be acceptable to both communities in the province. This has been interpreted to mean both that the government of Northern Ireland should contain representatives of both communities, and that the aspirations of the nationalist minority should be recognized through the Irish Dimension, some form of institutionalized connection with the Irish Republic.

Such an approach involves a striking departure from the Westminster model of government, which is based on the possibility of alternating governments. This model, it is clear, is unsuitable for societies divided by religion, language, or ethnicity. Societies of this kind must be governed by a different principle of democracy, the principle of power-sharing. That is the principle which operates, with more or less success, in other divided societies such as Belgium and Switzerland. Indeed, one commentator on the politics of Northern Ireland has declared as a political scientist who has specialised in the study of divided societies, that some kind of power-sharing has *always* been a feature of government in such societies which have successfully overcome their internal divisions. I do not claim that power-sharing will succeed—it broke down in Cyprus and Lebanon. But I know of *no* case where a divided society has been stable without power-sharing. As cases where it has been successful, I would point to Switzerland, the Netherlands, Belgium, South Tyrol, certain provinces of Canada, Malaysia, Fiji. The detailed arrangements in these countries differ . . . But in all of them there is some set of arrangements whereby the different segments of the population share power roughly in proportion to their numerical strengths, so that no segment feels permanently left out in the cold.[95]

Before the Belfast Agreement of 1998, British governments legislated for devolution on three occasions as part of their long-term objective of securing government by agreement in Northern Ireland—1973, 1975, and 1982. In 1973, the Northern Ireland Constitution Act provided for an assembly—not a parliament as in the 1920 Government of Ireland Act—of seventy-eight members to be elected by the single transferable-vote method of proportional representation. Devolution, however, was to be dependent upon the formation of a broadly based executive which appeared to the Secretary of State for Northern Ireland to be widely accepted throughout the province. He was required to ensure that the government of Northern Ireland included representatives of both communities. In addition, the Assembly would be required to establish consultative committees which reflected the balance of parties in the Assembly. The new Assembly and Executive would thus be very different from the former Northern Ireland Parliament, whose central principle had been majority rule.

The 1973 Act, by contrast with the Act of 1920, excepted franchise and anti-terrorist powers for Westminster, and reserved powers over law and order. There was provision, however, for these latter powers to be transferred to the Assembly at a later date with the agreement of the British government. The main powers transferred were health and social services, housing, education, environment, and agriculture.

Elections to the new Assembly were held in June 1973, and the leading unionist and nationalist parties agreed on a power-sharing executive, which took office in January 1974. In December 1973, at Sunningdale, agreement was reached between the British and Irish governments and the members of the new Northern Ireland executive-designate on the creation of a Council of Ireland with some executive functions, to comprise seven ministers from the Republic of Ireland and seven from the Northern Ireland Executive.

The Council of Ireland was, however, unacceptable to the majority of the Ulster Unionist Council, which repudiated the Unionist leader Brian Faulkner, who in consequence resigned from the Ulster Unionist Party. In February 1974, before Faulkner had a chance to regroup his forces, a British general election was held. In that election, eleven out of the twelve Northern Ireland seats were won by the United Ulster Unionist Coalition, a grouping pledged to oppose the Sunningdale Agreement. This helped to deprive the Assembly of democratic legitimacy. In May 1974, the Ulster Workers Council, supported by loyalist paramilitaries and by other unionists opposed to the Assembly, called a general strike. This led at the end of the month to the resignation of Faulkner as leader of the Executive and the prorogation of the Assembly. The Northern Ireland Act of 1974 dissolved the Assembly and restored direct rule in the province. It also proposed the election of a Northern Ireland Convention, elected by the single transferable vote, to produce new proposals for devolution. However, this failed to reach agreement and was dissolved in 1976.

In 1982, a new Northern Ireland Act provided for another assembly, once again elected by the single transferable vote.[96] The functions of this assembly, by contrast with those of the assembly of 1974, were to be those of scrutiny, consultation, and deliberation. It would in particular be able to scrutinize proposals for draft legislation and make reports and recommendations to the Secretary of State for Northern Ireland. Provision was, however, made for the 'rolling' devolution of functions, on either a partial or a total basis, to the Assembly if at least 70 per cent of its members were to agree on it, or if the Secretary of State were satisfied that particular proposals were acceptable to both communities. Full devolution would have to contain recommendations for the composition of an executive acceptable to both communities, and that almost certainly meant a power-sharing executive. An Order would then be laid at Westminster to provide for devolution. It would, therefore, be up to the Assembly whether devolution took place; but the actual decision to transfer powers would be taken by Parliament and not, as in 1974, by the Secretary of State.

In 1982, the SDLP and the other parties representing the nationalist community refused to participate in the Assembly because insufficient recognition was given, in their view, to the Irish Dimension, i.e. the creation of links between the minority community and the Irish Republic. There was, therefore, no chance of the cross-community requirement being met, and it proved impossible to devolve any functions to the Assembly. In consequence, 'Rather than rolling along the road to devolution and power-sharing, the Assembly ran into the sands of unionist factionalism and nationalist abstentionism and was dissolved in June 1986, four months before the expiry of its statutory term.'[97]

A crucial step forward in achieving devolution occurred when the IRA announced a ceasefire in August 1994, thus allowing for the representation of Sinn Féin, its political wing, in all-party talks. In 1996 multi-party talks began in Northern Ireland between the elected representatives of the parties in the province, under three independent chairmen led by Senator George Mitchell, a former majority leader of the United States Senate. These talks culminated in the Belfast or Good Friday Agreement of 1998.[98]

The Agreement provides for a 108-member assembly to be elected by the single transferable vote for a four-year fixed term. The Assembly enjoys specific powers devolved in finance, personnel, agriculture, education, health, social services, economic development, and the environment. The Agreement also states that the British government is ready in principle to consider devolving responsibility for policing and justice in due course. The Assembly is to have no tax-raising powers. As in the 1998 Scotland Act, the question of whether the provision of an Assembly bill is within its legislative competence can be referred by a government minister to the Judicial Committee of the Privy Council. By contrast with the 1920 legislation, however, there will be no Lord Lieutenant or Governor of Northern Ireland, an office which ceased to exist in 1972.

The crucial features of the Agreement, however, relate to the proposals for power-sharing. By contrast with 1973, the appointment of the executive is not to be made by the Secretary of State, nor is the coming of devolution to be dependent on a 70 per cent vote in the Assembly as it was in 1982. Instead, the executive is to be formed through a novel cross-community voting mechanism. At the first meeting of the Assembly, members are required to register a declaration of identity—unionist, nationalist, or other. For key decisions, which are to be designated in advance, instead of majority voting, cross-community consent will be required. This is to be achieved either by parallel consent, i.e. a majority of those members present and voting, including a majority of the unionists and nationalists present and voting; or, alternatively, a weighted majority of 60 per cent members present and voting, including at least 40 per cent of unionists present and voting and 40 per cent of nationalists present and voting. Those designating themselves as 'Others'—in 1998 only the Alliance Party of Northern Ireland and the Women's Coalition—do not count in either case.

By contrast with the arrangements in 1973, the First Minister and Deputy First Minister are to be elected jointly by the Assembly by means of a particular form of cross-community support, namely a majority of the members voting, a majority of the designated unionists voting, and a majority of the designated nationalists voting. This system provides an incentive for each community to nominate a candidate acceptable to members of the other community. Thus, even if Sinn Féin were to gain more votes than the SDLP in an Assembly election, it might not be wise for the nationalists to nominate Gerry Adams, since his nomination could be blocked by the unionists. In fact, the First Minister elected in 1998 was David Trimble, leader of the Ulster Unionist Party, and his Deputy was Seamus Mallon of the SDLP. The First Minister and the Deputy First Minister hold office jointly as a dyarchy and if one resigns the other also loses office. They are semi-presidential figures in the sense that they cannot be removed by the Assembly. But they do not, unlike most chief executives, appoint the other ministers, who take office in proportion to party strengths in the Assembly.

The requirement that members of the Assembly declare their identity had not been present in 1973 nor in 1982, and the former Irish Taoiseach John Bruton, in a debate in the Dáil in April 1998, while accepting that the requirement was 'necessary', added:

I hope it does not entrench division by defining parties on the basis of ultimate aspirations, which conflict with one another, rather than short-term aspirations which may coincide with one another. The rules may aggravate this by making it disadvantageous for a member to designate himself or herself in the 'other' category, where his or her vote will only count in initial votes but not in determining a minimum level of support in either community. I am worried that this new institutionalisation of two labels will also institutionalise old divisions.[99]

Although a novel requirement in the United Kingdom context, however, similar provisions have been put forward in other divided societies. Under the new Belgian Constitution of 1994, for example, Article 43 (1) provides that, for certain issues affecting the two communities, the elected members of each legislative chamber are divided into a French language group and a Flemish language group. Under Article 55, a motion signed by at least three-quarters of the members of one of the linguistic groups can delay legislation which would affect community relations. In Northern Ireland, in addition to the requirement for cross-community support, every minister is required, on the assumption of office, to take a Pledge of Office in place of the Oath of Allegiance to the Crown, which requires him or her, *inter alia*, to promise to abstain from violence and to act in accordance with the general obligation to avoid discrimination.

The Agreement, however, provides for more than devolution within the United Kingdom. For it also recognizes the Irish dimension in the politics of Northern Ireland and a confederal relationship between the United Kingdom and the Irish Republic. The Assembly is required, before powers are transferred to it, to make proper arrangements for the effective working of two new bodies established by the Agreement. The first is a North–South Ministerial Council to bring together representatives of the Irish government and the executive of the Northern Ireland Assembly to develop co-operation on matters of common interest in the island of Ireland, all decisions to be by agreement between the two sides. It is noticeable that the new body is not to be called 'Council of Ireland', a term with unfortunate overtones for unionists who refused to activate the 1920 Council, and whose opposition to the 1973 Council was largely responsible for the failure of the power-sharing experiment the following year.

The Agreement provides, under Article 1 (vi) for both the British and Irish identities of the people of Northern Ireland to be respected. Accordingly, anyone living in Northern Ireland is allowed to hold Irish citizenship, as well as British citizenship if he or she should so choose. Were Northern Ireland ever to be joined, by consent, with the Irish Republic, those living in Northern Ireland would be allowed to retain their British citizenship if they so chose.

The second new body is the British–Irish Council. This will bring together representatives of the British and Irish governments, and of devolved institutions in Northern Ireland, Scotland, and Wales (and in England, if devolved institutions are established there), as well as representatives of the Isle of Man and the Channel Isles, to consider matters of mutual interest. Because it links the Northern Ireland Assembly with other devolved institutions in Britain, the British–Irish Council might well succeed in defusing fears amongst unionists that the North–South Council is a step towards a united Ireland. For the unionists are more likely to countenance closer links with the Republic if both parts of Ireland are in turn linked together in an organization which includes the rest of the United Kingdom.[100]

The Belfast Agreement was approved in a referendum held on 22 May 1998 when, on a turnout of 81.1 per cent, 71.1 per cent voted 'Yes' and 28.9 per cent 'No'. The size of the 'Yes' majority indicated that the Agreement enjoyed majority support in both communities in Northern Ireland, the unionist and the nationalist. In a referendum held in the Irish Republic on the same day, the Agreement was endorsed by 94 per cent of those voting on a 56 per cent turnout. Elections, accordingly, were held for the new Assembly in June 1998, as provided for in the Northern Ireland (Elections) Act 1998, and Parliament implemented the Belfast Agreement in the new Northern Ireland Act 1998. This Act reiterates the constitutional guarantee to Northern Ireland, as in the Northern Ireland Constitution Act of 1973, with plebiscites to be held whenever the Secretary of State considers that a majority for change exists, but at intervals of not less than seven years, by contrast with the minimum ten-year period specified in the 1973 Act. The Act, however, repeals the Government of Ireland Act of 1920, most of the Northern Ireland Constitution Act of 1973, and the whole of the Northern Ireland Acts of 1974 and 1982. It provides for the final end of direct rule in Northern Ireland.

The Belfast Agreement offers, by contrast with previous attempts to secure devolution in Northern Ireland, a novel scheme of power-sharing designed to overcome the deep-seated communal conflict in the province; and also provisions designed to minimize the scope for boycott and obstruction by determined minorities. The Agreement has a double significance for the government of the United Kingdom since it proposes not only a solution to the Irish problem, but also recognition of the process of devolution to the non-English parts of the United Kingdom. It offers, in essence, a return to the original Gladstonian conception of Home Rule in a form suited to modern conditions. Gladstone's particular conception of the British–Irish relationship—a united Ireland enjoying Home Rule within a United Kingdom of Great Britain and Ireland—was breached in 1920 and 1921 by partition and by secession, and cannot of course be restored. But the proposals for devolution, together with the North–South Council and the confederal implications of the British–Irish Council, offer a chance of realizing the underlying theme of Gladstonian thinking—recognition both of the various and distinctive national identities within these islands, but also of the close and complex links between them.

Scotland

Up to date the Scottish Nationalist movement seems to have gone almost
unnoticed in England. . . . It is true that it is a small movement, but it could
grow, because there is a basis for it.

(George Orwell, 1947)

I

The Union brought political stability and economic progress to Scotland, and this helped to ensure its acceptance. Scotland was at first
administered by a Scottish Secretary, but this post was abolished
after the Jacobite revolt of 1745, and between 1782 and 1885 the
Home Secretary was the minister nominally responsible for Scottish
affairs, although the actual administration of Scotland was still
undertaken by Scots. Nevertheless, assimilationist feeling probably
reached its peak after the suppression of the Jacobites, at a time when
Scotland was making considerable economic advances. During these
years, it was coming to be believed that union might imply assimilation after all. In 1754, Lord Chancellor Hardwicke wrote to Lord
Kames:

I am extremely obliged to your Lordship for . . . that zeal which you express
for improving and perfecting the union of the two Kingdoms, to which nothing can contribute more than an uniformity of laws. Those great men who
conceived and framed the plan of the Union [had sought uniformity] . . . but
found it impracticable in the outset; but I have reason to think that they never
imagined near half a century would have passed after their articles were
established, without a greater advance being made towards it than has hitherto been attempted—an evil which I have often lamented, and should
rejoice to see remedied, because, without it, an incorporating union must be
very defective.[1]

Hardwicke and Kames, both lawyers, seem to have taken it for granted that an incorporating union implied assimilation. During the nineteenth century, Scotland was often referred to as North Britain, and

it was by no means clear that she would be able to retain her separate identity, rather than becoming a mere province of England. That this did not happen may be ascribed to two factors: first, Scotland's separate legal and administrative system which compelled government and Parliament to take account of her particular needs; and second, the influence of the Irish Home Rule agitation which stirred national feeling in both Scotland and Wales.

In the 1880s, Scotland's claims were championed at Westminster by Lord Rosebery, a young Liberal peer who was a favourite of Gladstone's. Rosebery was not a Home Ruler but he urged the establishment of a separate minister for Scotland, and, partly as a result of his efforts, the Scottish Office was resurrected in 1885. 'The whole object', Lord Salisbury told its first holder, the Duke of Richmond and Gordon, 'is to redress the wounded dignities of the Scotch people—or a section of them—who think that enough is not made of Scotland.'[2] Gladstone, in the 1886 Irish Home Rule debate, called the recreation of this post, 'a little mouthful of Home Rule'.[3]

At its inception, the Scottish Office was seen as something of a sinecure. 'The work is not heavy,' Salisbury had told the Duke. 'It really is a matter where the effulgence of two Dukedoms and the best salmon river in Scotland will go a long way.'[4] From 1892, however, the Scottish Secretary was always to be in the Cabinet except in wartime; and in 1926, he was made a Secretary of State. In 1939, the office was moved to Edinburgh, although a branch office remains in London.

The Scottish Office began, in 1885, with hardly any functional responsibilities; but from then on it saw a continual accretion of functions until, by the 1960s, the Secretary of State was expected to take an interest in all matters affecting Scotland and to put the case for Scotland in the Cabinet. Before devolution, he was responsible for a wide range of statutory functions which in England are the responsibility of nine or ten departmental ministers. These statutory functions were, until 1999, administered by five main departments within the Scottish Office: the Agriculture, Environment and Fisheries Department; the Development Department; the Education and Industry Department; the Department of Health; and the Home Department. The Scottish Office thus became the department of government administering Scotland's domestic affairs and the real heart of executive government in Scotland. Moreover, the Secretary of State became the focus of Scotland's political identity. He came to be seen in a wider sense as 'Scotland's minister' and thus held accountable for all government decisions affecting Scotland, whether or not they lay within his area of statutory responsibility.

In 1954, the Royal Commission on Scottish Affairs, the Balfour Commission, laid down two criteria to assess the effectiveness of governmental arrangements in Scotland. The first was that 'the machinery of government should be designed to dispose of Scottish business in Scotland', and the second that Scottish needs and the Scottish point of view should be borne in mind 'at all stages in the formation and execution of policy'.[5]

The wide range of statutory powers conferred on the Secretary of State undoubtedly satisfied the first criterion. Indeed, it is difficult to think of any specifically Scottish matter which had not already been transferred to the Scottish Office. It seems likely, therefore, that the limits of administrative decentralization had been reached.

The second requirement laid down by the Balfour Commission was met by governmental arrangements which allowed Scotland to be formally represented on any policy-making committee whose decisions might affect her, even where those decisions lay outside the Secretary of State's area of statutory responsibility. When the membership of Cabinet committees was first published by John Major's government in 1992, it became apparent that the Secretary of State was a member of all of the key economic and social committees of the Cabinet. Secretaries of State of both major political parties have used this influence to further Scotland's interests. Perhaps the first Secretary of State to make full use of his position was Thomas Johnston, the Labour Secretary of State in the wartime coalition government between 1941 and 1945. Johnston was, in the words of Herbert Morrison:

One of the most able men in the technique of getting his own way at cabinet committees . . . He would impress on the committee that there was a strong nationalist movement in Scotland and it could be a potential danger if it grew through lack of attention to Scottish interests . . . by dint of cajoing, persuasion, plus some slight exaggeration of the grievances fertilising the Scottish

Nationalist movement, he got his schemes through after three or so commit-tee meetings.[6]

Johnston was by no means the last Secretary of State to adopt this tactic and it may be for this reason that public expenditure in Scotland appears in the post-war years to have been higher than its needs would warrant. This important issue is further discussed in Chapter 7, in the section 'Financing devolution'.

Yet the very effectiveness of the system of Scottish administration only brought into greater prominence the conflict between the Secretary of State's role as 'Scotland's minister', and the convention of collective Cabinet responsibility. For this convention made it dif-ficult for the Secretary of State to initiate policies creating new precedents which might be unwelcome in England. Any new depar-tures would be noticed by other ministers, who would be very con-scious that they might have implications for their own 'English' departments. The Cabinet did not, under these circumstances, find it difficult to overrule one not very senior minister in a Cabinet of around twenty.

The Secretary of State's autonomy thus tended to be limited to matters, such as the reform of local government, where English min-isters did not particularly care what happened in Scotland, and where there seemed no implications for policy across the border. Many of the differences in administration between Scotland and England are in fact probably more the result of the legacy of history than of delib-erate governmental decisions to legislate specifically for Scottish conditions.

The consequences of this system have been well summed up by a former Scottish Office civil servant:

It was therefore possible to create a semblance of Scottish distinctiveness and autonomy which went beyond the reality. The same process made it pos-sible to enforce uniformity, or near uniformity, beyond what was necessary or desirable, when there seemed a risk that a distinctive Scottish line might raise embarrassing questions for another Minister concerned with the same field of policy elsewhere.[7]

In recent years, however, the main objective of the Scottish Secretary was less to take separate Scottish initiatives than to extract more resources for Scotland from the government. But the Barnett formula, introduced in 1980 to regulate the shares of increments in identifiable public expenditure between England and Scotland, reduced the extent to which the Secretary of State could negotiate to Scotland's advantage. (This formula is discussed in detail in Chapter 7, in the section 'Financing devolution'.) This made it more difficult for the Secretary of State to defend his position. He seemed to be able to provide neither distinctive attention to Scotland's needs, nor extra money for Scotland. His position became particularly embarrassing during the years of Conservative government between 1979 and 1997, when he enjoyed the support of only a minority in Scotland. It was hard for him to represent Scottish opinion effectively in Westminster, and he became, in reality, more like the ambassador of a hostile power than Scotland's spokesman in the Cabinet.

It is sometimes argued that the Scottish Office suffered from an especial lack of accountability in comparison with other Whitehall departments. The crucial difference, however, is that, when Parliament is sitting, the Secretary of State is unable to spend more than half of the week in Scotland, and he has to include in this period his constituency business and meetings with Scottish Office officials as well as the numerous interest groups which demand an audience with him. It was because the minister was 400 miles away from Edinburgh for much of the time that the degree of control he could exercise on the *implementation* of decisions and on day-to-day administration was bound to be very limited.

Moreover, the wide range of responsibilities enjoyed by the Scottish Office, covering matters for which nine or ten Whitehall departments were responsible, led to the overloading of the executive in Scotland. Education, for example, which in England is the responsibility of five ministers, was in Scotland just one of the responsibilities of the Secretary of State, aided by a Minister of State whose responsibilities included industry as well as education. This meant that fewer decisions were taken by ministers and more by civil servants than would have been the case in England. It also made it difficult for the House of Commons to hold the Scottish Office accountable, since Questions over this wide range of functions were held just once a month. Thus the arrangements for disposing of government business in Scotland did not meet the canons of accountability which were taken for granted in other government departments. The Scottish Office, it has been held, 'stimulates rather than satisfies the appetite for self-government. It has made Scottish government at once more Scottish and less subject to parliamentary control.'[8] It was in a sense the very success of the Scottish Office that made so powerful a case for devolution.

Just as it has long been recognized that Scotland is a separate unit for executive purposes, so also special arrangements have been made for the conduct of Scottish business in the House of Commons. The committee stage of bills certified by the Speaker as relating exclusively to Scotland is taken by one of two Scottish standing committees. These committees comprise between sixteen and fifty MPs and must include at least sixteen Scottish MPs. They are constituted, like other standing committees, to reflect the party balance in the House. Until 1987, only Scottish MPs could be members, but since 1987, there have never been more than eleven Conservative MPs returned in Scotland, so that, during the remaining period of Conservative government until 1997, it was found necessary to include MPs from English constituencies in order to give the government a majority. There is also a Scottish Grand Committee, comprising all of Scotland's seventy-two MPs. In contrast to other legislative committees and to select committees, the government does not necessarily enjoy a majority on the Scottish Grand Committee, and did not do so in the years of Conservative government between 1979 and 1997. The Grand Committee often meets in Scotland, and has power to take the second and third reading debates and the report stage of non-controversial Scottish bills. It also holds debates on secondary legislation for Scotland, and a question time at which it can question Scottish ministers. As with the Scottish standing committees, however, it is difficult to refer controversial matters to the Grand Committee, since such a reference can be blocked if ten MPs indicate their objection in the House. Moreover, the Grand Committee does not vote on legislation and has no legislative powers. It is an arena for discussion, not for scrutiny. Finally, there is a Select Committee on Scottish Affairs, one of the departmentally related select committees established in 1979 to scrutinize government departments. The Select Committee's remit is to enquire into the expenditure, administration, and policy of the Scottish Office and other public bodies in Scotland. After 1987, however, the Conservative government found it impossible to find sufficient Scottish MPs to serve on this Committee and it fell into abeyance until 1992, when it was reconstituted with eleven members and an opposition MP as chairman. As there were only ten Conservative MPs, five of whom were ministers, the problem of Conservative representation was resolved by appointing Conservatives from south of the border to serve. The Select Committee has performed a valuable inquisitorial and deliberative function in questioning Scottish Office ministers, and in scrutinizing projections of public expenditure in Scotland and the activities of the various non-departmental public bodies in Scotland under the authority of the Secretary of State.

The arrangements for considering Scottish legislation in the Commons have served to separate Scottish legislation and administration from non-Scottish MPs, most of whom are quite uninterested in it, and expected not to interfere. In 1968, Richard Crossman had it in mind to attend a second reading debate on the Social Work (Scotland) Bill, but

Just as we were going in we realised that the Scots would suspect some poisonous English conspiracy so we would have to keep out, come what may. I quote this to show how deep is the separation which already exists between England and Scotland. Willie Ross [the Scottish Secretary] and his friends accuse the Scot. Nats. of separatism but what Willie Ross himself actually likes is to keep Scottish business absolutely privy from English business. I am not sure this system isn't one that gets the worst of both worlds which is why I'm in favour of a Scottish Parliament.[9]

There was then already a Scottish subsystem in the House of Commons. Devolution transfers that subsystem to Edinburgh and places it under direct electoral control.

It is clear, then, that the distinctiveness of Scotland as a political unit was recognized, both at the executive level of government and in the arrangements for the dispatch of parliamentary business. But the conventions of the Constitution were bound to limit the extent to which Scotland could be treated as a distinctive unit even within the framework of the union state.

Collective Cabinet responsibility, as we have seen, limited the extent to which the Secretary of State for Scotland could act as a genuine minister for Scotland; while, in the Commons, the unwillingness of the House of Commons, which is jealous of its authority, to delegate that authority to committees, restricted Scottish control over Scottish business to relatively uncontroversial matters. For the working of Scottish committees has been conditioned by the principles on which the House of Commons operates. These committees cannot approve legislation without the agreement of the whole House; and while ministers took part in the debates of the Grand Committee and could be questioned there, they could not be required by the committee to change their policies. When, in November 1995, MPs asked whether the Scottish Grand Committee could block the imposition of nursery vouchers in Scotland, the Secretary of State, Michael Forsyth, declared that 'the absolute Westminster veto over Scottish business remains', adding that 'the Scottish Grand Committee is not a Scottish Parliament'.[10] That was a correct statement of the constitutional position.

Thus Scotland was in the anomalous if not unique position of having a separate legal system, together with separate arrangements for the handling of executive business, but no separate legislature to which the Scottish executive could be held responsible. 'It would be hard throughout the familiar world', Lord Kilbrandon, the Chairman of the Royal Commission on the Constitution, argued, 'to find a parallel for a country which had its own judicature and legal system, its own executive and administration, but no legislature, its laws being made within another and technically foreign jurisdiction, by an assembly in which it had only a small minority of members, but to which its executive was democratically responsible.'[11]

This anomaly might not have mattered when the party system transcended the border, as it did between 1945 and 1959, the party with a majority in the United Kingdom also enjoying a majority in Scotland (except in 1951 when the two major parties were level north of the border). Since 1959, however, Labour has won the majority of Scottish seats. This has meant that in years of Conservative government—the years between 1959 and 1964, 1970 and 1974, and 1979 and 1997—government was even less willing to devolve important business to Scottish parliamentary committees; while the Secretary of State for Scotland was handicapped in acting as Scotland's minister by the fact that the majority of Scots had indicated that they did not want him or the policies of the government of which he was a member. The distinctive arrangements for the handling of Scottish business, both at executive and at parliamentary level, could, it might be argued, work only within a very limited range of election results. That limit was breached between 1979 and 1997.

Thus the mainspring of the case for devolution was a democratic one, the need to repair a relationship which had been seriously undermined. The arrangements for handling Scottish business, both at executive and at parliamentary level, had become unsatisfactory and could hardly have been improved within the unitary framework. The Treaty of Union between England and Scotland had envisaged Scottish identity being preserved through her legal system and system of church government. These institutions, however, have long been displaced from their central position as guarantors of Scottish identity. In the modern world, Scottish identity is determined far more by the institutions of government than by the legal system or the church. Thus, it could be argued that it was only possible to preserve the spirit of the Union if the government of Scotland were able to reflect Scottish interests and needs more effectively.

Yet the machinery of government in Scotland proved unable to resist the centralizing pressures of modern government, since the machinery of Whitehall is inevitably geared towards standardization; the pressures towards uniformity could be resisted only by providing constitutional protection for Scotland in the form of a directly elected legislature. Part of the case for a devolved legislature in Scotland was that it would provide a corrective to the pressures of Whitehall. The great increase in the functions of government since 1945, only partially reversed by the Conservative governments of Margaret Thatcher and John Major, made the maladjusted arrangements for the government of Scotland of greater consequence than they had been before. When the scope of government was limited, it mattered less whether government was situated in London or in Edinburgh, since its decisions did not affect the individual as much as those of indigenous Scottish non-governmental institutions. Today, however, it is the institutions of government which, for good or ill, affect the lives of individuals. The need was to make the governmental arrangements providing for Scottish distinctiveness real rather than merely symbolic. Scottish devolution may be seen, from this perspective, as a means of renegotiating the terms of the Union so as to make them more palatable to Scottish opinion in the conditions of the late twentieth century. Such a renegotiation may be the only way to re-establish the kind of relationship between England and Scotland envisaged in 1707, a relationship which has been eroded by developments in government and in electoral behaviour in the latter part of the twentieth century. Seen in this light, Scottish devolution may be regarded analogously to Gladstonian Home Rule in the nineteenth century, as a policy of a strikingly conservative character.

II

Without the rise and electoral success in the 1970s of the Scottish National Party, the SNP, it is doubtful whether devolution would have assumed as prominent a place on the political agenda of the United Kingdom as in fact it has done. But nationalism in Scotland has not displayed the emotional hostility to the British connection which animated the Irish nationalists, and it has adhered strictly to constitutional methods.

The first distinctively modern political nationalist movement in Scotland, the Scottish Home Rule Association, was set up in May 1886, just one month after Gladstone introduced the Irish Home Rule bill into the Commons. It emphasized not the injustice of British rule, after the fashion of the Irish, but 'the legislative neglect of Scotland' and the need to reform the licensing laws and the land, game and fishery laws.[12] The emphasis was thus not separatist but integrationist, the securing of national equality with England. At the end of the nineteenth century, Home Rule was supported by such future Labour leaders as Keir Hardie and Ramsay MacDonald, and it also enjoyed the support of many Liberals. Between 1890 and 1914, measures proposing Scottish Home Rule appeared thirteen times before the House of Commons, being accepted in principle by the House on eight occasions and securing the support of a majority of Scottish

MPs on eleven occasions. But none of the bills was successful in reaching the committee stage, and this reflected the low priority attached to Scottish Home Rule even amongst MPs sympathetic to the cause.

Moreover, it would be wrong to suppose that the frequency of appearance of Scottish Home Rule bills corresponded to any great degree of popular feeling in Scotland at the time. They seem rather to have been introduced as ritual gestures on the part of Liberal and Labour MPs who felt duty-bound to argue that Scotland had claims no less important than those of Ireland. There was, however, no Parnell in Scotland, nor even a Tom Ellis, since Scottish grievances did not seem powerful enough to form the basis of a larger political programme. Before 1914, indeed, Scottish nationalism had the character of an imitative and rather artificial movement.

The founder of modern political nationalism in Scotland was John MacCormick who, while a student at Glasgow University, left the Labour Party to form a university Nationalist Society. He was the first leader of the SNP, which was born in 1934, but his aim was to secure Home Rule, a Scottish parliament within the United Kingdom rather than independence. He sought, moreover, to work in collaboration with other parties rather than in electoral competition with them, and so the SNP did not at first contest elections. MacCormick, however, was ousted from the leadership during the war and the SNP then became an explicitly separatist party committed to contesting elections against the other parties. It succeeded in winning Motherwell in a by-election in April 1945, during the period of the wartime electoral truce between the major parties, but the seat was lost in the general election just three months later when party politics was resumed. The SNP achieved little success in the immediate post-war years, and seemed to many to be little more than a merely picturesque grouping of cranks and faddists.

From 1955, however, the SNP's electoral performance improved steadily if unspectacularly until, in the general election of 1966, its twenty-three candidates secured 5 per cent of the Scottish vote, an average of 14 per cent per opposed candidate (Table 4.1).

After the 1966 general election, in the atmosphere of disillusion with Harold Wilson's Labour government, the SNP began to make

Table 4.1 SNP results in the elections of 1955–66

Election	Candidates	Total votes	% of Scottish total
1955	2	12,112	0.5
1959	5	21,738	0.8
1964	15	64,044	2.4
1966	23	128,474	5.0

spectacular progress. In March 1967, in a by-election in Glasgow, Pollok, the SNP gained 28 per cent of the vote in a marginal seat gained by the Conservatives from Labour. Then, in November 1967, the party won a by-election in Hamilton, hitherto a Labour stronghold. In the municipal elections of 1968, the SNP became a major force in local government, winning nearly a hundred seats, and gaining the balance of power in Glasgow, depriving Labour of overall control for the first time since 1952; and its average performance in the four parliamentary Scottish by-elections of the 1966–70 Parliament was 29 per cent of the vote.

In the general election of 1970, the SNP fought on a broader front that ever before, contesting sixty-five out of the seventy-one Scottish seats. Since then, the SNP has contested at least seventy seats in every election in Scotland. Its progress between 1970 and 1974 is shown in Table 4.2.

In February 1974, the SNP gained six seats, four from the Conservatives and two from Labour. In October, it gained a further four

Table 4.2 SNP results in the elections of 1970–4

Election	Candidates	Seats	Total votes	% of Scottish total
1970	65	1	306,802	11
February 1974	70	7	633,180	22
October 1974	71	11	839,617	30

seats, all from the Conservatives. The October 1974 election made the SNP the second largest party after Labour, overtaking the Conservatives, in terms of its percentage of the vote in Scotland. The SNP's percentage of the vote in October 1974 made it, indeed, the second strongest ethnic minority party in Western Europe.[13] It had by this time eleven seats, and was second in a further forty-two constituencies, including thirty-five of Labour's forty-one seats. A further swing of 5 per cent to the SNP from the sitting incumbent would give it sixteen more seats. The SNP, then, threatened not only the hegemony of Labour in Scotland, but also Labour's chances of continuing to be a governing party in the United Kingdom. But the rise of a strong nationalist party in Scotland posed a challenge, not only to Labour, but to all of the parties which sought to preserve the United Kingdom.

III

The spectacular growth of support for the SNP in the early 1970s not only caused problems for the British parties; it also posed difficult questions for those whose task it was to explain electoral behaviour, forcing them to readjust many of their preconceptions. The conclusions of psephology had, until that time, very much reflected the social democratic consensus of the immediate post-war years; and the social sciences had given little attention to those historical and geographical factors which made one part of the United Kingdom different from another. 'Class', it had been said in 1967, 'is the basis of British politics: all else is embellishment and detail'.[14] Regional differences in electoral behaviour, declared Butler and Stokes in the first professional analysis of British voting behaviour in 1969, were but 'variations upon the central theme of class'.[15] Paradoxically, class, being a nationwide factor, made for national unity. Such an analysis made it difficult, however, to explain the advance of the SNP as being anything other than a 'protest vote' against the two major parties, a temporary departure perhaps, from a stable political norm. The modicum of truth in the 'protest' explanation was that, until the late 1960s, the SNP performed well only in years such as 1961 and 1962, when disillusionment with government was strong enough for the Liberals to do well in England also. In the 1966–70 parliament, however, disillusionment with government led, in England, not to support for the Liberals, but to massive Labour abstentions and very large swings to the Conservatives. The Liberals were unable to attract Labour abstainers in England, but in Scotland, and also in Wales, disillusioned Labour supporters had an alternative to abstention; they could vote instead for a nationalist party.

In the 1970–4 parliament, the SNP did not perform well until after the Liberal breakthrough at Rochdale in October 1972. From then until the general election in February 1974, the Liberals gained five seats in England, four from the Conservatives and one from Labour. In addition, a Labour defector, Dick Taverne, succeeded in holding his seat at Lincoln, standing as a Democratic Labour candidate against official Labour opposition. During the same period, the SNP gained 30 per cent of the vote in Dundee East, 42 per cent of the vote in Glasgow, Govan, winning the seat from Labour; and 19 per cent of the vote in Edinburgh North. In February 1974, the SNP gained 21.9 per cent of the Scottish vote as compared with the Liberals' 23.6 per cent average share of the vote per opposed candidate in Britain as a whole; in October 1974, however, the SNP made further gains, its vote going up to 30.4 per cent while the Liberal vote declined to 18.9 per cent per opposed candidate. At this election, the advance of the SNP could no longer be explained by the mobilization of those who had previously not voted, since turnout was 4.2 per cent lower than it had been in February. Nor did it seem plausible any longer to describe the vote simply as a 'protest'. For the concept of a 'protest' vote did not seem to explain why it was that support for the SNP continued to increase while support for the Liberals in England and Plaid Cymru in Wales had begun to fall.

It seemed that the SNP was about to break the constraints of the two-party system in Scotland, something that the Liberals had never succeeded in doing. What might perhaps originally have been a protest vote appeared to be solidifying into something much deeper. It seemed that a new alignment was developing in Scottish politics, something that could be explained only by the powerful sense of Scottish nationality, strongly buttressed by history, which gave to economic and other grievances a shape unmatched in other parts of Britain. It was this strong sense of Scottish identity which provided the basis for the electoral success of the SNP. Indeed, the potential for nationalist revival in Scotland had perhaps existed for some time. In 1966, just before the SNP upsurge, Budge and Urwin in their study of Scottish political behaviour, perceptively put 'one awkward question' which 'has not been faced by our discussion'. The question was: 'If Scottish feeling is so widespread through all groups and both classes, why have the Conservative and Labour parties not lost more ground to the SNP and the Liberals who have promised to implement Home Rule?'[16]

The answer seems to be that, until the late 1960s, when the age of affluence ended, it had appeared that the major British parties— Conservative and Labour—would be able to secure Scotland's interests. Although Harold Wilson's Labour government, which came to power in 1964, showed little interest in Scotland's national claims, this might not have mattered if centralized government had been accompanied, as it had been in the 1940s, by economic progress. During the late 1960s, however, the combination of centralized government and economic failure led to disillusion in Scotland with Labour, as it did also in England. In Labour seats in England, voters found it difficult to cross class lines and support the Conservatives. But in Scotland, disillusioned Labour voters sympathetic to self-government could turn to the SNP which seems not to have been perceived, as the Conservatives were, as a class party.

Thus nationwide economic grievances were beginning to break up traditional party allegiances. But the strong sense of nationality in Scotland meant that the reaction to economic failure when it came would take a different form from that in England. The SNP gained support, not so much perhaps as the party of independence or separatism, but as the party that could speak for Scotland against the London parties, the party of Scottish identity. The SNP came to be seen as a pressure group for Scottish interests. In its Scottish general election manifesto in October 1974, Labour proclaimed how much it had done for Scotland in its seven months of office. It had doubled the

Regional Employment Premium, bringing Scotland an extra £40m. a year in revenue; it had given Edinburgh and Leith development-area status, bringing in a further £8m. a year; it had moved the Offshore Supplies Office to Glasgow; it had agreed to establish the British National Oil Corporation in Scotland; it had promised to move 7,000 civil service jobs to Scotland by the early 1980s; and it had tightened the limit for industrial development certificates, so improving Scotland's chances of attracting new industry. There were also further promises—to establish a Scottish Development Agency and a Centre for Oil Drilling Technology in Scotland, to halt rail closures in Scotland, and to modernize the Glasgow underground system at a cost of £11.8m. In addition, Labour promised to create a directly elected Scottish assembly. It does not require very much cynicism to ask how many of these reforms and promises would have been made in so short a time without the electoral threat posed by the SNP.

During the early 1970s, there were two developments which increased still further the credibility of the SNP and seemed to shift the balance of the argument significantly in the direction of Scottish independence. The first was the discovery and commercial exploitation of oil in the North Sea. This seemed to destroy the central unionist argument that the union was essential to Scotland's economic health. The choice could now be presented by the SNP as one between rich Scotland and poor England. It could now be argued that the union in fact placed Scotland under an economic handicap, for Scots could claim that their interests required a slower rate of extraction than was demanded by the British government, so as not to exhaust the country's resources too rapidly. The priority of the British government, on the other hand, seemed to be to use the oil revenues to pay off its debts as quickly as possible. Moreover, a rapid rate of extraction of the oil might have serious effects on the environment in the north-east of Scotland. Admittedly, a slower rate of extraction would lessen the immediate benefits of North Sea oil to Scotland, and would, in particular, mean a slower increase in employment. Nevertheless, it could be argued that the British balance of priorities, as between British energy needs and Scottish environmental needs, was not necessarily the right one for Scotland.

A further problem was the use to which the oil revenues would be put. The long-term benefits of oil lay in the gain to the balance of payments and the revenues accruing to government, rather than the immediate effects on incomes and employment, which were likely to be small. An independent Scotland, the SNP argued, if her legal claim to ownership of the oil fields was conceded—and this itself was a highly contentious point, most international lawyers being hostile to the SNP claim—could herself enjoy the benefits of the revenues. But, remaining in the United Kingdom, Scotland might not benefit at all unless the British government were to make a positive attempt to use the revenues to revive Scotland's industrial structure.

It would, however, be a mistake to put too much weight upon the discovery of oil as an explanation for the rise of Scottish nationalism. The increase in support for the SNP in the late 1960s pre-dated the discovery of oil, and surveys showed that support for Scottish independence remained fairly stable at about 20 per cent from around 1968 to the end of the 1970s, there being no dramatic increase in support for this option after the commercial exploitation of oil began. One account of support for the SNP found that 'attitude to self-government was clearly much more influential than attitude to oil revenues', for 'oil and, by extension, the feeling that Scotland could "go it alone economically" cannot be seen as more than a constraint breaking influence that reduced the perceived costs of an already desirable objective'.[17] Voting choices between 1974 and 1979 were determined much more by attitudes to devolution than by attitudes to oil. The feeling that Scotland should have a major share of the oil revenues inclined voters to support the SNP only if they were already favourable to devolution or independence.[18] Thus oil reinforced electoral support for the SNP; it did not create it.

The second factor which altered the nature of the political argument in Scotland was Britain's entry into the European Community in 1973, which both emphasized the disadvantages for Scotland of remote government, but also seemed to lessen the benefits to be derived from remaining in the United Kingdom. With important areas of decision-making being removed from London to Brussels, Edinburgh would become even more remote from the centres of power. Scotland was already part of the British periphery; how much more peripheral it would be when viewed from Brussels.

Economically, Scotland was at some distance from the European 'golden triangle', centred on the Rühr. High transport costs would make it more difficult for industry located in Scotland to penetrate European markets, and Scotland might find it hard to attract a skilled supply of labour or to persuade new industries to locate there. Thus Britain's entry into the European Community was likely to accentuate even further the economic advantages of the south-east core of the UK to the disadvantage of Scotland.

But if Scotland gained her independence, all this might be changed. An independent country would still retain the prime advantage which membership of the United Kingdom gave her: access to a duty-free market. Scotland could now avoid what had hitherto been seen as the main disadvantage of independence, namely that England would be able to ruin Scottish industry by imposing a tariff on Scottish goods. Such a policy would now be forbidden by the rules of the European Community. The very limits which the Community placed upon independence ensured that England could no longer threaten Scotland with disruption of markets and loss of trade in the event of independence. The Community, therefore, seemed to offer Scotland the economic advantages of union even in the absence of union. Moreover, an independent Scotland would, through its representation in the institutions of the Community, be able to argue powerfully for her interests and perhaps secure more favourable treatment for Scotland than the British government had been able to do. During the 1970s, the European Community was dominated by the so-called Luxembourg Compromise of 1965–6, according to which member states enjoyed a veto on matters essential to their national interest. This meant that Scotland could not be outvoted by the larger member states. She would enjoy a veto in the Community, and, so it could be argued, be in a stronger position to protect her interests than by remaining part of the United Kingdom.

IV

The rise of the SNP confronted the major parties with a dilemma: should they resist nationalist pressures, or, by offering devolution, appear to be appeasing them? How would the parties react? Their attitudes would reflect a complex mixture of tactical consideration and principled commitment, with conceptions of party self-interest jostling with ideologies inherited from long ago. Labour's philosophy of social democracy presented it with the problem that devolution might undermine the centralized allocation of economic resources, to be decided upon grounds of need rather than regional or national pressures. The Conservatives—who had called themselves Unionists between 1886 and 1921—had a long tradition of resisting national claims within the United Kingdom. Moreover, they were becoming increasingly an English party, and therefore more susceptible to the prejudices of their English members. Neither the Labour nor the Conservative party in Scotland enjoyed much autonomy; the Labour Party's Scottish Council was merely a regional branch of the Labour Party, possessing little more autonomy than, for example, the East Midlands Labour Party; while the Scottish Conservatives' role in policy-making was entirely subordinate to that of the leader of the party as a whole.

The Liberals would seem to have been in the most favourable position to take the nationalist tide at the flood. For devolution had, since the time of Gladstone, lain at the very forefront of Liberal policy. The Liberals had been strong supporters of Home Rule for Scotland and Wales, and had advocated parliaments in Edinburgh and Cardiff at every general election since 1950. Since surveys of Scottish opinion during the 1960s and 1970s showed that the majority of Scottish voters preferred devolution or federalism to either the separatism of the SNP or the status quo, the Liberals would seem to have been well placed to capitalize upon the politics of locality as the basis for a new Liberal breakthrough.

The difficulty was, however, that the Liberals found it difficult to decide upon the relative priority of Scottish claims. For the Liberal commitment to Home Rule for Scotland and Wales was within the context of a federal United Kingdom. Did this mean, however, that Scotland was to be equated with an English region and would she have to wait for devolution until the English regions also wanted it? The Scottish Liberal Party regarded Scotland as a nation and favoured a federal system of government for the United Kingdom, which included an English parliament with similar powers to the Scottish one. Some English Liberals, primarily from the south of England, shared that view. Most English Liberals, however, and especially Liberals from the north of England, took the view that a federal system should comprise regional assemblies in England with roughly similar powers to those of a Scottish parliament. In 1976, in a desperate attempt to reconcile these conflicting views, the Liberal Assembly committed itself to a federal United Kingdom which comprised both subordinate English provincial assemblies as well as an English assembly.

During Jo Grimond's period of leadership—between 1956 and 1967—the Liberals had sought the support of 'the new middle class' and the affluent worker, in the hope that these groups might be willing to support a radical, non-socialist alternative to the Conservatives. So, although the Liberals were trying to break up the two-party system in British politics, they were still relying upon the traditional assumption that class was the central motivating factor in voting behaviour. They were unwilling to commit themselves to a strategy based upon exploiting locality. The Grimond strategy, however, failed to yield a breakthrough for the Liberal Party. The 'new middle class', evenly spread as it was in the south-east, did not constitute a sufficiently concentrated grouping of support to enable the Liberals to win seats. There was, however, according to the historian John Vincent, writing in 1967, room in Britain, 'for a party which puts locality before party conflict',[19] a party which focused the resentments of provincial England, Scotland, and Wales against the metropolis. That had, Vincent believed, been a large part of the *raison d'être* of the Liberal Party from the time of its formation in the 1850s.[20] The early Labour Party had assumed this role also. In the 1960s, the Liberals might well have been able to secure a new electoral base in the peripheral areas of Britain, areas reacting against excessive centralization. In 1964, they had gained three seats in the Scottish Highlands—Caithness and Sutherland, Ross and Cromarty, and Inverness; and in a by-election in 1965, they gained Roxburgh, Selkirk, and Peebles, a border constituency, 'to some extent a second Scottish periphery',[21] suffering from many of the same problems as the Highlands—remoteness, poor communications, migration, and disruption of community values. By 1966, of the twelve Liberal seats, five were in Scotland, one in Wales, two in Cornwall and one in Devon—that is, six in the 'Celtic fringe' and three in the south-west, leaving just three seats in English suburbia.

In Scotland, the Liberals faced competition from the SNP. Should they seek, at the cost of a few deposits, to destroy the SNP? Or should they, alternatively, ally themselves with the SNP on a Scottish self-government platform? The Liberals might well have been able to destroy the SNP had they put forward Scottish Home Rule as an absolute priority from the 1960s. An alliance with the SNP, however, was probably never possible because liberalism and nationalism were such different philosophies. The basic cause of lack of agreement remained that, during the 1960s, the SNP was nationalist while the Liberals were not. The SNP took the view that it was not logical to seek federalism as an initial goal, and that it was for the Scottish people, and not Westminster, to decide what kind of constitution they wanted for Scotland. The Liberal Democrats, together with Labour, had come round to this view by the time of the Scottish Convention in 1989, which argued that the Scottish people, and not Westminster, were sovereign; but by then it was too late for the Liberal Democrats to present themselves as a specifically Scottish party.

Thus the Liberals failed to make an electoral breakthrough by championing the peripheral areas of the United Kingdom. Indeed, despite their longstanding commitment to devolution, they had given so little attention to the details of the subject that during the period of the Lib–Lab pact in 1977–8, when they were invited to produce proposals for resurrecting the legislation, they were forced to rely upon an outside policy unit, the Outer Circle Policy Unit, for their ideas.

'The Liberals', John Vincent commented in 1967, 'have been obsessed for ten years with the belief that they, like the Congregational Church, have a vocation to serve the "new" middle class. . . . The Liberals set their cap at the London commuter and ended up with the Ross and Cromarty crofter. They tried to win by spotlighting a particular social group. They should have spotlighted place.'[22] It is difficult to quarrel with this verdict.

V

Neither of the other two United Kingdom parties would appear to have been in as strong a position as the Liberals to meet the SNP challenge. The Scottish Conservative Party had called itself the Unionist Party between 1912 and 1965. It had opposed Scottish as well as Irish Home Rule. The Conservatives therefore seemed much less likely than Labour or the Liberals to prove sympathetic to Scottish aspirations. But there was another tradition in Scottish conservatism, which had become unionist to defend Pitt's union with Ireland, rather than the 1707 settlement with Scotland. This latter settlement was, after all, not under challenge, and was in any case a triumph of Whig rather than Tory statesmanship. If conservatism meant reverence for tradition, then Conservatives could well regard themselves as guardians of that sense of Scottish identity which Scotland's institutions sustained. Indeed, in Scotland, it had been the Tories who had in a sense been the nationalists, and the Whigs who appeared as the anglicizers and assimilationists. Sir Walter Scott has been called 'the outstanding example of what Scottish nationalism meant both in its depth of feeling and in its practical good sense'.[23] In 1808, after a debate in which he had fiercely opposed alterations in the procedure of the Scottish judicial system, his companions began to joke about it: ' "No, no," cried Scott, " 'tis no laughing matter; little by little, whatever your wishes may be, you will destroy and undermine until nothing of what makes Scotland Scotland shall remain." And so saying, he turned round to conceal his agitation— but not until Mr. Jeffrey saw tears gushing down his cheek.'[24]

Conservatives could thus respect the feelings which animated the national movement in Scotland, and they supported reforms designed to decentralize administration to Scotland. In the twentieth century, the expansion of the role of the Scottish Office, in 1926 and 1939, took place under Conservative governments. In opposition in the late 1940s, the Conservatives sought to harness Scottish feelings against the Attlee government, and the Churchill administration, in office from 1951, pursued a programme of further administrative devolution to Edinburgh.

By the late 1960s, however, the Conservatives were a sharply declining electoral force in Scotland. In 1955, they had secured a majority of Scottish seats and a majority of the Scottish vote—the only time that this result has been achieved by either major party since the war. But, by 1966, the Conservatives had been reduced to twenty seats in Scotland and 37.7 per cent of the vote. Within eleven years, they had lost sixteen seats and one-eighth of their vote. The traditionalist approach of the Scottish party appeared deeply unattractive to an electorate becoming increasingly concerned at the economic difficulties facing Scotland. The Scottish Conservatives were therefore eager to inject some element of Scottish awareness into their policies, and in the summer of 1967 they set up a committee under the chairmanship of Sir William McEwan Younger to consider how the structure of government could be made more responsive to Scottish needs. At the same time, a parallel investigation into Scottish government was being carried out by a new Conservative 'ginger group' called the Thistle Group, which was to become identified as a pro-devolution pressure group.

Both of these investigations were begun some time before the Hamilton by-election of 1967 and were motivated more by a concern for the reform of Scottish government than by fear of the SNP. The two groups came to strikingly similar conclusions, agreeing that the existing structure of government in Scotland was inefficient, because the range of functions for which the Scottish Office was responsible was too wide to be scrutinized properly either by Parliament or by ministers. As a result, too much power rested in the hands of civil servants.

Edward Heath, the Conservative leader, was not unresponsive to the argument for devolution in Scotland. He told Richard Crossman, leader of the House of Commons, a week before the Hamilton by-election, that 'nationalism is the biggest single factor in our politics today'.[25] Moreover, devolution would allow Heath to contrast Conservative sensitivities to different parts of the country with the centralizing tendencies of the socialists and the separatism of the SNP. The Conservatives, therefore, became the first of the two major parties to commit themselves to devolution.

At the Conference of the Scottish Conservatives in 1968, Heath, in a speech known somewhat grandiloquently as the Declaration of

Perth, proposed a directly elected Scottish assembly. He explicitly recognized the need for devolution as a counterweight to the central-izing tendencies of the European Community, and his speech dis-played a far-sightedness which, in different circumstances, might have done much to pre-empt the rise of the SNP in Scotland. Heath emphasized the contrast between the Conservative Party's stand for diversity and a 'world of mass industrialisation, mass communica-tions, and increasingly complex organisation' in which the strongest influences were those of 'uniformity and centralisation'. These pres-sures had led many to feel that they were losing control over their lives and there was, as a result, frustration and resentment with gov-ernment. The Labour Party, being the party of state control, was, Heath argued, unable to understand this new source of discontent. The SNP understood it, but proposed a wholly inappropriate remedy which involved sacrificing the gains Scotland derived from member-ship of the United Kingdom. 'The art of government', however, was 'to reconcile these divergent needs. The need to modernise our insti-tutions so as to cope with our complex changing society. And the need to give each citizen a greater opportunity to participate in the decisions that affect him, his family, and the community in which he lives.' The reconciliation of these needs involved finding a balance between two contrasting principles—the one being the unity of the United Kingdom, and the other being 'our belief in the devolution of power'. Heath ended his speech with a quotation from Quintin Hogg's *Case for Conservatism.* 'Political liberty is nothing else but the diffusion of power. If power is not to be abused, it must be spread as widely as possible throughout the community.'

Heath set up a Scottish Constitutional Committee under Sir Alec Douglas-Home, the function of which was to consider whether, while preserving 'the essential principle of the sovereignty of Parliament', it was possible to meet the desire of the majority of the people of Scotland to have a greater say in the conduct of their own affairs.[26] The Constitutional Committee reported in March 1970, and advocat-ed a directly elected Scottish assembly, a Convention, to take those bills certified by the Speaker as exclusively Scottish measures and considered by the Scottish Grand Committee and a Scottish standing committee. The Convention would thus consider the second reading, committee, and report stages of Scottish bills, leaving only the third reading and House of Lords stages to be taken at Westminster. The Secretary of State for Scotland, however, would remain responsible to Westminster and not to the Convention.

The great advantage of this scheme was that it could be presented as 'a natural evolution and extension of parliamentary practice as we know it'.[27] The Scottish Convention would take its place as a part of the Westminster machinery. Awkward questions, such as the future of Scottish representation at Westminster under devolution, could be entirely avoided. The Douglas-Home proposals offered the maximum degree of devolution possible within the existing parliamentary framework. The proposals were also constitutionally innovative in that they provided for legislation to be scrutinized by those who were not members of either House of Parliament.

It was not difficult of course for critics to find weaknesses in the Douglas-Home report. The proposed Convention, critics claimed, would do little to make the Scottish Office more accountable, since the Scottish Office would remain responsible to Parliament, not to the Convention. Moreover, decisions of the Convention could still be overturned at Westminster, and difficulties would arise when a Scottish majority, represented at the Convention, came into conflict with a majority of a different political colour at Westminster. The Douglas-Home committee denied that the Convention would cause conflict, since it would discuss only Scottish legislation which 'in the main consists of legislation which is not unduly controversial'. But, if controversial legislation were to be kept from the Convention, it was difficult to see what value it could have, and in particular whether it would have enough powers to deal with the serious weaknesses in Scottish government which the Douglas-Home committee had diagnosed. The committee, for example, had deplored the slow pace of decision-making on Scottish industrial matters. 'Long delays in deciding on matters which seriously affect the level of Scottish employment and generally influence the Scottish standard of living cannot be tolerated', the committee declared; and it found itself 'particularly impressed by the working of the Northern Ireland Ministry of Commerce—and especially by the speed of its decision-making'.[28] Yet what was proposed fell far short of the Northern Ireland model and the Convention, since it would lack executive powers, would be able to do nothing to speed up the process of administration.

These criticisms, however, were, in a sense, beside the point. For the Convention proposal would, it was hoped, be seen by the Scots as a signal that Westminster would henceforward take more notice of the Scottish point of view. It would give Scotland a political forum within which her problems would be discussed; and it would not be easy for Westminster to overrule the settled wish of the Scottish people as expressed in the Convention. Even if it did not provide the final answer, therefore, to the problems of Scottish government, the Convention might serve as a practical point of departure for further evolutionary development. Politically, moreover, the report isolated Labour, now the only major party opposed to devolution.

The Douglas-Home report was accepted by the Conservative leadership, and the Conservative election manifesto of 1970 promised that its recommendations, including the Scottish Convention sitting in Edinburgh, 'will form a basis for the proposals we will place before Parliament, taking account of the impending re-organisation of local government'. The Queen's Speech of 1970 promised that measures would be produced 'for giving the Scottish people a greater say in their own affairs'. Yet the Heath government made no move to establish a Scottish assembly. For this omission, two explanations have been given.

The first is that the Heath government did not want to legislate in advance of the report of the Royal Commission on the Constitution, which had been established by the Labour government in 1969, and did not in fact report until October 1973, when Britain was in the grip of the rise in oil prices which followed the Yom Kippur War. Had the Conservatives simply gone ahead with devolution in 1970, some at least of the members of the Royal Commission would have resigned, and this would have been an embarrassment for the government. Possibly the Heath government could have pressed the Commission to issue an interim report, as a basis for rapid action, but it did not do so.

The second explanation is that the Conservatives decided, without waiting for the report of the Royal Commission, to proceed with local government reform in Scotland, and this was hardly compatible with establishing an assembly in Scotland as well. Heath in fact argued that local government reform was a more important priority than devolution, writing to John Mackintosh, a pro-devolution Labour MP, in May 1973:

We for our part have always held that reform of local government is a matter of importance and urgency for the people of Scotland and that there should be no avoidable delay in putting in hand the complex arrangements needed to implement it. The question of devolution, while clearly a related matter, has always seemed to us one which should be pursued separately, and *later*, in a United Kingdom context . . . [emphasis added.]29

The government appears to have believed that local government reorganization might defuse Scottish grievances so that devolution would be unnecessary. Reorganization, however, created a cumbrous two-tier structure in Scotland, the upper tier of which consisted of regions, with the largest—Strathclyde—containing over half of the population of Scotland. This meant that if ever a Scottish assembly was set up, local government would have to be reorganized again, since the assembly would not easily be able to coexist with Strathclyde. It would have been better, if devolution had been in prospect, to have created a unitary system in Scotland; better still to have established an assembly first, and to have allowed it, as the representative body of Scotland, to put forward its own proposals for local government reform. The future shape of government in Scotland should have been decided first, and the new local government system could then have taken its place within that framework. For devolution was hardly, as Heath suggested in his letter to Mackintosh, an issue 'which should be pursued separately', after local government reform.

The probability is that devolution had ceased to be an important priority for Heath after 1970. The nationalist threat seemed, until 1973, to have evaporated and the energies of the Heath government were exercised elsewhere, on matters such as industrial relations legislation, incomes policy, and the European Community, itself a major constitutional issue. Thus, while the formal commitment to devolution remained, nothing was done about it. Nor were Scottish Conservatives particularly enamoured of devolution. Indeed, the Scottish Conservative Conference rejected the Douglas-Home proposals in 1973 and the only reference to devolution in the February 1974 election manifesto declared that the Conservatives were studying the report of the Royal Commission, although the Scottish manifesto declared that 'We are preparing proposals taking into account the different recommendations' made by the Royal Commission on the Constitution and that 'Our commitment to present proposals still stands.'

In the two elections of 1974, the Conservatives lost eight seats, all of them to the SNP, and 13 per cent of their vote. In twenty years they had lost no less than twenty seats in Scotland and a quarter of their vote. Following the success of the SNP in the elections of 1974, the Conservatives reiterated their support for devolution, but the election of Margaret Thatcher to the leadership of the party in 1975, as successor to Heath, replaced a supporter of devolution by someone whose instincts were hostile to it. 'Ted', she wrote, 'had impaled the Party on an extremely painful hook from which it would be my unenviable task to set it free. As an instinctive Unionist, I disliked the Devolution commitment.'[30]

Thus, when the Labour government presented its devolution proposals, in the form of a Scotland and Wales Bill, to Parliament in December 1976, the Conservatives, against the advice of the majority of Scottish Conservative MPs, opposed it. In May 1977, the Conservative spokesman on devolution, Francis Pym, announced that the party's commitment to a directly elected assembly was now 'inoperative'. The Conservatives had become the party of the Union again. The decline of the Conservatives in Scotland continued until, in the general election of 1997, they were completely wiped out, failing to return a single MP for a Scottish constituency.

VI

In the 1960s, however, it seemed as if it was the Labour Party which was in the most danger from the rise of Scottish nationalism. For

Labour had only twice in its history—in 1945 and 1966—succeeded in securing a majority of English seats. Not only, therefore, was Labour's industrial heartland in Scotland threatened by the SNP, but separatism foreshadowed the possibility of Labour becoming a permanent minority at Westminster.

It has been said of the Independent Labour Party, forerunner of the Labour Party, that it was 'in many respects a rebellion of the provinces and intrinsically regional in character'.[31] The Scottish Labour Party, founded in 1888, and influenced by men such as Keir Hardie and Cunninghame Graham, inherited the radical mantle of Scottish Home Rule. At Scottish Labour Party conferences between 1916 and 1923, Home Rule for Scotland was regularly passed without dissent, and the Scottish party helped to draft a Home Rule Bill in 1924. Indeed, many Scottish socialists wished to go further. For by 1922 Labour had become the largest party in Scotland. Why should it wait for the rest of the United Kingdom to be converted to socialism? Could not Labour establish a socialist bridgehead of its own in Scotland? Such were the thoughts of a number of Scottish socialists, amongst whom John Maclean was the most prominent, in the early 1920s.

With the onset of mass unemployment, however, socialists came to believe that economic progress depended upon a strong central government. The search in the 1930s was for measures of state control to cure the slump. National ownership by the state would be better than ownership by the capitalists of Scotland. Tom Johnston, Secretary of State for Scotland during the years of Churchill's wartime coalition, and a former Home Ruler, warned, after the Second World War, that a Scottish parliament might have nothing to administer but 'an emigration system, a glorified Poor Law and a graveyard'.[32] During his tenure as Secretary of State between 1941 and 1945, moreover, Johnston had shown what could be done for Scotland by using the machinery of a powerful centralized state to lobby for Scotland's interests.

In the years between the wars, the trade-union wing of the Labour Party had also come to be hostile to devolution because of its belief that national wage bargaining was needed to maintain wage levels in Scotland. Indeed, even as they claimed to support Home Rule, the

Scottish trade unions pressed for national bargaining, prompting J. H. Thomas, Labour's minister in charge of policy for unemployment in 1929, to remark that 'Scotsmen are far-reaching people. They want Home Rule in everything that does not cost anything'.33

In the immediate post-war years, Scotland benefited from the Attlee government's regional policies and it was natural that the Scottish Labour Party should be unwilling to put this at risk by a policy of Home Rule. In 1945 the Scottish Council for Labour rejected by 113 votes to five a motion by the nationalist, Douglas Young, calling for Home Rule; and Arthur Woodburn, a future Secretary of State for Scotland, argued that agitation for a Scottish parliament would drive industry away from Scotland. Home Rule suffered a further setback in the Labour Party when it came to be used by the Conservatives in their campaign against the Attlee government. For the Conservatives, 'London government' became a euphemism for the Labour government. In Scotland, Walter Elliot, a former Conservative Scottish Secretary, declared nationalization meant denationalization.34 John MacCormick, standing in 1948 as a Liberal candidate at Paisley, with Conservative support, went even further, declaring that the issue was 'one between freedom and totalitarianism. If the Government is allowed to pursue its present course our retrogression towards State tyranny is inevitable.'35 Such overheated rhetoric did not endear Labour to the nationalist cause.

The interventionist state seemed to be yielding benefits to Scotland in the form of social welfare and economic aid, and yet, by integrating her more closely into Britain, it perhaps meant that Scotland was coming to lose something of herself. In reaction to this centralization, MacCormick launched, in 1949, the Scottish Covenant, and it attracted over two million signatures in favour of a Scottish parliament. Attlee, understandably, regarded the Covenant as a move to embarrass Labour, and refused to meet a delegation from the Convention. Churchill, however, during the 1950 general election, sought to draw the connection between interventionist government and Scottish nationalism and to harness the new Scottish mood to the Tory cause.

The principle of centralisation of government in Whitehall and Westminster is emphasised in a manner not hitherto experienced or contemplated in the

Act of Union. The supervision, interference and control in the ordinary
details of Scottish life and business by the Parliament at Westminster has not
hitherto been foreseen, and I frankly admit that it raises new issues between
the two nations. . . . If England became an absolute Socialist state, owning
all the means of production, distribution and exchange, ruled only by politicians and their officials in the London offices, I personally cannot feel that
Scotland would be bound to accept such a dispensation. . . . I would never
accept the view that Scotland should be forced into the serfdom of Socialism
as the result of a vote in the House of Commons. It is an alteration so fundamental in our way of life that it would require a searching review of our
historical relations.[36]

Attlee himself 'was not inclined to give much time to Scottish problems' and he 'was intolerant of any regional variations that might
impede progress'.[37] What might be called the ideology of the welfare state was to conflict sharply with the view that Scotland enjoyed
a special status within the United Kingdom, which was guaranteed
by the Treaty of Union. Thus, the traditional unionism of the
Conservatives which attacked Home Rule as a threat to national
unity came to be complemented by a unionism of the Left which
stressed that only a strong central government in London could
secure equity of treatment between the different parts of the United
Kingdom.

The centralist approach continued through the 1960s, and whereas in the Conservative Party grass-roots pressure had created a
favourable climate for devolution proposals, in the Labour Party
pressure came from the top. For the instinct of Labour, as shown by
the opposition of Left-wing MPs such as Eric Heffer and Neil
Kinnock to the devolution legislation in the 1970s, was that devolution would make the task of socialists more difficult. They were concerned less perhaps with the loss of *sovereignty* involved than with
loss of the *power* of central government, a power which was needed,
amongst other reasons, to remedy the very territorial disparities and
inequalities which so concerned advocates of devolution.

The first reaction of the Labour Party's Scottish Council to the
rise of Scottish nationalism in the 1960s was that it was a product of
economic setbacks, and that with the return of prosperity, nationalism would disappear. Devolution, the Council held, would threaten

the position of the Secretary of State for Scotland, and also Scotland's over-representation at Westminster, both of which enabled Scotland to gain advantages when it came to the allocation of public expenditure. In 1968, therefore, the Scottish Labour Party Conference rejected devolution by a large majority, and in its evidence to the Royal Commission on the Constitution, the Scottish Council declared, 'We think that legislative devolution would damage Scotland's economic development. Labour's record in this respect . . . is something we cannot afford to lose.' And the secretary to the Scottish Labour Party told the Commission that 'There is . . . no such thing as a separate political will for Scotland.'[38] These attitudes were reinforced in the Cabinet by the determination of William Ross, Secretary of State for Scotland, who, in the 1960s, was adamantly opposed to devolution. Ross, Richard Crossman believed, was 'determined to treat nationalism as a mere emotional attitude which can be cured by economic policies alone'.[39]

The Labour election manifesto of February 1974 said nothing about devolution, although its Welsh manifesto promised a directly elected council for Wales. After the election, however, in which the SNP had gained six seats, two of them from Labour, the issue of devolution was one which the party could no longer ignore, especially since, in office as a minority government, it would be forced to go to the polls again shortly. At its conference in March 1974, the Scottish Council came out in favour of a directly elected assembly. In June, however, the executive of the Scottish Council, meeting with one-third of its members absent watching a World Cup football match, rejected devolution by six votes to five as 'irrelevant to the real needs of the people of Scotland', because:

The essential strategy for the Labour Party is to bring about a fundamental and irreversible shift in the balance of power and wealth in favour of working people. Public ownership and control of North Sea oil is a vital element . . . constitutional tinkering does not make a meaningful contribution towards achieving our socialist objectives.

This decision caused considerable embarrassment to Labour's National Executive in London, which was preparing the party's programme for the next general election, and was convinced that, unless

Labour committed itself to devolution, it would suffer further losses to the SNP.

The Scottish organizer of the Labour Party was therefore summoned to London and pressure was put on constituency parties and trade unions in Scotland to call a special conference to reverse the decision of the Scottish Executive. At this special conference on 16 September 1974, two days before the general election was announced, 'the devolutionists', in the words of one commentator, 'got their way by arm-twisting', the union block vote being swung to the government's policy on devolution as a quid pro quo for the social contract on wages.[40] Tam Dalyell, the leading Labour opponent of devolution in Scotland, wondered how one union leader, 'believing what he does about the assembly will be able to look at himself in his shaving mirror'.[41] In the general election of October 1974, Labour made an official commitment to devolution, and published, for the first time, a separate manifesto for Scotland, although 'there were complaints, nonetheless, that the Scottish manifesto had been written in London and shown to the Scottish Executive only when it was too late to make any major changes.'[42]

It is ironic that Labour became a devolutionist party under pressure from London. The parties indeed had reversed their positions, the Conservatives beginning as devolutionists and ending as supporters of the status quo, Labour beginning as supporters of the status quo, and ending as devolutionists. In each case, the shifts were made on grounds of tactics rather than principle. All the same, these tergiversations of the 1960s and 1970s were to prove of vital importance for the future not only of Scottish, but also of British politics. For they were to determine party positions on devolution for many years to come. The parties were to become frozen in the positions of the mid- and late 1970s. The Conservatives would be the party of the constitutional status quo and Labour the party of constitutional change.

From the late 1970s, Labour began to recover its electoral position in Scotland, even while it was losing support in the rest of the country. In 1979, although defeated in the general election, Labour actually improved its performance in Scotland, while the SNP lost nine of its eleven seats (Table 4.3).

Table 4.3 Labour results in Scotland, October 1974 and 1979

Election	% of Labour vote	Labour seats in Scotland
Oct. 1974	36.3	41
1979	41.6	44

During the long years of opposition, between 1979 and 1997, Labour retained its position as the majority party in Scotland. Labour, whose support for devolution had begun by being halting and uncertain, would become the strongest political force arguing that only devolution could keep Scotland within the United Kingdom.

Wales

Britain is the creation of the state. Wales the creation of providence.

(Gwynfor Evans, *Wales Can Win*)

I

Following the incorporation of Wales with England in the sixteenth century, the Welsh people did not find it easy to maintain their identity. For governmental purposes, indeed, Wales came to be treated as if it were part of England. Section 3 of the Wales and Berwick Act of 1746, provided that 'in all cases where the Kingdom of England, or that part of Great Britain called England, hath been or shall be mentioned in any Act of Parliament, the same has been and shall from henceforth be deemed and taken to comprehend and include the Dominion of Wales.'[1] This Act remained in force until 1967. By the nineteenth century, Gladstone could claim that 'The distinction between England and Wales . . . is totally unknown to our constitution.'[2] For Wales, unlike Scotland, did not enjoy those independent institutions which not only ensured separate treatment, but, more crucially, preserved the memory of independent statehood.

Thus Welsh nationalism, lacking an institutional focus, had to build on less concrete factors—language, religion, and culture. It was left to writers, poets, and preachers to create 'the cultural form, the tracery of a nation where no state had existed'.[3] The Welsh faced the same uphill task as other ethnic minorities in Europe—the Corsicans and the Bretons, for example; they were seeking to create a national movement on the basis of symbols such as language and religion whose importance was declining in the modern world.

The crucial difference between Scotland and Wales has been summed up by Marxists in the distinction between a 'historic' nation and a 'non-historic' nation, between a nation which had succeeded in retaining the institutions of statehood and one which had not. For nations of the latter sort, Engels at least had little sympathy. They were merely:

remnant people, left over from an earlier population, forced back and subjugated by the nation which later became the repository of historical development. These remnants of a nation, mercilessly crushed, as Hegel said, by the course of history, this *national refuse*, is always the fanatical representative of the counter-revolution, and remains so until it is completely exterminated or de-nationalised, as its whole existence is in itself a protest against a great historical revolution.[4]

Wales, however, has always been very far from being a 'fanatical representative of the counter-revolution'. Indeed, the politics of Wales in modern times has been characterized by its consistent and powerful support for the Left, first for the Liberals and then for Labour. Before the First World War, Wales was the most anti-Conservative area in Britain; during the years 1885–1914, there were only two Welsh constituencies where the average Conservative vote was higher than the average Liberal vote, and the Conservatives performed appreciably worse than the Liberals in rural constituencies, 'at a time when in Britain as a whole the Conservatives were regarded as the party representing most effectively the interests of both landlord and farmer'. Indeed, during the six elections between 1885 and 1914, the average vote for the Conservatives was 38.6 per cent in Wales, but 52.7 per cent in the predominantly working-class constituencies of inner London. There can be little doubt therefore that, during these years, 'nationalism contributed something to political feeling which went beyond the mere sense of economic grievance'.[5] The prime reason for the minority position of the Conservatives in Wales was that they were seen as the political representatives of the Anglican church, the church of a minority in Wales, and the landowner—influences which seemed hostile to the national as well as the social aspirations of Wales. 'A Welsh nonconformist who is a Conservative in politics', it was said in 1914, 'is considered by his co-religionists a traitor to his sect, and almost a traitor to his country.'[6]

The Liberal ascendancy began with the general election of 1857, and coincided with a remarkable reawakening of Welsh national consciousness. The Liberals sought to have this consciousness recognized. Their first success came in 1881 with the Sunday Closing (Wales) Act, the first time that a legislative principle was applied to Wales but not to England. For many Welsh Liberals, indeed, radicalism and nationalism were indistinguishable. Tom Ellis declared in his election address at Merioneth in 1886, 'I solicit your suffrages as a WELSH NATIONALIST'; and Lloyd George characterized himself in Dod's Parliamentary Companion until 1923 as a Radical and Welsh Nationalist.

In 1866, the *Cymru Fydd* (Wales of the Future) movement was founded. It began as a cultural movement, but became nationalist in the 1880s. Its nationalism, however, entailed not separation from England, but equality with England. This was because, in the words of one account of *Cymru Fydd*, it was

recognised, not only that union with England is inevitable, but that it provides the best opportunity that Wales could have to deliver her mission . . . to the world. The closer the connection the better it will be for the purposes of *Cymru Fydd*; for it is by influencing England that Wales can influence the world. The one condition which is insisted upon is that the connection shall not be closer at the expense of Welsh nationality or at the sacrifice of some national qualities. The voices of England and of Wales should be joined, not in unison, but in harmony.[7]

Home Rule was in no way crucial to the Welsh claim for equality. Indeed it was, as we shall see, a divisive issue in Wales; and for Tom Ellis, 'it was the nonconformity of Wales that created the unity of Wales, rather than any spontaneous demand for Home Rule.'[8]

The agitation for Irish Home Rule gave an impetus to national sentiment in Wales, but there are a number of reasons why Home Rule did not play as crucial a role in Welsh politics as it did in Ireland. Wales, it is true, shared with Ireland an agrarian problem and resentment at English domination; but its experience of English rule had been very different, and there was no equivalent in Welsh history to the Irish famine and emigration which had so embittered Irish attitudes.

In Wales, unlike Ireland, the agrarian problem was not complicated by the existence of an alien and absentee landlord class belonging to the dominant nation. However much the landlords had become anglicized, they were still either Welsh or linked in marriage to the native Welsh, and many of them were nonconformist and Welsh-speaking. It was impossible to feel for them the same depth of antagonism which the Irish peasant felt for his English landlord. Moreover, Wales, unlike Ireland, had not been a colony of settlement, nor had it been 'planted' with those of an alien religion. There was, furthermore, no agrarian violence or crime in Wales. Altogether, therefore, conditions in Ireland and Wales were very different.

In addition, the effects of the gradual democratization of life were felt more tangibly in Wales than they had been in Ireland. In the first elections to the Welsh county councils in 1889, 'the Welsh national feeling' was 'very strongly brought out' and the Liberals succeeded in winning every county except Brecknock. Precisely because these new local authorities succeeded in undermining the rule of the landowner and the gentry, it was apparent that reform in Wales did not depend upon Home Rule. Indeed, the results of the elections 'created a social transformation more striking even than the extension of democracy at the national level'. 'It is not', Gladstone told his friend Stuart Rendel, MP for Montgomery, in 1892, 'the Irish case over again.'[9] In Wales, unlike Ireland, there was no desire for separation and little doubt that Home Rule could be killed by kindness.

Home Rule, moreover, was a divisive issue in Wales, and schemes for establishing Welsh national institutions were continually to founder 'on the same rock, the balance of representation between Glamorgan and Monmouth and the rest of the country'.[10] In 1892, for example, a proposal for a Welsh national body to take over the powers of the Local Government Board, the Board of Guardians, Commissioners for Works, and the Charity Commissioners for Wales, was considered. But Welsh opinion failed to agree on what the basis of representation on this new national body should be. Glamorgan favoured representation on a population basis under which it would secure twenty-five of the fifty-nine seats. This meant, however, that Merioneth and Radnor would secure only two seats each. Radnor therefore sought equal representation by county on the lines of the American Senate. But to this Glamorgan would not agree; so the proposal came to nothing.

Shortly afterwards, Lloyd George attempted to create a centralized democratic political leadership in Wales. This involved the abolition of the North and South Wales Liberal Federations and their replacement by one central body. Lloyd George was defeated, however, by opposition from the South Wales Liberal Federation which refused to merge its powers, one English-speaking Liberal from Cardiff, Alderman Bird, declaring that 'a cosmopolitan population from Swansea to Newport' would 'never bow to the domination of Welsh ideas'.[11] Nationalism in Wales proved, as it was to do in 1979 and in 1997, divisive, not integrative as it was in Scotland. The Liberal Party, therefore, concentrated on measures designed to secure 'equality for Wales within the British and imperial framework, not exclusion from it'.[12]

The development of industrialism in south Wales served further to weaken the pressure for Home Rule. It did so in two ways. First, it helped to relieve the growing pressure on the land, and thus provided an alternative to migration of a kind not available to the Irish peasant. Second, industrialization introduced a new element into Welsh politics, threatening not only the Liberal Party, but that radical nonconformist nationalism which had first triumphed in 1857. For class conflict was to cut across the old Liberal–Conservative and Welsh–English cleavages. This meant that a Welsh nonconformist industrialist such as D. A. Thomas, later Lord Rhondda, who had found himself on the progressive side of politics when the cleavage had been a religious and cultural one, came to be branded as a class enemy by the Labour Party. Moreover, industrialism, by tying the economy of south Wales more tightly to the English economy, made nationalism appear not only sociologically irrelevant, but also economically foolish.

It was for these reasons that the collapse of the *Cymru Fydd* movement in 1896 proved to be the end of political nationalism in Wales for seventy years until the Welsh nationalist party, Plaid Cymru, together with changes in political culture in Wales, once more put Home Rule onto the political agenda.

II

The failure of *Cymru Fydd* made it seem as if the sentiment of nationality in Wales was not powerful or unified enough to sustain a strong Home Rule movement. Accordingly, Welsh Liberals concentrated their efforts upon winning recognition for Welsh cultural aspirations and religious distinctiveness. Rather than a Welsh parliament, they sought national educational institutions and the disestablishment of the Welsh church. The first of these aims proved easier to achieve than the second. In 1889 the Intermediate Education Act made Welsh county councils the first local education authorities in Britain. They were empowered to raise a halfpenny rate for secondary education, with a Treasury grant being made available to the local authorities equivalent to the sum raised in the rates. This was the system later adopted in England in A. J. Balfour's Education Act of 1902. In 1893, a charter was granted to the University of Wales, and in 1896, a Central Welsh Board was established to administer examinations. The Welsh educational system was thus in the process of becoming 'a national system, the first and most striking expression in institutional terms of the reawakened consciousness of nationhood'.[13]

But Welsh Liberals sought, above all, disestablishment of the Welsh church, the church of a minority of the Welsh people, to which no Welsh-speaking bishop had been appointed between 1715 and 1870, and yet a church to which Welsh tenant-farmers were compelled to pay tithes. The 'tithe war', under which tithes were withheld, linked together the issues of land and church, class and religion, powerfully strengthening the Welsh Liberals; and in Wales it was disestablishment rather than Home Rule which served to unify national opinion.

Welsh disestablishment, however, was a highly contentious issue in British politics, and when Gladstone embarked on his Home Rule crusade, it took second place to the Irish demand. For this reason, Gladstone, in his final ministry of 1892–4, failed to carry disestablishment, while the short-lived Rosebery government of 1894–5 fell before a Welsh disestablishment bill could complete its passage through Parliament. Welsh Liberals could, in theory, have reacted to this setback by forming an independent party on the Parnellite model, threatening to withhold support from any government which did not meet their wishes. But it never occurred to them to do so. They well appreciated that liberalism could not survive in Wales

merely as a vehicle for Celtic claims. They sought primarily not separation but recognition. 'The ideal of Wales was to be recognised as
a part of the British political and social structure: the ideal of Ireland
was to be severed from it. The object of the one was equality: the aim
of the other was exclusion.'14

But if Welsh Liberalism was a political instrument fashioned to
meet the challenge of recognition, it was less well equipped to meet
the challenge of industrialism. Too many of its policies assumed a
social homogeneity that was rapidly disappearing in Wales. Indeed,
both Welsh Liberalism and Welsh nationalism came to be tied to symbols—the land, religion, and the language—whose importance in
Welsh life was diminishing. In 1895, the *Cymru Fydd* programme had
placed 'labour and industrial' questions seventh, well behind such nos-
trums as Home Rule for Wales, temperance reform, and security for
the tenant-farmer. Lloyd George himself 'remained an Old Liberal in
Wales, although a "New Liberal" in England', and for Wales he argued
that 'the land question, the temperance question and the question of
disestablishment were equally matters of interest to labourers as an
Eight Hours bill'.15 National claims came increasingly to be focused
on the limited aim of disestablishment, and when that was achieved in
1914—although it did not come into effect until 1920—the movement
faded and Welsh Liberalism lost much of its vitality. Disestablishment
in Wales was an end in itself and not, as it was in Ireland, a prelude to
the demand for political change. There was to be no Welsh Parnell.

In 1918, most Welsh Liberals allied themselves with Lloyd
George and the Conservatives in the 'coupon election', and this
proved fatal to the claims of the Liberal Party to be the radical party
in Wales. By 1922, Labour had replaced the Liberals as the dominant
party in Wales, and by 1951 there were only three Liberal MPs left
in the principality, all of whom held their seats through tacit
Conservative support. The Liberals had ceased to be the party of
Welsh aspirations. That title now went to Labour.

III

Labour always held an ambivalent attitude to Welsh national claims.
It inherited the mantle of Liberalism as the party of the provinces and

the periphery, but it was also a British-wide movement which saw class rather than community as the basis of political action. Thus, 'To the old pattern of Welsh solidarity, expressed in the Liberal Party and closely allied to Nonconformity, [Labour] opposed a new philosophy—one of secular Socialism, British rather than Welsh in content.'[16] The trade unions, the industrial wing of the Labour movement, saw themselves as national bodies, and feared that if they allowed themselves to be divided by geography, employers would have an excuse to cut wages in the less prosperous parts of the country. The trade unions, therefore, protested when, as a concession to national sentiment, Lloyd George, in his National Insurance Act of 1911, agreed to set up separate administrations for National Health insurance in Scotland and Wales as well as in Ireland.

During the early years of the century, however, Labour proved a unifying force in Welsh politics. Like the Liberals, Labour enjoyed a broad cultural appeal, based as much upon the chapel and the Sunday school as upon class-consciousness. Labour, in the words of Tom Jones, was 'not bound by a narrow economic doctrine; our approach was ethical or rather we were striving to bring the economic and religious factors into a right relation . . . we wanted a classless society but not a class war'.[17] This cultural dimension, much influenced by Keir Hardie, implied recognition of ethnic diversity in the fashioning of the state, and Labour, in its early years, espoused the Liberal doctrine of 'Home Rule All Round', which of course implied a Welsh parliament.

But, as we have seen, Home Rule and the redress of nonconformist grievances were becoming more peripheral to Welsh politics. After the First World War there was a brief flurry of interest in regionalism and nationalism, but this soon died away. A conference on devolution in Wales held at Shrewsbury in 1922 failed disastrously, the industrial counties of Glamorgan and Monmouth not even bothering to send representatives.

During the inter-war years, faced with mass unemployment and migration from south Wales to the Midlands and London, nationalism seemed to have nothing to offer. Instead, the unemployed looked 'fixedly, if resentfully, to the government in London, apparently seeing no prospect of salvation under a separate system of government in Wales'.[18] The solution to the problems of Wales was to be found in a Labour government, able to plan the economy from the centre, not in a Welsh parliament.

In office from 1945, Labour's main concerns lay with economic policy and social reform, and this tended to reinforce its centralist outlook. On the first Welsh Day debate in the House of Commons in 1944, Aneurin Bevan declared that 'My colleagues, all of them members of the Miners' Federation of Great Britain, have no special solution for the Welsh coal industry which is not a solution for the whole of the mining industry of Great Britain. There is no Welsh problem.'[19] On devolution, Bevan said in 1946:

Is it not rather cruel to give the impression to the 50,000 unemployed men and women in Wales that their plight would be relieved and their distress removed by this constitutional change? It is not socialism. It is escapism. This is exactly the way in which nation after nation has been ruined in the last 25 to 50 years, trying to pretend that deep-seated economic difficulties can be removed by constitutional changes.[20]

Bevan in the 1940s, like Eric Heffer and Neil Kinnock in the 1970s, saw socialism as a doctrine which required control of the levers of economic power. It would be madness for socialists, having after so many years achieved power at Westminster, to dissipate it by dividing it up between subnational units. In the 1960s, Labour was to become even more committed to central planning of the economy and to a regional policy run from London. Thus, with Labour the dominant party in Wales in the post-war years, 'Welsh nationalism seemed as dead as the druids.'[21]

Yet Labour was still electorally dependent on the peripheries, and, in 1964 and 1974, would not have been able to form a government without support from Wales. It is not surprising, then, that Labour's approach to Wales should have been so ambivalent, its centralist philosophy clashing with its traditional role as the party of peripheral protest, and with its electoral self-interest.

IV

The Welsh nationalist party, Plaid Cymru, was born in 1925 in the midst of an era of disillusion and depression in the principality. As with the SNP, so also with Plaid Cymru—its birth was a sign not of the strength of peripheral nationalism but of its weakness. For both movements were founded on a recognition that neither national self-government nor even devolution were to be obtained from the other parties. The Conservatives had always opposed Welsh Home Rule, the Liberals were no longer in a position to offer it, while Labour seemed uninterested.

Plaid Cymru, however, faced problems far more daunting than those of the SNP. For in Scotland, nationalism was a unifying and integrative force, the institutions of nationhood eliciting feelings of sympathy from nearly every Scot. In Wales, by contrast, the symbols of nationality—the land, religion, and the church—seemed symbols of a dying culture, while the language, the most obvious badge of Welsh identity, was for many years to prove a deeply divisive force, tending to confine Plaid Cymru to 'Welsh' Wales in the north-west, as opposed to the industrial south-east.

In the twentieth century the Welsh language was in steady retreat until, by 1981, only 21 per cent of Welsh people spoke Welsh. By 1991, the figure had fallen to 18 per cent, but there were signs of a revival in Welsh-speaking amongst young people, on whom the future of the language depends. Nevertheless, if language were to be the criterion of Welshness, around 80 per cent of the inhabitants of Wales would have to be dismissed as not truly Welsh. The English-speaking majority could hardly be expected to vote for a party whose main platform was the promotion of a language which they could not speak. If, on the other hand, Plaid Cymru were to underplay the language issue, it might lose its central core of support from those who saw the preservation of the language as the main purpose of self-government. The party was placed, therefore, in a cruel dilemma and it has never succeeded in resolving it.

Plaid Cymru began as a movement to preserve the language, and it was originally more of a 'cultural conservationist society' than a political party.[22] Admittedly Saunders Lewis, its president from 1926 to 1939, believed that only self-government could save the language; but, in a radio broadcast in 1962 he modified his position, proclaiming that the language 'is the only political question deserving of a Welshman's attention at the present time', and that it was:

more important than self-government . . . if we were to have any sort of self-government for Wales before the Welsh language is recognised and used as an official language in all the administration of State and local authority in the Welsh areas of our country, it would never attain official status, and the doom of the language would come more quickly than it will come under English government.[23]

Saunders Lewis hoped that just as English was the official language of England, so also Welsh would become the sole official language of Wales. However, a later generation of Plaid Cymru's leaders adopted a more moderate stance on the language problem. In his book, *Plaid Cymru and Wales*, published in 1950, Gwynfor Evans, president of the party, insisted that: 'since common membership of the Welsh community rather than language or descent is the test of nationality in Wales, nationalists are proud to know them [English-speaking Welshmen] as fellow-Welshmen. Wales has no finer patriots than some who have no knowledge of the national tongue'.[24]

The party dissociated itself from the extremists of the Welsh Language Society, which one of Plaid Cymru's leaders, Dr Phil Williams, accused of 'alienating increasing numbers of the population' and creating 'hostility to the Welsh language'.[25] In 1968, Plaid Cymru adopted a policy of bilingualism, but it did so somewhat reluctantly. Since then, however, it has moved further in the direction of seeking to accommodate English-speaking Wales, and in 1998, it decided to change its name to Plaid Cymru the Party of Wales. Its electoral successes, however, have remained largely confined to the Welsh-speaking north-west of the principality.

In its early years, Plaid Cymru was so preoccupied with the language question that it devoted little attention to the economic changes which were visibly altering the face of Wales. Since the early 1960s, however, there has been 'a campaign of attrition by a growing band of Modernists to bring the party into the world of modern Wales, to drag the movement, however reluctantly, away from total preoccupation with the cultural strongholds of the north and west'.[26] The party has put forward ideas based on the thought of E. F. Schumacher, author of *Small is Beautiful*, and Leopold Kohr, an *émigré* social scientist at Aberystwyth University College, who sought to put some of Schumacher's prescriptions into concrete form. Crucial to Plaid Cymru's vision is a means of strengthening the identification of the individual with his ethnic community. This, according to Gwynfor Evans, means preserving the heritage of the Welsh past:

Adaptation requires a hold of the past, of traditional life. The past lives in the tradition of the national community; if it is destroyed no adaptation is possible. Therefore, although they are a radical party which seeks fundamental changes in Wales, nationalists have been conscious of the necessity for roots and continuity in human society and of the importance of identity and community in human life.[27]

During the parliamentary debates on devolution in the 1970s, Evans argued for a federal system within which Wales would take its place, rather than for separatism, although he was not clear whether England or the English regions should be the units in the system. Plaid Cymru's concern seemed to lie less in setting up a classic nine-teenth-century nation state as the SNP was seeking to do, than in transcending the notion of sovereignty altogether. Plaid Cymru was and is as much a communalist and decentralist party as a separatist one, and, whereas the debate in Scotland has been primarily one about nationalism, in Wales it has been about how to restore the lost spirit of community.

As with the SNP, Plaid Cymru found itself unsuccessful at the hustings for many years, although in by-elections in Ogmore and Aberdare in 1946, it was able to secure 29 per cent and 20 per cent of the vote. Between 1950 and 1956, Plaid Cymru took part in an abortive all-party campaign to press for a Welsh parliament. A petition was drawn up which received a quarter of a million signatures, equal to 14 per cent of the Welsh electorate, but it was ignored both by the government and by the Labour opposition, while the Labour MPs who were associated with the campaign—including Cledwyn Hughes, a future Secretary of State for Wales—were carpeted by Labour's National Executive Committee for defying official party policy on the issue.

Until 1959, Plaid Cymru concentrated its electoral forces on the Welsh-speaking areas. As late as 1969, seven constituencies in Glamorgan and Monmouth had never seen a Plaid Cymru candidate.

Yet, ironically, Plaid Cymru's breakthrough, when it came, occurred not in the rural Welsh-speaking areas of Merioneth or Carnarvon, but in the areas of industrial decline in the valleys—Rhondda and Caerphilly—and in Carmarthen, where in a by-election in July 1966 Gwynfor Evans overturned a Labour majority of 9,233 to win the party's first seat. In a by-election in Rhondda West, one of the safest Labour seats in the country, in March 1967, Plaid almost won, slashing a Labour majority of 16,888 to 2,306. In the third and last by-election in Wales in the 1966–70 parliament, in Caerphilly in July 1968, Plaid Cymru also ran a close second. 'In the Midlands', the journalist David McKie commented, 'the slump in the Labour vote looked merely like the collapse of a habit: in South Wales, it looks like the death of a religion.'[28]

In the two general elections of 1974, however, Plaid Cymru failed to emulate the SNP and its percentage of the vote remained static (Table 5.1).

In October 1974, although Plaid Cymru won three seats, there were only five seats where its vote exceeded 20 per cent, and the party succeeded in saving only four deposits outside the six predominantly Welsh-speaking constituencies. In Wales, by contrast with Scotland, the demand for a third force in Welsh politics found its outlet not in the nationalists, but in the Liberal Party, whose share of the vote increased from 6.8 per cent in 1970 to 15.5 per cent in October 1974.

However, because Plaid Cymru gained *seats* in both of the two elections in 1974, Westminster politicians and commentators believed that there was increasing support for nationalism in Wales

Table 5.1 General election results in Wales, 1970 and 1974

Election	Total votes in Wales	% of vote in Wales	Candidates	Elected
1970	175,016	11.5	36	0
February 1974	171,374	10.7	36	2
October 1974	166,321	10.8	36	3

as well as in Scotland. It was common for politicians and commentators in the mid-1970s to speak of 'the rise of nationalism in Scotland and Wales', ignoring the fact that Plaid Cymru's support had fallen from its high point in 1970; and this mistaken diagnosis was to play its part in the events that led to the débâcle of the 1979 referendum.

V

Welsh nationality, however, did not depend primarily upon a nationalist party for its expression. During the twentieth century, Welsh distinctiveness came to be underlined, in an almost unnoticed way, by a series of reforms whose effect was to decentralize administration from London to Cardiff. Whereas Scotland already had its own institutions and distinctiveness which the establishment of the Scottish Secretary in 1885 merely recognized, in Wales, by contrast, governmental institutions were established by Westminster and Whitehall, not so much to meet national claims as to meet the needs of central government itself.

The first recognition by any government department that separate treatment was necessary for Wales occurred in 1907, when a Welsh Department of the Board of Education was established. This innovation showed that administrative devolution in education could yield valuable benefits, for the Welsh Department was able to secure 'a unified approach to the educational problems of each individual authority so that, at any one time, officials of the Welsh Department were able to see the whole range of educational services provided in a particular area'. The Department, unlike the Board of Education in London, was able to shift funds from primary to secondary education and vice versa, and it had the added advantage that 'it was possible for the officers of the local authorities to establish a close personal relationship with the Department's officials'.[29] The Department was also given a free hand to encourage education in the Welsh language, and the outstanding feature of the Board's work in its first two years was 'the definite recognition of the Welsh language and Welsh literature in the curriculum of the schools and training colleges of Wales'.[30]

The next instalment of administrative decentralization in Wales occurred in 1911 with Lloyd George's National Insurance Act. The Irish demanded a separate national commission, and Scotland and Wales then sought a similar concession. Lloyd George, who had originally hoped for a unified system of administration, gave way, saying 'you have got to defer to sentiment'.[31] The Welsh commissioners came to exercise 'an influence and authority which nobody sitting in and operating from London could have hoped to exercise'.[32] The Act, therefore, proved, 'not only a necessary but a very successful experiment in applied home rule'.[33]

The third area of administrative decentralization was in agriculture. In 1912, a year after the Scottish Board of Agriculture had been set up, the office of Agricultural Commissioner for Wales was established, together with an advisory Agricultural Council for Wales. However, as the Welsh Land Enquiry Commission reported in 1914, 'the problem of land in its varied features is so vast and complicated that it is impossible to deal effectively with Wales by a department located in Whitehall and staffed by men out of touch, and more often than not, out of sympathy with the special needs of Wales'. In consequence, a Welsh office of the Board of Agriculture and Fisheries was set up in 1919.[34]

This process of administrative decentralization continued until, by the 1950s, no fewer than seventeen departments had established administrative units in Wales.[35] This did not, however, reflect any overall plan of devolution. The process of decentralization was entirely pragmatic, and the extent of decentralization differed from department to department. There was no obvious reason, for example, why the Welsh Board of Health, the successor to the insurance commissioners, which, by 1950, was exercising most of the major powers of the Ministry of Health in Wales, should have come to enjoy more autonomy than the Welsh Department of the Ministry of Agriculture. Were there, however, to be a minister whose responsibility it was to concern himself specifically with Wales, then, it could be argued, it might be possible to shape policy more effectively to meet Welsh needs. There would then be an overall approach towards administrative devolution to Wales as there had been in Scotland, in place of the piecemeal approach of earlier years. The logical next step seemed to be a Minister for Wales. This proposal was rejected in the 1930s by Neville Chamberlain and in the 1940s by Attlee, but in 1951, Winston Churchill appointed his Home Secretary, Sir David Maxwell-Fyfe, as also the first Minister for Welsh Affairs. Sir David was to be answerable to the Commons for the general effect of government policy in Wales and for the annual White Paper on government action in Wales, and he was also to lead in Welsh Day debates. But he was given no executive powers and, as he lacked a departmental machine, his effectiveness was bound to depend upon the degree of influence which he could secure over his Cabinet colleagues. Moreover, Sir David suffered from the handicap of sitting for an English constituency.

In 1957, Harold Macmillan announced that the Minister of Housing and Local Government, Henry Brooke, would in future also be the Minister for Welsh Affairs, since this Minister, unlike the Home Secretary, had executive responsibility for a wide range of matters affecting Wales. He would therefore be in a position to take the initiative through the use of his own departmental powers. But Brooke too sat for an English constituency, and his credibility was shattered when he approved the acquisition of water in the Tryweryn Valley in Merioneth by Liverpool, even though it was opposed by twenty-seven of the thirty-six MPs in the principality.[36] Macmillan refused, however, to consider the appointment of a Secretary of State for Wales, and from this point on, the initiative in the process of administrative decentralization passed to Labour, which had advocated a full-time Minister for Welsh Affairs since 1954. When in 1956 James Griffiths, MP for Llanelli, was elected deputy leader of the party, Welsh interests were given greater prominence in Labour's policy-making; and in its 1959 and 1964 election manifestos, the party promised to create a Secretary of State for Wales. Griffiths duly became the first Secretary of State when this commitment was honoured following Labour's election victory in October 1964. At a meeting of the Welsh Grand Committee on 16 December 1964, Griffiths declared that the establishment of the Welsh Office was 'recognition of our nationhood'.

Nevertheless, the Secretary of State's powers were at first extremely limited; he was given executive powers only over the functions of the Ministry of Housing and Local Government in Wales, and responsibility for roads. In addition to these powers, however, the Secretary of State was to participate in the process of policy-formulation in the economic plan for Wales in conjunction with the newly established Department for Economic Affairs, and he was given powers of 'oversight within Wales of the execution of national policy' by other domestic departments in Wales, which in Harold Wilson's view would enable him 'to express the voice of Wales'.[37] Gradually, the responsibilities of the Office were extended. In 1968, the Secretary of State was given powers over health functions in Wales, and in 1970 powers with respect to primary and secondary education. Since that time, the responsibilities of the Welsh Office have been further extended so that its responsibilities have become nearly as great as those of the Scottish Office.

The establishment of the Welsh Office gave to Wales advantages not enjoyed by the regions of England; for not only did Wales have a representative in the Cabinet, but she was also represented at the crucial interdepartmental committees involved in policy-formation. However, the scope of the Welsh Office was limited, as was that of the Scottish Office, by the conventions of British government, and in particular by the convention of ministerial responsibility. Any divergence in policy in Wales might create unwelcome precedents in England, and so there were limits to the discretion which civil servants could exercise as they strove to meet Welsh needs. The Welsh Secretary, moreover, is far junior in rank in the Cabinet to his predecessors, the Home Secretary and the Minister for Housing and Local Government. It was for this reason that Sir Keith Joseph opposed the setting up of the Welsh Office, arguing that 'a minister who speaks for a large department has slightly more of a chance of getting his case put or heard, than a minister who speaks for a smaller department'.[38] In general, moreover, the Welsh Office, since Wales lacks a separate system of law, which has allowed the Scottish Office to argue for distinctively Scottish legislation, has tended to follow the policies laid down by the London-based departments. It has not played a large part in creating policy, but has, at best, been able to modify agreed policies to ensure that the interests of Wales are taken into account. There are very few instances where the Welsh Secretary has challenged an important policy presumption or worked out a major policy from basic principles dictated by specifically Welsh patterns of need.

Devolution to Wales, as we shall see, divorces the execution of policy from law-making in Wales. Yet it might be argued that such a divorce existed before devolution if the role of the Secretary of State in the formulation of laws for Wales was in practice minimal, since law-making normally emanated from the 'English' departments. Of course, putting the legislative and executive responsibilities in separate elected bodies raises new and important problems. But the divorce between law-making and execution in Wales is perhaps in itself nothing new.

As with the Scottish Secretary, there was some danger that the more responsibilities the Welsh Secretary accumulated, the more, in the words of Sir Goronwy Daniel, the first Permanent Secretary at the Welsh Office, Wales would come to be governed 'by an élite civil service'. There were, Sir Goronwy believed, two ways in which this might happen: 'One might be that if accountability is only to Westminster, the amount of parliamentary time which can be made available is limited. The other factor would be that as the functions of the Secretary of State grow it becomes more necessary to delegate more and more work to officials.'[39] The powers of the Welsh Office have expanded greatly since Sir Goronwy issued his warning, and before devolution it had the responsibilities of seven English departments.

The position of the Welsh Secretary became particularly difficult under Conservative governments, since the Conservatives have never, in modern times, gained a majority in Wales. Indeed, only one of the six Conservative Secretaries of State for Wales—Nicholas Edwards, Welsh Secretary between 1979 and 1987—actually sat for a Welsh constituency. Under Margaret Thatcher, the Welsh Secretaryship was used as a form of internal exile for Tory dissidents—Peter Walker, Welsh Secretary between 1987 and 1990, and David Hunt, Welsh Secretary between 1990 and 1993; while John Redwood, Welsh Secretary between 1993 and 1995, appeared to be using Wales as a laboratory for his particular form of free-market economics, a doctrine which enjoyed very little support in the principality.

The distinctive parliamentary arrangements devised for Wales by no means overcame the dangers to which Sir Goronwy Daniel had drawn attention in his evidence to the Royal Commission on the Constitution. Welsh question time lasts for a little over an hour every month, and the Welsh Grand Committee, established in 1960, is a far weaker body than its Scottish counterpart, since there is so little legislation which relates exclusively to Wales. It was given new standing orders in 1996 allowing it to hold question time, second reading debates, and various other debates, but met only twice in the 1996–7 parliamentary session. It has, admittedly, enjoyed a revival since the 1997 election since, under a Labour government, the majority in Wales is of the same political colour as the majority at Westminster. Nevertheless, the Welsh Office, like the Scottish Office, came to be seen as unaccountable. Thus, once the principle had been accepted of a separate minister with responsibility for Wales, it naturally came to be asked why Wales should still be accountable for her domestic affairs to Westminster, rather than to an assembly directly elected by her own voters.

VI

Because Labour has been the dominant party in Wales for so long, the recent history of devolution in Wales is very largely the history of an internal Labour Party debate. But the debate has had a very different flavour from that in Scotland. In contrast to the Scottish Labour Party's gradual yet grudging concessions on devolution, the Welsh Council of Labour committed itself to an assembly in the mid-1960s; but it had to fight hard to maintain this commitment against increasingly recalcitrant MPs and constituency parties, especially in the south-east of Wales.

The initial response in Wales was more enthusiastic than in Scotland for two reasons. The first was that the plethora of non-departmental public bodies or quangos in Wales gave the Conservatives a means of retaining a hold over Welsh public life even though they remained very much a minority in Wales. An assembly would be able to render these quangos democratically accountable. A more important reason, however, was that in Wales, unlike Scotland, devolution could be linked to local government reform, and the case for devolution was first presented in the mid-1960s as part of a broader argument for the reform of Welsh local government on a two-tier basis—a lower tier of district bodies and an upper, all-Wales tier. This was first proposed by the Executive Committee of the Welsh Council of Labour in 1965, and also, at the same time, by an interdepartmental working party set up by the Welsh Office to advise the Secretary of State on local government reform. Thus, the idea of an all-Wales body was put forward some time before Plaid Cymru appeared to threaten Labour. It is best understood perhaps, together with the rise of Plaid Cymru, as an illustration of the revival of feelings of Welsh identity in the late 1960s. Whereas in Scotland, local government reform and devolution seemed conflicting priorities, in Wales they seemed complementary. Indeed, as originally conceived, the all-Wales body would not have been a devolved admin-istration at all, but rather an upper tier of local government which would not have assumed any of the functions of central government in Wales. It would, however, have been able to control Welsh-nominated bodies.

The first two Welsh Secretaries, James Griffiths and Cledwyn Hughes, were sympathetic to an elected Welsh Council, and they had an ally in the Labour Cabinet of the late 1960s in Richard Crossman, who asked, 'Why not accept this local government reorganisation as a political necessity and then go for a really ambitious plan for a Welsh Council or Parliament?'[40] When, however, the proposal for an elected council reached the Cabinet, it met, ironically, the deter-mined opposition of William Ross, the Scottish Secretary, who feared that it would become impossible to resist the demand for a Scottish parliament if an all-Wales body were to be set up; it was also opposed—a further irony—by James Callaghan, the Home Secretary, who sat for a Cardiff constituency and believed that the Welsh Council would provide a powerful forum for Plaid Cymru. The proposal was thus watered down in Cabinet, and the Welsh Council was converted into a nominated body with purely advisory and promotional powers. This prompted the *Western Mail* to make the tart comment that Cledwyn Hughes 'had been placed in charge of a Government department which though set up to deal with Wales's unique problems is forbidden to propose uniquely Welsh solutions, because of the repercussions in England and in Scot-land.'[41]

If Labour in Wales was more sympathetic to devolution than its Scottish counterpart, it was desperately anxious to avoid the taint of separatism. MPs who might be perfectly prepared to vote for a new local government structure would not support proposals which appeared as a concession to separatist feeling. That was why the rise of Plaid Cymru in Wales in the late 1960s undermined Welsh Labour's commitment to devolution. In Scotland, by contrast, where there appeared a real threat to the Union in the 1970s, the SNP helped push Labour into a devolution commitment. The advocates of an all-Wales body were placed in an even more difficult position when, in 1968, Cledwyn Hughes was replaced as Welsh Secretary by George Thomas, a strong anti-devolutionist who, in Crossman's words, 'regards Cledwyn's views as sheer treason',[42] and did his best to frustrate the devolutionists.

In retrospect, it is clear that an excellent chance to secure an all-Wales body was lost in the 1960s through a specifically Welsh reform of local government. The Conservative government which came to power in 1970 reorganized local government in Wales, in an Act which applied both to England and Wales, establishing a two-tier structure in Wales. But the top tier consisted not of an all-Wales council, but of eight county authorities, and this was bound to make devolution more difficult, since an elected council for Wales on top of two tiers of local government would, in the Welsh Council of Labour's view, be 'like a jellyfish on a bed of nails'.[43] 'No responsible government', declared Dr Phil Williams of Plaid Cymru, 'would totally reorganise local government in Wales without first deciding the pattern of devolution. Unfortunately we underestimated the total irresponsibility of the Heath government.'[44]

Labour moved an amendment to the 1972 Local Government Bill calling for an elected Welsh Council; it was moved by George Thomas, who had undergone what one Conservative member called a conversion 'faster than recent conversions to North Sea Gas'. Thomas, however, declared that Labour were '100 per cent in support of this motion . . . that there shall be established from 1 April 1976 an elected Council for Wales'.[45]

Just as the commitment to an elected all-Wales body arose from an internal Labour Party debate, so also did the particular form which devolution was to take. When preparing its evidence for the Royal Commission on the Constitution in 1969, a Labour research group had argued for a legislative Welsh assembly. George Thomas, however, as Welsh Secretary, pressed for an indirectly elected body. Labour in Wales compromised by committing itself to a directly elected assembly, but without tax-raising or legislative powers. Its evidence to the Royal Commission in 1970 declared: 'We anticipate that the Assembly would work within the legislative decisions of the House of Commons.'[46] The Welsh Council's evidence to the Royal Commission, therefore, contains the germ of the notion of executive devolution for Wales: an assembly with powers to alter only secondary legislation, an innovation in British constitutional experience which was nevertheless to be the central principle of the abortive Wales Act of 1978 and the Government of Wales Act of 1998. The commitment was made when it appeared that Labour in Scotland was not interested in devolution at all. When, in a panic, Labour offered legislative devolution to Scotland in 1974, Labour in Wales pressed for her devolution commitment to be upgraded to parity with Scotland (legislative devolution), to be met with the argument that they had not originally asked for it. 'Labour's decision to grant legislative powers to its proposed Scottish Assembly but only executive powers to a Welsh Assembly, had as much to do with political compromise and accident as with any rational argument.'[47]

Yet even the limited form of devolution on offer came to be opposed by many in the Welsh Labour Party. During the 1970s, the anti-devolutionists in the Welsh Labour Party, led by Neil Kinnock, conducted a powerful rearguard action against devolution, demanding a referendum before it was implemented. The political climate in Wales was also changing from the optimistic years of the 1960s when institutional reform had been seen as the remedy for so many ills. Thus Labour entered the Welsh devolution debate unhappy and divided. Wales, having lost the opportunity of establishing an all-Wales body in the 1960s, would have to wait thirty years for the establishment of an assembly; and when it came, it did so with a narrow and half-hearted mandate given by a bare majority of the 50 per cent of Welsh electors who had taken the trouble to vote.

Devolution
Challenge, Defeat, and Renewal

England is not governed by logic but by Parliament.

(Benjamin Disraeli)

I

After the settlement of the Irish problem in 1920–1, devolution disappeared from the British political agenda. Indeed, it had seemed to be an important issue in the years between 1885 and 1921 largely because it appeared to offer an equitable method of dealing with the Irish problem. Once Lloyd George had decided to deal with Ireland separately from the remainder of the United Kingdom, the impetus behind the movement for devolution elsewhere collapsed. Moreover, the decline of the Liberal Party not only removed from the centre of politics a party for which devolution and constitutional reform were vital issues; it also corresponded with an important change in political alignments.

Before 1914, politics was based as much upon locality as it was upon class. The Conservatives were the party of the nation-builders, of the established church, and of the land; the Liberals the party of the periphery, of the dissenting churches, and of the urban middle class. The politics of locality had most force where the grievances of peripheral areas of the United Kingdom could be linked with nationality. That was most obviously the case with Ireland; but it was true also for Scotland and Wales where, as we have seen, the strength of the party of the Left, the Liberals, is difficult to explain merely in socio-economic terms. The two general elections of 1910, for example, were dominated not only by reform of the House of Lords, but also by Irish Home Rule and the disestablishment of the Welsh church. These were explicitly core-periphery issues, Welsh disestablishment pitting the core religion, Anglicanism, against the beliefs, practices, and languages of the periphery. These core-periphery issues had been at the very heart of politics since 1886, when Gladstone had first espoused Home Rule.

After the First World War, however, the democratization of the franchise and the growth of class feeling turned national and regional resentments into class politics, and the Liberal Party, the party of the provinces against the metropolis, was eclipsed by Labour, the party of the working class; and the working class, as Marx and Engels had declared in *The Communist Manifesto*, had no country. The transition is symbolized by changing perceptions of the mineowners of south Wales, some of whom were Welsh-speaking nonconformists. From being perceived as on the progressive side of politics as nonconformists, they now came to be perceived as being on the reactionary side because they belonged to a hostile class. Representing the organized working class, Labour came to adopt the same centralized structures as the trade unions:

Like the unions the Labour Party was national in its organisation and centralised in its institutions. It deliberately over-rode regional boundaries and local interests ... In its formal organisation, the Party had consistently imitated the great unions. With its national executive secretariat and pyramidal structure it was (and is) quite unlike any other British party.[1]

But Labour, as well as representing the politics of class, also represented, as the Liberals had done, the periphery, and articulated the old radical grievances against the centre, thus inheriting Liberal strength in Wales and in Scotland. There had been a powerful decentralist tradition in the early Labour Party, symbolized by the commitment of Keir Hardie to Scottish and Welsh Home Rule. Indeed, Hardie saw socialism, as 'at bottom ... emerging from a rooted local culture'.[2] The Webbs and Laski had also displayed much sympathy with decentralist ideas during the Labour Party's early years. Nevertheless, Labour, while continuing to represent the interests of the periphery, had become, by the mid-1920s, a centralizing party, because the periphery wanted policies which, so it was thought, could only be achieved by central government. Thus, while the Liberals had emphasized the dispersal of power, Labour came to emphasize nationalization and centralized economic planning. This meant that Labour in office might well come to disappoint those who still looked upon it as the party which would return power to the peripheries. In the late 1940s, there was, as we have seen, a mild nationalist revolt in Scotland; but its support, although wide, was not deep, because Labour's policies of full employment and social welfare contrasted so markedly with Scotland's experience in the inter-war years of mass unemployment and depression. In the late 1960s, however, the centralization of power under Labour was combined not with economic success, but with economic failure, and the politics of class came once again to be complemented by the politics of locality. Labour was, however, ideologically ill equipped to deal with the revival of nationalism.

It has been argued that 'European socialists inherited the tradition, deriving from Louis XIV but reinforced by the French Revolution and Napoleon, that large centralised states were progressive and small regional autonomies reactionary.'[3] Labour had proved an exception to this generalization in its early years, but it gradually came to conform to it, for it came to see peripheral nationalism as a force splitting the working-class movement. It was reinforced in this view by the trade unions who, even when they supported Home Rule, demanded national wage bargaining and were fearful lest decentralized bargaining allowed employers to lower wages in the less prosperous areas of the country. In a devolution debate in 1975, Neil Kinnock gave powerful expression to this outlook:

If I had to use a label of any kind, I should have to call myself a 'unionist'. However, I am a unionist entirely for reasons of expediency. I believe that the emancipation of the class which I have come to this House to represent, unapologetically, can best be achieved in a single nation and in a single economic unit, by which I mean a unit where we can have a brotherhood of all nations, and have the combined strength of working-class people throughout the whole of the United Kingdom brought to bear against any bully, any Executive, any foreign power, any bureaucratic arrangement, be it in Brussels or in Washington, and any would be coloniser, either an industrial or a political coloniser. I believe that the organised strength of the working-class people has brought the only benefits to have been secured by those whom I came here to represent. Their misfortunes are not the result of being British, Welsh or Scottish.[4]

Here too, as with Joseph Chamberlain and Aneurin Bevan, there is the anti-Home Rule, anti-devolution motif from the Left, based not on Conservative fears concerning the undermining of sovereignty, but on radical or socialist fears about the dissipation of power.

From the 1920s, Labour came to believe that economic efficiency required centralization. The unemployment of the inter-war years could be cured only if the state retained control of the instruments of economic management. To devolve economic functions, therefore, would threaten centralized planning and was inconsistent with Keynesian demand management, an orthodoxy in British politics until the mid-1970s.

But in addition an effective social policy also required centralization. For it would be inequitable if benefit rates varied in different parts of the country as a result of political vicissitudes in a decentralized state. Benefits should depend on need, not on geography. 'The underprivileged child in Eastbourne is as important as the child in Glasgow', declared one Labour MP, Colin Phipps, in the devolution debates.5 It would be inequitable if the deprived child in Glasgow received a higher level of benefit simply because he or she lived in a part of the country which had a strong parliament able to press for higher standards. The devolution of social policy, however, implied just that—different standards of social welfare in different parts of the country, and it threatened, therefore, the very foundations of the Welfare State.

Thus devolution would undermine the twin pillars of Labour's programme, full employment and the Welfare State. Social democracy, therefore, was only to be achieved through centralized government. During the debates on devolution, Colin Phipps once again gave eloquent voice to this attitude: 'Any Labour Government who gave up central power to decide on matters such as comprehensive education and the moving of money around the United Kingdom would be foolish . . . If comprehensive education is right in Glasgow, it is right in the South of England'.6 During the inter-war and immediate post-war years, socialists in Scotland and Wales shared this perspective. Like their counterparts in the industrial areas of England, they demanded not autonomy, but a government which took more notice of their grievances. They sought to strengthen the government in London, not to undermine it.

By the time of the general election of 1951, the issues had become overwhelmingly class based—nationalization, the future of the welfare state, and so on. The manifestos of the two major parties said nothing about Scotland or Wales, while the now shrunken Liberal Party offered just one paragraph promising Scottish and Welsh parliaments.

From the late 1960s, however, core-periphery issues were to spring up once more. This was a result of the gradual and steady emergence of a new cleavage between the parties, with the Conservatives gaining strength in the south-eastern core, while Labour increased its strength in Scotland and Wales as well as in the northwest. From the time of the two general elections of 1974, core-periphery issues began to play an important if still subordinate part in general election campaigns. But this, by contrast with the period before the First World War, was occurring *as the result of* a change in voting behaviour. It was not itself a cause of that change. And, in the four general elections of 1979 to 1992, the victorious Conservatives fought on the basis that the core-periphery cleavage was fundamentally irrelevant to British politics. Nevertheless, a major issue in the general elections of the past twenty-five years has been the geographical distribution of political power. The overwhelming Labour victory in the general election of 1997, therefore, would decide the future shape of the polity as well as which party would win power at Westminster. It would decide the issue in favour of the non-English parts of the United Kingdom, whose power would increase at the expense of that of England.7

II

In the late 1960s, Labour's ideological inheritance meant that it would respond with considerable caution to the rise of nationalism. For concessions to nationalism would threaten Labour's economic and also its social philosophy. Moreover, devolution might also threaten the position at Westminster of Labour MPs from Scotland and Wales, and also the Secretaries of State for Scotland and Wales. Labour had far more to lose than the Conservatives from a weakening of the Scottish and Welsh presence in London.

It would, however, have been foolish to dismiss the claims of

Scotland or Wales out of hand, for this might further alienate disillusioned Labour supporters, encouraging them to believe that Labour was insensitive to their problems. The Wilson government, therefore, resorted in the late 1960s to that favourite expedient of a harassed administration, a Royal Commission. This would contain any demand from devolutionists in the party to meet the nationalist threat with radical new measures. Indeed, by the time the Royal Commission reported, it might be that the nationalist threat would have disappeared in which case its findings could be quietly pigeonholed. It seemed, therefore, that nothing would be lost by playing for time.

The decision to set up the Commission was taken in the autumn of 1968, but its members were not actually appointed until April of the following year. The terms of reference of the Commission were extremely wide-ranging, and the government's levity was shown by the fact that it did not seek to co-ordinate the work of the Commission with the work of the Redcliffe–Maud Commission on Local Government in England, nor with that of the Wheatley Commission on Local Government in Scotland, both of which reported in 1969. Yet the proposals of these two Commissions, and especially those of Wheatley, were bound to impinge upon devolution.

The Royal Commission on the Constitution was beset by difficulties. Its chairman was Sir Geoffrey, later Lord Crowther, a former editor of *The Economist*, but he died suddenly in April 1972, and was replaced by Lord Kilbrandon, a Scottish judge. Three other members resigned from the Commission during its deliberations. The Commission reported in October 1973, but its Report was not unanimous, and was accompanied by a Memorandum of Dissent signed by Lord Crowther-Hunt, a Labour peer and Fellow of Exeter College, Oxford, and by Professor Alan Peacock, professor of economics at the University of York and an adherent of the free-market school of economics.

The Report and the Memorandum of Dissent differed not so much on specific proposals as on the interpretation of the very wide-ranging terms of reference given to the Commission which required it to 'examine the present functions of the central legislature and government in relation to the several countries, nations, and regions of the United Kingdom', and to consider 'having regard . . . to the interests of the prosperity of Our people under the Crown whether any changes are desirable in those functions or otherwise in present constitutional and economic relationships'. This, as the Memorandum of Dissent pointed out, meant 'that virtually every aspect of the central legislature and government is subject to our scrutiny . . . Indeed, only if we recommend the abolition of the Monarchy would we be in conflict with our terms of reference.'[8] The signatories of the main Report, however, took the view that 'the main intention behind our appointment was that we should investigate the case for transferring or devolving responsibility for the exercise of government functions from Parliament and the central government to new institutions of government in the various countries and regions of the United Kingdom'.[9] The Report, therefore, might be more accurately described as a report on devolution rather than on the Constitution, and the Commissioners who signed it were perhaps guilty of assuming that devolution was the only plausible response to the dissatisfactions with government which they found.

The Memorandum of Dissent, on the other hand, interpreted the terms of reference far more widely, and produced a far-reaching scheme of constitutional reform, involving not just devolution, but also the reform of Parliament and of the political parties. Broadly, it recommended that Britain adopt the German model of federal government; but there were various nuances of that model which escaped the authors of the Memorandum, who devoted insufficient thought to the problems involved in transposing a system of government from one country to another which had different historical traditions and methods of law-making.

It has been said that Royal Commissions are not suitable bodies to evaluate controversial proposals for change, since they are likely to be composed of representatives of different outlooks, unwilling to thrash out their differences in order to reach positive agreement on what should be done. Instead, they are likely to compromise in a report which will not only be 'vague, general, ambiguous,' but which 'perhaps even expresses conflicting views in different corners'.[10] Such a description is certainly applicable to the Report of the Royal

Commission on the Constitution, a diffuse and long-winded document in which it is difficult to disentangle the essential arguments. Indeed, the division between the signatories of the Report and the Memorandum of Dissent is itself misleading, since the signatories, even of the Report, were divided. They were in fact able to agree on very little. All, however, rejected separatism; and also federalism, to which they gave less space than separatism, on the somewhat inadequate grounds of 'very little demand . . . and people who know the system well tend to advise against it . . . if government in the United Kingdom is to meet the present-day needs of the people it is necessary for the undivided sovereignty of Parliament to be maintained.'[11] The signatories all supported a directly elected assembly for Scotland—although they disagreed on whether it should have legislative, executive, or advisory powers. The Commission was, however, unanimous in recommending that elections to any devolved assemblies that were set up should be by the single transferable-vote method of proportional representation rather than by the first-past-the-post system.

The real division between the Commissioners cut across that between the signatories of the Report and the Memorandum of Dissent. The division was in fact threefold, between nationalists, regionalists, and sceptics.

The nationalists, who comprised six members of the Commission, were not in favour of independence for Scotland and Wales, but believed that they deserved special treatment on the grounds of nationhood. They therefore recommended devolution for Scotland and Wales, but were opposed to directly elected regional assemblies for England. This group included all five of the Commissioners from Scotland, Wales, and Northern Ireland, including the Chairman, Lord Kilbrandon, but only one English Commissioner.[12]

The regionalists comprised Lord Crowther-Hunt and Professor Peacock, the two signatories of the Memorandum of Dissent, and Lord Foot and Sir James Steel, who indicated their views by means of footnotes to the Report. All four believed that the causes of dissatisfaction with government were common to all parts of Britain, even if, in the absence of nationalist parties, they could not be so easily expressed in England as in Scotland and Wales.[13] They insisted also, as a basic constitutional principle, that devolution must be based upon equality of political rights, and that the claims of Scotland and Wales to separate nationality did not, in the words of the Memorandum of Dissent, 'entitle the people in Scotland and Wales to be better governed or to have more participation in the handling of their own affairs than is offered to the people of Yorkshire or Lancashire'. Indeed, for Professor Peacock, the principle of equality of rights was 'not only an important matter of principle, but also a reasonable prediction of what would be politically acceptable in the long run'. For, without equality of rights, 'there would no longer be any reality to the concept of the practical unity of the United Kingdom'.[14] The regionalists favoured, therefore, devolution, not only for Scotland and Wales, but also for the English regions, so giving to Scotland and Wales nothing which was to be denied to England. They believed that all of these assemblies should possess executive, but not legislative powers.

There were, however, two obvious difficulties with this position. The first is that many, if not most, of the English regions did not want devolution, while it seemed that Scotland did. The second was that it did not take sufficient account of the special features of Scottish legislation which resulted from the existence of a separate legal system. The Crowther-Hunt and Peacock scheme would have led to the absurdity that, after devolution, Scottish laws would still have been made by Westminster, continuing to legislate for an alien legal system, while in Edinburgh, Scottish ministers, familiar with the Scottish legal system, would not be able to legislate for it.

Significantly, the four members of this group all had strong regional ties and none of them hailed from London or the south-east. Lord Crowther-Hunt, although an Oxford academic, had been born in the north of England, while Professor Peacock had spent much of his academic life at the University of York. Sir James Steel was an industrialist from the north-east concerned lest Scotland gain advantages through devolution denied to his own area, and Lord Foot was a prominent solicitor living in the south-west. There was only one Commissioner with a personal background in the north of England who did not share the regionalist position.

The third group, the sceptics, consisted of Sir David Renton, Conservative MP for Huntingdon, whose roots lay in East Anglia and the south-east, Nancy Trenaman, a former civil servant and Principal of St Anne's College, Oxford, and Harry Street, professor of law at Manchester University. They were entirely against devolution to Wales, favouring only a Welsh Council with deliberative and advisory powers, but two of them—Mrs Trenaman and Professor Street—thought that there was a case for legislative devolution to Scotland; although Nancy Trenaman was later to retract her support for devolution in Scotland, and to argue that the issue at stake was solely whether or not Scotland wished to remain in the United Kingdom.[15] Sir David Renton favoured a Scottish assembly with primarily deliberative powers.[16]

Professor Street and Nancy Trenaman were the only two members of the Commission to favour different treatment for Scotland and Wales. No member of the Commission proposed the precise mix of legislative devolution to Scotland and executive devolution to Wales which was to form the basis of the devolution proposals both of the 1974–9 Labour government and the 1997 government.

It is not surprising that, faced with so wide a range of differing views whose significance was concealed rather than brought out by the form of the Report, most MPs greeted its publication with bafflement and even mirth. The Report appeared in October 1973, shortly after the Yom Kippur War in the Middle East, and at a time when there seemed to be a serious threat to Britain's oil supplies. It seemed, therefore, quite irrelevant. The Report was debated briefly in the Commons. Both government and opposition promised to consider its findings carefully, but it was then forgotten. Neither the Labour nor the Conservative manifestos for the February 1974 election, fought on the issue of the miners' strike and Edward Heath's question—who governs: the government or the miners?—made any proposals for devolution.

When, however, devolution once more became a serious issue, the Commission's Report came to take on a new significance. MPs and opinion-formers remembered not the careful qualifications, but the main message, which was taken as being in favour of directly elected assemblies in Scotland and Wales. The fact that the Commission's members recommended no less than three different types of assembly was less noticed. The majority of members of the Commission, moreover, had taken the view 'that it is not necessary to have a uniform system of government in all parts of Great Britain'.[17] It seemed, therefore, that the Commission had shown that devolution to Scotland and Wales was possible without major constitutional consequences in England and without breaking up the United Kingdom. The nationalists on the Commission had not considered the implications for England of their proposals, and in particular the problem of the role and number of Scottish and Welsh MPs in Westminster after devolution—the problem of representation which had so baffled Gladstone nearly ninety years earlier. The Commission indeed contented itself with the following anodyne reflection:

We have, for example, noted the thorny problem of the representation of Scotland and Wales at Westminster if they alone were to have legislative assemblies of their own; the difficulties are not, however, in the view of most of us so great as to make legislative devolution to Scotland and Wales impracticable unless it is extended to England.[18]

It was not until the proposals for devolution were debated in Parliament that these implications were noticed. But by then it was too late to do anything about them, as the government had become committed to its policy, and it used the Commission as authority for not coming to terms with the problem. In 1977, Francis Pym, the Conservative spokesman on devolution, asked Michael Foot, Leader of the House:

Will the right honourable Gentleman explain why there is no mention of, let alone any solution to, the single most contentious problem to arise in our debates on the bill; that is, the role and the number of Members of Parliament representing the Scottish and Welsh constituencies? . . . Why is it that, in spite of the Government's recognition of the profound implications upon England of their devolution proposals, they have failed after nearly a year of consideration to put before the House their conclusions in relation to England?

Foot replied:

The right honourable Gentleman said that the most contentious question to arise in our earlier debates was that of representation in this House and the form that that representation should take. I am sure that by this time the right honourable Gentleman must have studied the Kilbrandon Report, which came to the same conclusion as we reached on the major in-and-out question which has sometimes been advocated. We have taken that conclusion into account.[19]

This view—that devolution to Scotland and Wales would not entail repercussions in England—was the legacy of the Royal Commission of the Constitution, and it was to colour thinking on devolution for many years to come.

III

Following the result of the general election of February 1974, devolution returned rapidly on to the political agenda. The result of that election is shown in the Table 6.1.

Harold Wilson took office as Prime Minister of a minority Labour government, seventeen seats short of a majority, in circumstances such that a second general election could not be long delayed. Meanwhile, Wilson desperately needed the support of the nine nationalist MPs as well as the fourteen Liberals who were strongly committed to devolution. The Labour manifesto had contained no reference to devolution, yet in the Queen's Speech it was announced that the government would 'initiate discussions in

Table 6.1 General election results, February 1974

	Seats
Labour	301
Conservatives	297
Liberals	14
United Ulster Unionist Council	11
SNP	7
Plaid Cymru	2
SDLP	1
Others	2

Scotland and Wales on the Report of the Royal Commission on the Constitution, and will bring forward proposals for consideration'. But, in reply to an interjection from Winnie Ewing, leader of the SNP, Wilson, in the debate on the Queen's Speech, went further, declaring that 'Of course we shall publish a White Paper *and a bill*'.[20]

With another election in the offing, time was short. A consultative document, *Devolution within the United Kingdom: Some Alternatives for Discussion*, setting out the various options proposed by the Royal Commission, was published on 3 June 1974. Comments were invited from the public, but the deadline was 30 June. The summer months were spent in ensuring that the Labour Party in Scotland came out in support of devolution, and on 17 September 1974, three weeks before polling day, the government published a White Paper, *Democracy and Devolution: Proposals for Scotland and Wales* (Cmnd. 5732).

This White Paper laid out various decisions of principle with regard to devolution. They were as follows:

1. There would be directly elected assemblies in Scotland and Wales.
2. The Scottish Assembly would have legislative powers, the Welsh Assembly only executive powers.
3. The assemblies would be elected by the first-past-the-post system.
4. The assemblies would be financed by a block grant allocated by Parliament. There would be no devolution of revenue-raising powers.
5. There would be no reduction in the number of Scottish or Welsh MPs at Westminster.
6. The offices of Secretary of State for Scotland and Wales would remain, and the office-holders would continue to sit in the Cabinet.
7. Devolution in England would be postponed for further consideration.

These 'decisions of principle' had been hurriedly formulated. They were determined more by the fear of electoral losses to the SNP than by any particular conviction of the merits of devolution. Senior ministers were either sceptical or definitely opposed. At a ministerial meeting in July 1974, Roy Jenkins, the Home Secretary, despairing of the levity with which the issue was being treated, burst out, 'You cannot break up the United Kingdom in order to win a few seats in an election.'[21] After the last draft of the White Paper had been agreed in Cabinet, Harold Wilson issued his benediction, 'And God help all who sail in her'. Civil servants were, according to Barbara Castle, 'deeply alarmed at the whole exercise'.[22]

Nevertheless, through all the long debates on devolution, the government never departed from its hurriedly formulated 'decisions of principle'. They formed the basis of the Scotland and Wales Acts of 1978. In the 1998 Scotland Act and Government of Wales Act, the Blair government at last departed from the principles, but in a very limited way: it abandoned the third principle and marginally altered the fourth—since a small tax-varying power was proposed for Scotland, and the fifth—since provision was made for a reduction in the number of Scottish MPs to be returned to Parliament. With regard to the seventh principle, on English devolution, although no specific proposals were presented, provision was made for devolution to the regions if and when there was a demand for it. On the whole, however, it is the similarities and not the differences which are remarkable when comparing the legislation of 1978 with that of 1998. Decisions made hastily in the 1970s were thus fundamentally to determine the shape of devolution in the 1990s.

Following the October 1974 general election, in which Labour gained an overall majority of three, a further White Paper, *Our Changing Democracy: Devolution to Scotland and Wales*, (Cmnd. 6348) was published in November 1975, turning the general principles of devolution into detailed proposals. This White Paper put forward a minimalist conception of devolution circumscribing the proposed assemblies with seemingly powerful restraints to prevent them undermining the policy of the British government. In addition, the government declared that it would not devolve major economic and industrial powers or matters related to energy or agriculture.

The government also decided that, although Scotland and Wales were to be offered quite different types of devolution, it was, in the words of Michael Foot, Leader of the House of Commons, 'logical that the matter should be dealt with in the same bill'.[23] The Scotland and Wales Bill was given its second reading in the Commons on 13 December 1976, by which time James Callaghan had replaced Harold Wilson as Prime Minister. In introducing the bill, Callaghan declared that it would promote 'a new settlement among the nations that constitute the United Kingdom'.[24]

The bill passed its second reading comfortably by 294 votes to 249, a government majority of forty-five. But there was a considerable amount of cross-voting amongst MPs from the major parties. On the Labour side, ten MPs voted against the bill, while forty-five abstained or were paired. On the Conservative side, five MPs voted for the bill and forty-two abstained or were paired, including the former Prime Minister Edward Heath.

The composition of the majority on second reading was ominous and showed that the bill would not enjoy an easy passage through the Commons. For the government, if it were to succeed, would need to obtain a majority for a guillotine motion during the committee stage of the bill. Otherwise it would be filibustered to death by its opponents. But, on a guillotine motion, the Conservative dissidents, having made the point that they favoured devolution in principle, would rejoin their party, while the Labour dissidents were mainly irreconcilables whom it would be difficult to win back. Equally ominous was the attitude of the Liberals on whose support the government was relying. For David Steel, the Liberal leader, made it clear that his party was voting for the second reading only on the understanding that the bill would be fundamentally amended in committee, so as to provide for proportional representation in elections to the assemblies and the devolution of revenue-raising powers. Concessions to the Liberals, however, and in particular proportional representation, would make devolution even more unpalatable to Labour back-benchers, whose commitment to devolution was already only lukewarm. The government seemed caught in a revolving-door situation. It decided, therefore, to offer a political concession to Labour dissidents, in the form of referendums on devolution.

One of the reasons for introducing the devolution proposals in a bill covering both countries had been to disarm Welsh Labour opponents of devolution, who would not then be able to oppose devolution in Wales without also opposing devolution in Scotland, where it was thought to be essential to overcome the threat of the SNP. The Welsh dissidents, led by Leo Abse, MP for Pontypool, sought to circumvent this tactic by putting down an amendment proposing that the implementation of the bill be made subject to referendums in Scotland and Wales.

The case in principle for referendums was that they would test the government's argument that there was a powerful popular demand for devolution in Scotland and Wales. Moreover, if devolution were to fail, it would be better for it to be rejected by the Scots and Welsh themselves, rather than by the House of Commons. For if an over-whelmingly English-dominated Parliament rejected devolution, the nationalists would undoubtedly be granted an extra grievance to help stoke their campaign for independence. But the referendum had a tactical point also, for it would enable the Welsh dissidents to support the bill in Parliament, but then argue against devolution in the refer-endum campaign in Wales.

It was at first thought that the Abse amendment could not be selected for debate at the committee stage of the bill on the grounds that it was unconstitutional. For, in the words of the nineteenth edition of *Erskine May*, published in 1976: 'Amendments to a bill proposing that . . . the provisions of a bill should be subject to a ref-erendum, have been ruled out of order as proposing changes in leg-islative procedure which would be contrary to constitutional prac-tice.'[25] The chair, however, declared that it would admit the Abse amendment, since it ruled that the European Community referendum had created a precedent. That referendum, however, had not been introduced as an amendment to an already published bill.

By the time the second reading debate of the Scotland and Wales Bill had begun, the Abse amendment had attracted eighty signa-tures. The government therefore decided to accept the amendment in committee; and, on 10 February 1977, it introduced a referendum clause amidst scenes of some procedural chaos. For a number of back-benchers bitterly objected to what they saw as a tactical manoeuvre by which a referendum was being introduced as a new clause on an already published bill in order to overcome resistance to it. By this time, the view was widespread that the government had lost its way. John Mackintosh, MP for Berwick and East Lothian, a fervent supporter of devolution, declared that the Scotland and Wales Bill was so bad that if the referendum result was Yes, the 'appalling difficulties' inherent in the bill 'could . . . endanger the unity of the country'. He continued:

Seldom have I seen the House or the Government in quite such a mess or in such difficulties as we are in over this bill . . . What has happened is that this house does not contain a majority for this bill. As a person who has supported devolution for twenty years, I would rather see this house have the courage of its convictions and reject this bill. It should be thrown out and the electorate should make their views known at a General Election, so that the government can come back with a better bill at a later stage.[26]

At this stage, only three clauses and the new referendum clause had been debated in a bill of 115 clauses. Debate on such important matters as the powers of the assemblies, the reserve powers of the Secretaries of State, and the financial provisions had not yet begun. The government therefore proposed an allocation-of-time motion— a guillotine—without which the bill could not be passed. It was, however, unable to attract its own dissidents back to the fold, nor keep the support of dissident Conservatives, while eleven of the thirteen Liberals now decided to vote against the government. Thus the only supporters of the bill outside the Labour Party were now the nationalists. In David Steel's words: 'The whole exercise started as a ploy to keep the nationalist wolves from the door, but the government find they have ended up in bed with them. The government have as their non-Labour supporters only those people in the House who know that the bill will not work and hope that it will not'.[27]

At 10 pm on 22 February 1977, the guillotine motion was defeated by 312 votes to 283. Twenty-two Labour MPs voted against the motion and twenty-three abstained. The Scotland and Wales Bill was in effect dead. It was the first defeat for any major item of government legislation since 1969, when the previous Labour government had been bogged down in committee on its bill to reform the House of Lords, and had been forced to abandon its plans. But abandonment of House of Lords reform had not endangered the survival of the government, for that government enjoyed a large majority in the Commons. Abandonment of devolution, however, did threaten the survival of the Callaghan government which was in a minority in the House of Commons by February 1977. It depended therefore on the support of the minority parties. With opinion polls seeming to show that the SNP was now the leading party in Scotland and had the support of 36 per cent of the electorate, the nationalist parties withdrew their support from the government in an attempt to precipitate a general election. The government, therefore, needed the support of the Liberals to survive. But part of the price of that support would be a new and improved devolution bill.

IV

The government's response to the defeat of the Scotland and Wales Bill was to propose all-party talks to resurrect devolution. The Conservatives agreed to talks, but wanted them to consider 'proposals for the better government of Scotland and Wales within the United Kingdom, including . . . the Scotland and Wales Bill and federalism'. The government, however, indicated that it was only prepared to discuss its own legislation. That ended any prospect of talks with the Conservatives.

But in March 1977 Labour agreed to a parliamentary pact with the Liberals, the terms of which included negotiations to produce better legislation on devolution. Yet the Liberals failed to secure either of their two main aims—proportional representation and revenue-raising powers for the assemblies. The government offered a free vote on the electoral system, but this, predictably, led to its defeat in the Commons. The government remained adamant against revenue-raising powers, and indeed any concessions on this issue would have antagonized English back-benchers, making it even more difficult to pass the legislation through the Commons. So the Liberals had to accept devolution without proportional representation and devolution without revenue-raising powers, the alternative being no devolution at all.

In fact, the main difference between the first devolution exercise and the second was the division into two of the Scotland and Wales

Bill. Michael Foot, who on 18 January 1977 had declared that there was a logical case for dealing with devolution in one bill, argued in July that 'the House would welcome the separate consideration of what are dissimilar proposals'.[28] This was, ironically, unwelcome to the Liberal Party's Machinery of Government panel which believed it 'a major tactical blunder . . . bound to endanger the Welsh bill'; and if the Welsh bill were lost, this 'would completely scupper any chance of pressing the case for a measure of regional government in England. A Scottish assembly would be seen as *sui generis* and not inviting parallels elsewhere.'[29] The separation of Wales from Scotland seemed to put the Liberal idea of federalism even further into the remote distance. The Liberals, all the same, had no option but to support the resurrected Scotland and Wales bills unless they wished to force an election at a time when by-election results and survey evidence indicated that they would lose many of their seats.

The Scotland and Wales bills were given second readings in the Commons on 14 and 15 November 1977 respectively, and then immediately guillotined after second reading. The success of these guillotine motions was due not only to the accretion of Liberal support, but also to the return of Labour dissidents. Of the forty-five who had abstained or voted against the guillotine on the Scotland and Wales Bill, only sixteen were still prepared to withhold their support.

It was not that there had been significant Labour conversions to the cause of devolution. Rather, the consequences of the defeat of the first bill and the realization that the government could be driven from office if devolution were to be defeated for a second time, persuaded doubters to conform. Besides, there was always the possibility, especially in Wales that the bills could be defeated at the referendum stage. Eric Heffer, the left-wing Labour MP for Liverpool, Walton, rationalized his support for the bills in these terms:

I am in favour of sustaining the government. Therefore if I do vote for the government it will not be because I agree with the proposals, but merely to help sustain it. I have not become converted to devolution. I think it is unnecessary and a great mistake, and if the proposals are accepted, could lead to the break-up of the United Kingdom and ultimately of the Labour movement. If the bills do go through I shall offer my services to those in the Labour and trade union movements in Scotland and Wales who oppose the

proposals and speak and campaign in the referendums against the legislation. I hope that at that stage the people will vote the proposals down.[30]

In a speech at Bexhill on 25 November, Enoch Powell referred to this
tactic as:

without precedent in the long history of Parliament . . . that members openly and publicly declaring themselves opposed to the legislation and bringing
forward in debate what seemed to them cogent reasons why it must prove
disastrous, voted nevertheless for the legislation and for a guillotine, with the
express intention that after a minimum of debate the bill should be submitted to a referendum of the electorate in which they would hope and strive to
secure its rejection.

The referendum was becoming, in the words of one constitutional
authority, 'the Pontius Pilate of British politics', enabling MPs to
vote for a bill while washing their hands of it.[31] There can be little
doubt that, in free votes, the Scotland and Wales bills would not have
passed the Commons.

Even so the bills were passed with a small number of amendments. Two of them, however, were of fundamental constitutional
importance, including one which was to prove fatal to devolution in
Scotland.

The first amendment of constitutional importance which became
part of the bill had been proposed in the House of Lords by Lord
Ferrers, a Conservative front-bench spokesman on devolution. It was
rejected in the Commons on the casting vote of the Speaker, but
returned again by the Lords, and eventually, when it came back for a
second time to the Commons, carried by one vote against the advice
of the government. The Ferrers amendment, which became section 66
of the Scotland Act, provided that if any Commons vote on a matter
devolved to Scotland were passed through the votes of Scottish MPs,
an Order could be laid before the House requiring a second vote to be
taken two weeks after the first. The purpose of the amendment was to
deal with the question, which had baffled Gladstone, of whether MPs
from a devolved area, in this case Scotland, could after devolution
continue to vote on domestic affairs for England, Wales, and Northern
Ireland, when English, Welsh, and Northern Irish MPs would
no longer be able to vote on Scottish domestic affairs. The Ferrers

amendment may thus 'be regarded as a specific type of "in-and-out" clause'.[32] For its implication was that pressure would be exerted upon Scottish MPs not to participate in the second vote, held two weeks after the first. Then the House of Commons would become, for part of its life, an assembly for England, Wales, and Northern Ireland only. This was a change with profound consequences for the future of British government, especially when, as in 1964 or October 1974, a government depended upon Scottish MPs for its majority. In such a situation, ministers responsible for matters such as education and health which had been devolved to Scotland, would have found that their majority in the Commons had disappeared. There would then be a bifurcated executive, one majority when all MPs were voting, and another majority, of a different political colour, when the Scottish MPs were absent. It is not easy to imagine how effective Cabinet government could continue under such circumstances.

V

The second amendment of major significance to the Scotland and Wales bills was the so-called 40 per cent rule, requiring 40 per cent of the registered electorate to support devolution for it to be implemented. This was inserted into the bill against the wishes of the government by a Labour MP, George Cunningham, an expatriate Scot, who sat for Islington South and Finsbury. The genesis and constitutional status of this provision are of great interest and indeed it has some claim to be regarded as the most important back-bench initiative in British politics since the war.

Clause 82(2) of the Scotland Bill which provided for a referendum, declared: 'If it appears to the Secretary of State, having regard to the answers given in a referendum and all other circumstances, that this Act should not be brought into effect, he may lay before Parliament the draft of an Order in Council providing for its repeal.'

This clause gave the Secretary of State considerable discretion in interpreting the result of a referendum. Yet the argument for the referendum was that it would test the case that devolution met a powerful demand in Scotland. Would that case be vindicated by a narrow majority on a low turnout—or should a stiffer test be required?

The Cunningham amendment required a repeal order to be laid before Parliament if fewer than 40 per cent of Scottish electors voted Yes. Its rationale was stated by another Labour back-bench opponent of devolution, Bruce Douglas-Mann, who, however, favoured a 33⅓ per cent threshold.

I regard this amendment as absolutely central to the support I give to the bill. I abstained on second reading of the Scotland and Wales bill and I voted against the timetable motion for that bill. By the end of the summer, I had come to the conclusion that if—it is a large 'if'—a substantial majority of the people of Scotland were determined on this measure, it was not for English members to defeat it.[33]

George Cunningham added the powerful argument that devolution was, in effect, an irreversible constitutional change. In many countries with codified constitutions, there was some special method of validating such constitutional changes. Britain, Cunningham argued, ought not to make such a change without convincing evidence that it was sought by the people of Scotland.

The amendment, to the surprise of the government, was carried, ironically, on Burns night, 25 January 1978, by 166 votes to 151. The Conservative opposition front bench abstained, but a number of Conservatives voted in favour, while four Conservatives, led by Edward Heath, voted against. The amendment could not have been passed without at least the tacit support of Labour back-benchers, who refused to vote it down. Many Labour MPs had become profoundly indifferent to devolution, which seemed to be clogging the parliamentary timetable, while some Labour MPs 'who had been voting with the government, in a bored and listless way . . . were actually convinced or converted by George's speech which was a massive piece of advocacy'.[34] The government attempted at the report stage of the Scotland Bill to delete the amendment, but this time the Conservatives turned out in force to support it, and the motion to delete the amendment was defeated by 298 votes to 243. The fact that the Cunningham amendment was resisted by supporters of devolution showed that their confidence in the strength of the pressures for devolution in Scotland was not as strong as it appeared. But those who supported the amendment also displayed less than total confidence in their case—for they seemed to be conceding that devolution in Scotland would not be defeated on a straight referendum vote.

VI

The Cunningham amendment, which became section 85(2) of the Scotland Act, declared: 'If it appears to the Secretary of State that less than 40 per cent of the persons entitled to vote in the referendum have voted "yes" . . . he shall lay before Parliament the draft of an Order in Council for the repeal of this Act.' A similar provision was added to the Wales Act.

The amendment was widely seen as a device to prevent devolution. But it could not of itself achieve that aim. Had support in Scotland been sufficient to overcome the 40 per cent hurdle, devolution would have occurred. Parliament had accepted, perhaps grudgingly, that if Scotland wanted devolution, she could have devolution. What the amendment achieved was to ensure that Scotland did not have devolution in the *absence* of strong support for it. That support could be shown either by a high turnout or by large majority for a Yes vote.

The Cunningham amendment subtly combined two separate requirements: first, that a minimum percentage of the electorate should turn out to vote; and second, that there should be considerable support for devolution if the legislation were to come into force. The lower the turnout, the higher the majority that would be needed. In the unlikely event of an 80 per cent turnout, a majority of one would be sufficient. If the turnout were to be 70 per cent, a 57 per cent Yes vote would be needed, while if the turnout were only 60 per cent, a 67 per cent Yes vote would be required.

The amendment, however, was advisory and not mandatory. It required the Secretary of State only to lay a repeal order before Parliament if the Yes vote was less than 40 per cent. Parliament could, however, vote down the repeal order; and it would undoubtedly have done so if, for example, the outcome had been, say, 39 per cent Yes and 25 per cent No. Thus, as George Cunningham appreciated, the amendment did not 'decide whether devolution takes place or not, but only whether the matter goes back before Parliament in the event of an inconclusive referendum result'.[35]

A crucial problem with the amendment, however, was that the electoral register was not accurate enough to enable the definitive number of all those who might conceivably be 'entitled to vote' to be calculated. It was not in fact designed for that purpose, but for the very different purpose of *including* all those entitled to vote. The register might very well contain names which ought not to have been included and who would be unlikely to vote. The electoral registration officer for the Lothian Regional Council declared that 'in so far as the register may contain names that ought not to have been included, this is the result of deliberate policy'.[36] Moreover, errors and omissions in the register meant that it would be far from being completely accurate. In addition, hospital patients and the seriously disabled or ill, while entitled to postal or proxy votes, might well not claim them, while those who had moved home after the qualifying date for the register in October 1978 would find it difficult to vote in a referendum held in March 1979.

The government, however, took the view that the amendment bound it to discount the votes only of those not legally entitled to vote; it could not also discount the votes of those unable to vote, or very unlikely to vote. The government, therefore, made a discount for four categories. These were, with the numbers in Scotland:

1. Those on the electoral register, but below the age of 18 on 1 March 1979—49,802.
2. Those who had died between October 1978 and March 1979—26,400.
3. Students and student nurses living away from home but in Scotland and registered both at their home and at their college or hospital address—11,800.
4. Prisoners legally disbarred from voting, but registered at their home address—2,000.

The total discount, then, amounted to 90,002. It is, however, possible to suggest that a deduction of a further 535,226 voters could be justified to take account of errors in the electoral register, hospital patients, the seriously disabled, those ill at home, and removals.[37]

With the figure of 535,226 added to the government's figure of 90,002, the target for a 40 per cent Yes vote would have been reduced from 1,498,845 to 1,284,754 votes, only 31,252 more than the actual Yes vote in the referendum. Supporters of devolution, therefore, could complain that they were being handicapped by over 200,000 votes—the difference between the two targets.

The referendums on devolution were held on 1 March 1979. In Wales, devolution suffered a massive defeat:

Yes	243,048	20.2%
No	956,330	79.8%

The turnout was 58.8%.

In Scotland, however, the result was a narrow victory for devolution, on a turnout of 62.9 per cent:

Yes	1,253,502	51.6% of those voting: 32.85% of the electorate
No	1,230,937	48.5% of those voting: 30.78% of the electorate

This result destroyed the credibility of devolution. It had been pressed in Parliament on the ground that there was a surge of popular demand for it in Scotland, but the outcome of the referendum entirely undermined that claim. Not only was the Yes vote well below 40 per cent, but the closeness in the popular vote and the fact that the Yes majority was concentrated entirely in the central regions of Scotland, the Highlands, and the Western Isles, made it impossible for the government to implement the Scotland Act.

The Callaghan government, in a minority position in the House of Commons and so dependent on nationalist and Liberal support, strove manfully to avoid defeat, hoping that it could persuade the Commons to vote down the repeal order, a tactic which came to be known as the Frankenstein solution. According to ex-Prime Minister Harold Wilson, 'There had been some hope in the Cabinet that, having laid the repeal Order, their own supporters would vote the other way and keep devolution alive. But strenuous inquiries by the Government Whips revealed that some forty or so Government back-benchers would join the Conservatives in killing devolution.'[38]

When it was seen that the government could not implement devolution, the SNP put down a no-confidence motion. The Conservative opposition then put down its own motion of no confidence, and on 28 March, it was carried by one vote, the first time such a vote had been carried since the defeat of Ramsay MacDonald's first Labour government in 1924. The Liberals voted against the government as did the SNP, which declared that Labour MPs preferred Margaret Thatcher in Downing Street to a Scottish assembly in Edinburgh. Plaid Cymru, however, continued to support the government. It was thus devolution and not the industrial and economic troubles of the 'Winter of Discontent' of 1978–9 that was the immediate cause of the collapse of the government, and which was to inaugurate eighteen years of Conservative rule.

The new Conservative government, elected in May 1979, repealed the Scotland and Wales Acts in June 1979. The repeal of the Wales Act was passed by 191 votes to 8, and the repeal of the Scotland Act by 301 votes to 206, but of the Scottish MPs, 43 voted against repeal and 19 in favour with 9 absent. Devolution, which had probably never enjoyed a majority in the House of Commons, was now off the legislative agenda. Scotland had, all the same, voted for it, by however narrow a margin, while the vote on the repeal order showed that her representatives in the Commons remained committed to it.

VII

The devolution referendums had been held at the worst possible time for the Callaghan government, shortly after the 'Winter of Discontent', when Labour's standing in the polls was very low. Nevertheless, the policy had originally been put forward not because it was an essential part of Labour's ideology, but because it was believed that the Scots and the Welsh wanted it. By the time the proposals came to referendum, however, there was considerable disenchantment with institutional reform, the recent reorganization of

local government in Scotland and Wales being seen as a costly failure. Devolution, moreover, might require a further reorganization of
local government, since the two-tier local government structure set
up in the early 1970s would not co-exist easily with the new assemblies. Indeed the new local authorities in Scotland and Wales were to
survive for fewer than two decades, being replaced by unitary authorities in 1996. Paradoxically, the establishment of these new unitary
authorities by the Conservatives removed a major obstacle to devolution.

In 1979, however, it was argued that devolution would introduce
yet another layer of administration on top of two tiers of local government, and this would mean higher costs and more bureaucracy.
The argument that the assemblies would make government more
accountable fell on stony ground, since there was as much suspicion
of politicians as of officials. Many indeed feared that a Scottish
assembly would replicate the weaknesses of local government in
Scotland in that it would be dominated by machine politicians of the
Labour Party which would, under the first-past-the-post system, normally be in control of it.

In Wales, similar anxieties were expressed with regard to the
Labour machine in south Wales. The chairman of the Clwyd 'No'
Campaign argued in 1979 that: 'People in South Wales are very
charming, but as a crowd they are loud and coarse. We do not want
to be governed by Cardiff. The Assembly will be permanently dominated by Labour. It will be a dictatorship.'[39] Other opponents of
devolution used the contrary argument, that the Assembly would be
dominated by a Welsh-speaking clique from the north and the west.
The Welsh legislation, moreover, was criticized even by those who
had helped draw it up as muddled and confused. Lord Crowther-
Hunt, who had been a minister of state working on devolution, told
a Labour Party rally two days before the referendum that the Wales
Act was 'a dog's breakfast', and so badly drafted that 'it must
amount to sabotage by the drafters in London', although he still
invited the Welsh to vote for it.[40] It is not surprising, perhaps, that his
invitation was declined.

The Labour Party was divided on devolution and appeared to lack
enthusiasm for it. In Wales, indeed, the majority of constituency

Labour parties were opposed, while in Scotland, the most eloquent spokesman on the Labour side was an opponent of devolution, Tam Dalyell. His 'Labour Vote No' campaign may well have led some to believe that there was official Labour support for a No vote. The only real enthusiasts for devolution were the nationalists, but this served to deter Yes voters, since it fuelled fears that the assemblies would prove a stepping-stone to separation.

The Conservatives, in their eagerness to defeat the devolution proposals of the Callaghan government, had argued that the referendum in Scotland was a specific one, on the particular proposals put forward by the government, rather than a vote on the principle of devolution. Lord Home, the former Prime Minister, argued that the Scotland Act was flawed, but could be replaced by something more workable, and that, therefore, a No vote need not imply any disloyalty to the principle of devolution. 'A "No" vote does not mean the devolution question will be buried', declared Margaret Thatcher the day before the referendum, a promise which may have persuaded Scottish Conservatives not to vote Yes.[41] Once the Scotland Act was repealed, however, devolution was indeed buried, and the administrations of Margaret Thatcher and John Major, which governed Britain between 1979 and 1997, ensured that it was not resurrected. The defeat of devolution in 1979 was thus to prove a turning-point not only in Scottish, but also in British history. For, instead of beginning the task of dispersing power, Britain took a different path, moving, under the Conservatives, towards a more uniform and inflexible system of government, and one which accentuated the geographical and social conflicts between different parts of the country.

Throughout the period of opposition, however, Labour continued to support devolution, its commitment growing stronger as the years passed. Thus, while its belief in devolution had been hesitant in the 1970s, by 1997 it had become one of the main items on Labour's programme. Paradoxically, the defeat of devolution, far from destroying what had seemed a merely tenuous commitment, served instead to reinvigorate it. The explanation is not difficult to find. Devolution had been pressed by its advocates as a means by which the distinctive voice of Scotland and Wales could be expressed through government. But it seemed unnecessary during the 1974–9 period because the voices of Scotland and Wales were already being heard by a government so dependent on Scotland and Wales for its majority. When, however, in 1979, 1983, 1987, and 1992, England voted for the Conservatives, Scotland and Wales remained loyal to Labour (Tables 6.2, 6.3).

There had never been so prolonged a period of geographically one-sided government in Britain in the twentieth century. After 1987, the government was supported by fewer than one-seventh of Scottish MPs and fewer than a quarter of Welsh MPs. The Conservatives gained a large overall majority with the votes of less than a quarter of the Scots, and around three-tenths of the Welsh. Thus Scotland and Wales, instead of following England by swinging to the Right, were developing a specifically Scottish and Welsh consciousness of their own. This consciousness would prove incompatible with hitherto-accepted constitutional arrangements for governing Scotland and Wales.

Table 6.2 Scottish results in the elections of 1979, 1983, 1987, and 1992

		Seats	% of votes
1979	Conservatives	22	31.4
	Labour	44	41.6
	Liberals	3	9.0
	SNP	2	17.3
1983	Conservatives	21	28.4
	Labour	41	35.1
	Alliance	8	24.5
	SNP	2	11.8
1987	Conservatives	10	24.0
	Labour	50	42.4
	Alliance	9	19.2
	SNP	3	14.0
1992	Conservatives	11	25.7
	Labour	49	39.0
	Liberal Democrats	9	13.1
	SNP	3	21.5

Table 6.3 Welsh results in the elections of 1979, 1983, 1987, and 1992

		Seats	% of votes
1979	Conservatives	11	32.7
	Labour	22	48.6
	Liberals	1	12.8
	Plaid Cymru	2	8.1
1983	Conservatives	14	31.0
	Labour	20	37.5
	Alliance	2	23.2
	Plaid Cymru	2	7.8
1987	Conservatives	8	29.6
	Labour	24	45.1
	Alliance	3	17.9
	Plaid Cymru	3	7.3
1992	Conservatives	6	28.6
	Labour	27	49.5
	Liberal Democrats	1	12.4
	Plaid Cymru	4	8.8

The situation might conceivably have proved politically manageable had the Conservatives displayed the sensitivity to Scottish opinion of the Churchill or Macmillan governments of the 1950s, but it was made more intractable by the attitudes of Margaret Thatcher, an instinctive assimilationist, who saw little need to maintain the conventions of the union state. The Union with Scotland, she was to write in her memoirs, was 'inevitably dominated by England by reason of its greater population. The Scots, being an historic nation with a proud past, will inevitably resent some expressions of this fact from time to time.' Margaret Thatcher saw Scotland as an outpost of the dependency culture which she was determined to extirpate, while the 'very structure' of the Scottish Office 'added a layer of bureaucracy, standing in the way of the reforms which were paying such dividends in England'.[42] This outlook heralded the end of the 'dual polity' which had dominated territorial relations since at least the 1920s, 'a state of affairs in which national and local politics were largely divorced from each other', and which had allowed Scotland and

Wales a significant degree of autonomy whatever the political colour of the government in London.43

The Thatcher government's policies of competitive individualism were resented both in Scotland and Wales, where they were seen as undermining traditional values of community solidarity; and policies such as privatization and opting out from local authority control had little resonance there. But resented above all was the community charge, the poll tax, introduced into Scotland in 1989, a year before it was introduced in England and Wales. The Scottish Office, significantly, seems to have been 'excluded from all forums engaged with the detailed work of the review until it became de facto policy'.44 The new tax gave a considerable fillip to the SNP which urged non-payment, and indeed levels of non-payment in Scotland were higher than in any other part of the country. But, more generally, the fiasco of the poll tax seemed to prove to the Scots and Welsh that, in rejecting devolution, they had surrendered themselves to a government which cared little for their interests. Only devolution, so it seemed, could protect Scotland and Wales against future outbursts of Thatcherism.

In Wales, Labour did not renew its proposals for devolution until the late 1980s. When it did so, it kept devolution as an internal party issue, and did not seek to involve other parties in its work. In Scotland, however, the process was more complex. On the first anniversary of the devolution referendum, 1 March 1980, an all-party Campaign for a Scottish Assembly was established to renew the battle. It seemed to be making little headway, however, until, in 1988, it appointed a Constitutional Steering Committee which issued a Claim of Right for Scotland and called for the establishment of a Scottish Constitutional Convention which could draw up proposals for the reform of Scotland's government. A Convention was duly established in 1989, and declared that sovereignty in Scotland lay with the Scottish people and not with Westminster. Labour and the Liberal Democrats agreed to participate in the Convention, but the Conservatives refused, as did the SNP, which declared that it could support only a directly elected convention prepared to draw up a constitution for an independent Scotland.

The aim of the Convention was to translate what seemed like

widespread support for devolution into concrete proposals for legislation, for there seemed no other constitutional way by which Scots could have their demands recognized. Devolution was not a high priority at Westminster, even for Labour, and there were fears that a Labour government might not be willing to prepare new devolution legislation only to see it once again destroyed by hostile English back-bench MPs, as had occurred in 1977 with the Scotland and Wales Bill. Since Scottish issues were subsidiary to United Kingdom matters, there seemed no way in which the Scots could make known their support for devolution other than by voting for the SNP, and that would be regarded as a vote for separation. There was, therefore, a gap in the Scottish representative system. The Convention was intended to fill that gap. Its role was to draw up a specific scheme which could then be adopted by an incoming government sympathetic to devolution; and also to promote its chosen scheme.

Although not elected, the Convention comprised a large slice of Scottish opinion, not only Labour and Liberal Democrat MPs, but also trade unions, representatives of local government, the churches, and other representative bodies. The Convention produced two reports, the first, in 1990, *Towards Scotland's Parliament*, and the second, in 1995, entitled *Scotland's Parliament, Scotland's Right*. These reports laid out a scheme for devolution which was to form the basis of the Scotland Act in 1998. The most significant innovation was the agreement between Labour and the Liberal Democrats that the Scottish Parliament should be elected by the additional-member system of proportional representation. Labour appreciated that if it wanted to win support for devolution outside the party, that was the price which had to be paid. The Liberal Democrats, in turn, appreciated that Labour would never accept their favourite nostrum, the single transferable vote, and were prepared to compromise on another system. The outcome showed what could be achieved by co-operation between parties and perhaps prefigured the more general consultative arrangements on constitutional matters developed by the Blair government after 1997.[45]

The Convention did not, however, devote sufficient consideration to many of the other problems which had bedevilled devolution in the 1970s, in particular the relationship between a Scottish

Parliament and local government, the West Lothian Question, and, more generally, the future relationship between Edinburgh and London after devolution. The Convention would have liked to propose the devolution of revenue-raising powers to the Scottish Parliament, but was dissuaded from doing so by the Labour leadership, frightened of any apparent commitment to higher taxes. Moreover, just because the Convention's reports seemed, and no doubt were, supported by the bulk of Scottish opinion, it became difficult in 1997 for either the Blair government or Members of Parliament to suggest alternative proposals. Thus, although the Convention was to succeed in pre-empting English parliamentary hostility to devolution, it did so at the cost of also pre-empting serious scrutiny of the devolution legislation. There were no parallel debates on devolution in England.

The Convention's first report was produced in 1990 during the period of Neil Kinnock's leadership of the Labour Party. Kinnock had, as we have seen, been an opponent of devolution in the 1970s, but now agreed to support it. John Smith, who replaced Kinnock in 1992, had become a far more enthusiastic devolutionist, but Tony Blair, who succeeded Smith after the latter's untimely death in 1994, was more aware of the difficulties involved in getting so complex and controversial a constitutional measure through Parliament. In June 1996, therefore, he insisted that there be referendums on devolution in Scotland and Wales and that these be held before legislation was introduced into Parliament, rather than afterwards, as in 1979; and he also insisted that the Scots be asked not one question, but two: not simply whether they wanted a parliament but also whether that parliament should have income tax-varying powers. Blair was much criticized in Scotland and Wales for insisting on referendums, oddly perhaps, since the signatories of the Claim of Right, having celebrated the sovereignty of the Scottish people, now seemed to want to prevent the Scots from actually exercising it. Blair's tactic, however, was to succeed in disarming English back-bench parliamentary criticism of devolution; and it can be seen, in retrospect, that it was one of the factors ensuring that devolution would at last actually come to fruition.

Labour won a landslide victory in the general election of 1 May 1997 and, following the passage of a Referendum (Scotland and

Wales) Act, referendums were duly held. The Scottish referendum was held on 11 September 1997, two questions being asked on separate ballot papers. There was a 60.2 per cent turnout, as compared with a turnout of 62.9 per cent in 1979. The result in Scotland was a decisive victory for devolution and for tax-varying powers.

I agree that there should be a Scottish Parliament

    1,775,045   74.3%

I do not agree that there should be a Scottish Parliament

    614,000   25.7%

I agree that a Scottish Parliament should have tax-varying powers

    1,512,889   63.5%

I do not agree that a Scottish Parliament should have tax-varying powers

    870,263   36.0%

The proportion of the electorate voting Yes in 1997 was 44.7 per cent for a Scottish Parliament and 38.1 per cent for tax-varying powers. Thus, if a 40 per cent rule had been in operation, the Scottish Parliament would have been approved but without tax-varying powers.

The referendum in Wales was held on 18 September 1997, a week after the Scottish referendum, so that Welsh opinion might be influenced by a favourable result in Scotland. That might indeed have swayed the outcome, since the result was a very narrow victory for devolution by less than 7,000 votes out of over a million cast, on a turnout of just over 50 per cent.

I agree that there should be a Welsh Assembly

    559,419   50.1%

I do not agree that there should be a Welsh Assembly

    552,698   49.9%

The referendum was won through an alliance between Welsh-speaking Wales, the heartland of the north-west, and the industrial Wales of the valleys, the former coalfield areas. It seemed, by comparison with the 1979 result, to show that Welsh identity was becoming less divisive and that a sense of Welshness was growing irrespective of language, a sense of Welshness which may be more deep-seated than social analysts have noticed. Remarkably, the distribution of voting within Wales almost exactly replicated the political geography of the reign of Edward I over seven centuries earlier. The areas which he had succeeded in conquering—English Wales—voted No; while the rest of Wales voted Yes.[46] Thus, although narrow, the majority in Wales did reflect a real consciousness of Welshness, a consciousness which, no doubt, the Welsh National Assembly will strengthen and intensify.

Legislating for Devolution
The Constitutional Problems

The British Constitution presumes more boldly than any other the good faith of those who work it.

(W. E. Gladstone)

The basic structure

The Scotland Bill and the Government of Wales Bill were introduced into Parliament in 1997. They were the tenth major measures of devolution to have been introduced by governments since 1886. Eight of the previous ten had failed. The 1886 and 1893 Government of Ireland Bills never reached the statute-book. The 1912 bill reached the statute-book in 1914, but was suspended on the outbreak of the war. The 1920 bill also reached the statute-book but was implemented only in Northern Ireland. Devolution as provided by the Northern Ireland Constitution Act of 1973 lasted for just five months in 1974; and, under the Northern Ireland Act of 1982, for just four years. The 1976 Scotland and Wales Bill had been withdrawn after the government had failed to secure its guillotine motion. The Scotland and Wales Acts of 1978 had been repealed in 1979 after failing to win sufficient support in referendums. In 1998, by contrast, with devolution to Scotland and Wales having been endorsed in referendums *before* being introduced into Parliament, the legislation reached the statute-book without difficulty.

All previous devolution measures, except for the Government of Ireland Act of 1920, which replaced the Act of 1914, and the Acts of 1973 and 1982, were introduced in hung parliaments where the government of the day was dependent upon nationalist votes, either the Irish nationalists, as in 1886, 1893, and 1912, or the Scottish nationalists, as in 1976 and 1978. There are good reasons for believing that devolution legislation would not have been introduced had these governments not been so dependent. The 1997 Labour government, by contrast, was quite independent of nationalist votes. Far from there being a hung parliament, the government had a majority of 177 seats, the largest majority that Westminster has seen since 1935. The government, therefore, was free to introduce devolution and to shape the legislation as it thought best, rather than having to respond to outside pressures. Precisely because it enjoyed so large a majority, however, and because devolution had already been endorsed in the referendums, the legislation was little scrutinized in the House of Commons. Indeed, many of the key clauses were not discussed in committee.

The legislation received much closer scrutiny in the House of Lords, where all of the major clauses were discussed. But the Lords too were bound by the outcome of the referendum and also by the Salisbury Convention, which dictated that they could not reject or even amend in principle a measure which had been in the government's election manifesto. Thus, while the debates in the Lords highlighted many of the difficulties of devolution, they did not result in the legislation being altered to any significant degree. For all practical purposes, the Scotland and Government of Wales bills reached the statute-book in the same shape and form as when they were introduced into the Commons.

*

The Scotland Act provides in section 1 for the establishment of a Scottish Parliament. Section 28 provides that this parliament may make laws within its area of competence; subsection 7 declares that 'This section does not affect the power of the Parliament of the United Kingdom to make laws for Scotland'. This subsection succinctly lays out the central constitutional principle underlying devolution. It rejects both separatism, under which the Parliament of the United Kingdom would no longer have power to legislate for Scotland at all; and federalism under which the Parliament of the United Kingdom would have power to legislate for Scotland only in certain defined areas, other areas becoming the entire responsibility of the Scottish Parliament. The Act thus, in theory at least, preserves parliamentary supremacy, and Westminster can, if it wishes, continue to legislate on matters devolved to Scotland.

Devolution is not intended to affect the unity of the state or the form of government in the rest of the United Kingdom. The provisions of the Scotland Act, therefore, contain safeguards to ensure that the Scottish Parliament does not abuse its powers. The first is the supremacy of Westminster, reaffirmed in section 28 (7). The second consists of provisions limiting the legislative powers of the Scottish Parliament to domestic matters, and preventing it, in virtue of section 35 (1) (b), from legislating on such domestic matters so as to influence the administration of matters reserved to Westminster in a manner harmful to the public interest. The third consists of the limitation of the revenue-raising powers of the parliament to a variation of not more than 3 per cent in the basic rate of income tax from that determined for the rest of the United Kingdom by Westminster.

The Scotland Act provides for a Scottish Parliament directly elected by the additional-member system of proportional representation, similar to that used in Germany, and consisting of a total of 129 members. Seventy-three of these members will be elected from the seventy-two single-member parliamentary constituencies, with Orkney and Shetland being split to make two constituencies. The remaining fifty-six members will be elected proportionally, seven each in the eight regional constituencies used until 1999 for elections to the European Parliament.

There is to be a separate Scottish Executive led by a First Minister, and comprising other ministers appointed by the First Minister, together with two law officers, a Lord Advocate and a Solicitor-General for Scotland. The First Minister is to be appointed by the Queen following election by the Scottish Parliament. The Parliament will have a fixed term of four years. It can be dissolved, under the provisions of section 3, and an extraordinary general election held, only if a two-thirds majority of the Parliament as a whole votes for it, or if the Parliament is unable to nominate a First Minister within a period of 28 days. If it is dissolved, however, the general election that would have occurred at the end of the four-year period still takes place, unless such a poll is held within six months of a previously scheduled election. Thus, for example, if the first Scottish Parliament, elected in May 1999, were to be dissolved in May 2001, the general election in May 2003 would still be held. If, however, the first Scottish Parliament were to be dissolved in December 2002, the election of May 2003 would no longer be held, and the next election would be in December 2006.

By contrast with the abortive Scotland Act of 1978, the Scotland Act of 1998 lists, in schedule 5, the reserved, not the devolved, functions. Reserved functions are those which must be carried out at United Kingdom level, such as foreign affairs and defence, and those where significant anomalies are unacceptable for other reasons. The main reserved functions are:

(*a*) The Constitution, including the Crown, the succession to the Crown, the Parliament of the United Kingdom, and the Union of Scotland and England.

(*b*) Foreign affairs and the European Union.

(*c*) The civil service.

(*d*) Defence.

(*e*) Fiscal, economic, and monetary policy—although local taxes funding local authority expenditure, for example the council tax and non-domestic rates, are not reserved.

(*f*) The currency, financial services, and financial markets.

(*g*) Elections and the franchise for local government elections. Otherwise, however, local government elections are not reserved.

(*h*) Immigration and nationality.

(*i*) National security.

(*j*) Emergency powers.

(*k*) Extradition.

(*l*) Competition and import and export control.

(*m*) Telecommunications and the Post Office.

(*n*) The bulk of energy policy.

(*o*) Certain essentials of transport policy.

(*p*) The bulk of social security policy.

(*q*) Employment, industrial relations, and health and safety.

(*r*) Abortion.

(*s*) Broadcasting.

Anything not specifically reserved lies within the legislative competence of the Scottish Parliament, which will have power to legislate over a broad range of Scottish domestic affairs, and in particular, over home affairs, the legal system, local government, housing, agriculture, health, social, educational, and environmental policy.

The bulk of the funding for the Parliament will be derived from a block grant paid annually by the Secretary of State, but the Scottish Parliament will, as noted above, have the power to vary the basic rate of income tax in Scotland by up to 3 per cent of the rate in the rest of the United Kingdom. Moreover, since the Parliament will be responsible for the financing of local authorities, it will have the power to secure revenue for itself by withholding revenue-support grant from local authorities. The Parliament could moreover, if it so wished, abolish the council tax in Scotland, replacing it with another form of local taxation, and it could, if it so wished, return the power to fix the non-domestic rate, the uniform business rate, to local authorities. It could also abolish the capping of local authorities.

The Scottish Parliament and the Scottish Executive will, by contrast with the 1978 Act, enjoy a direct relationship with the Crown. Legislation passed by the Scottish Parliament will not need to go to the Secretary of State for approval, apart from the special circumstances associated with section 35 of the Act and mentioned below. Otherwise, the Secretary of State, again by contrast with the 1978 Act, is to have no governor-general functions and will not act as an intermediary between the Scottish Parliament and the Queen.

The Scotland Act contains provisions to ensure that the Scottish Parliament does not overstep its powers. First, the Presiding Officer of the Parliament must assure himself that any proposed legislation lies within its powers. This provision could easily prove controversial. It would be perfectly possible for the Presiding Officer to take the view that a proposed bill is *ultra vires*, while the majority in the Parliament takes a different view. It is not clear what would happen in the case of such a disagreement. The courts, clearly, could not give a verdict on whether proposed legislation was *ultra vires* or not, until it had actually been passed by the Parliament. Possibly, however, the courts might be asked for an advisory opinion in such a situation. Nevertheless, this provision could easily lead to conflict between the Presiding Officer and the Scottish Executive and Parliament.

Second, the Act provides that the Presiding Officer shall submit bills for the royal assent only after four weeks have elapsed following the passage of a bill. During this four-week period, the Scottish law officers may refer a bill or part of a bill to the Judicial

Committee of the Privy Council for a decision as to whether it lies within the legislative competence of the Scottish Parliament. The purpose of this provision is to ensure that the Queen is not offered conflicting advice, the Presiding Officer of the Scottish Parliament advising her to give the royal assent, but the British government advising her to reject it because it believes that it lies outwith the powers of the Scottish Parliament. The Act prevents such a situation arising since the Advocate General, a new Scottish law officer, would have secured a judicial verdict before the bill is submitted to the Queen. Nevertheless, this provision puts the courts and the Judicial Committee of the Privy Council in the position of deciding a question of *vires* in the abstract rather than in the context of a concrete case, without which there may be an incomplete understanding of the facts. Any opinion is bound to be in large part hypothetical, since it would be given before the Act had come into operation and without any real evidence as to the effect of the legislation.

The third provision ensuring that the Scottish Parliament does not overstep its powers is that of post-assent judicial review. An Act of the Scottish Parliament will be in the same position as the decisions of any other statutory body in that its legislation can be reviewed by the courts. Anyone with a *locus standi* may therefore challenge Scottish legislation in the ordinary courts, although the ultimate authority on the interpretation of the Act is to be the Judicial Committee of the Privy Council. There is thus both pre-assent and post-assent review. But to determine the validity, as opposed to the construction, of primary legislation within the United Kingdom will be a novel function for a British court—always excepting the Northern Ireland experience—and it will mean that an Act of the Scottish Parliament will be law only in so far as a court has ruled that it is valid, or if it has not yet been challenged. However, the Scottish Office Minister for Home Affairs and Devolution, Henry McLeish, has given as his opinion that 'the overwhelming majority of issues will be resolved in very early stages'.[1]

The Judicial Committee of the Privy Council will come to assume the function of a constitutional court for devolution issues. It is in fact rare for common-law countries to have a separate constitutional court since, under such jurisdictions, constitutional issues can arise from all kinds of litigation, often as side issues. These matters, therefore, are generally dealt with, in common-law countries, by the ordinary courts. The Judicial Committee is the final court of appeal for British dependent territories and for those independent Commonwealth countries which chose to retain this particular avenue of appeal on attaining independence. It does not deal with domestic matters other than appeals from the Channel Islands and the Isle of Man, some church matters and appeals, and appeals from the disciplinary and health committees of the medical and allied professions. It was, however, chosen as the final court of appeal rather than the House of Lords, which does not hear appeals from Scottish courts in criminal cases. For the House of Lords is a constituent part of the United Kingdom legislature, presided over by a member of the British government, the Lord Chancellor. It would not perhaps be the body best placed to adjudicate questions which may raise the issue of the relative competence of Westminster *vis-à-vis* the Scottish Parliament; for the British government might itself be a possible party to such a dispute. Moreover, the Appellate Committee of the House of Lords has a majority of English judges, while the composition of the Judicial Committee is more flexible, being open to any judge who is a member of the Privy Council and holds or has held high judicial office within the Commonwealth. It will thus be much easier to ensure that there are sufficient Scottish judges on the Judicial Committee than it is in the House of Lords. The Minister for Home Affairs and Devolution, Henry McLeish, has indicated that the government 'expect cases to be considered by five of the 12 Lords of Appeal in Ordinary and we would expect the two Scottish Lords of Appeal to be members of the Judicial Committee to consider devolution *vires* cases.'[2] It is to be hoped, however, that there are not too many occasions on which the two Scottish judges declare an Act of the Scottish Parliament *intra vires*, while the three non-Scottish judges declare it to be *ultra vires*. For, even though the judges will have acted in a perfectly professional manner, such a division would provide powerful ammunition for those in Scotland who sought to create conflict between Westminster and Edinburgh. The precise membership for any hearing of the Judicial Committee will in

practice be determined by the senior Law Lord. It is perhaps surprising that there is no provision regulating the constitution of the
Committee for hearings that may arise from the terms of the
Scotland Act. For a constitutional court, which is what the Judicial
Committee will in effect become, needs a stable membership, with
the same set of judges considering the various cases which raise
issues of *vires*, not a different membership for different cases. Since,
moreover, many people are not particularly aware of the role of the
Judicial Committee, it may take some time for its decisions to yield
the same legitimacy as those of constitutional courts in federal
countries.

Fourth, and finally, under section 35, a Secretary of State may
issue an Order prohibiting the Presiding Officer of the Scottish
Parliament from submitting a bill for royal assent if he has reasonable grounds for believing that it would be incompatible with
Britain's international obligations, including defence and security
obligations, the nature and extent of these obligations being matters
for the government to determine; or if, although the bill lies within
the legislative competence of the Scottish Parliament, it nevertheless
would have an adverse effect on some reserved matter. A Secretary
of State's use of this power will in general be subject to the negative-
resolution procedure of both Houses of Parliament, and will no
doubt, like other delegated legislation, be reviewable by the courts.
The purpose of this provision is to ensure that the Scottish
Parliament does not use its powers in an unacceptable manner. For
example, a Scottish Parliament dominated by unilateralists might
decide to build a housing estate near a military airfield, so rendering
the airfield inoperable. That would no doubt be thought by a
Secretary of State for Scotland to be unacceptable as affecting the
operation of a reserved matter, namely defence.

This provision also ensures that the Queen is not offered conflicting advice. The Secretary of State, if he believes that the Queen
ought not to sign a bill of the Scottish Parliament, when he has specific grounds for that belief in terms of section 35, may prohibit the
Presiding Officer of that parliament from submitting the bill in question to the Queen. Thus this provision and the provision for pre-
assent review ensure that the Queen will not be put in the position of

appearing to have to arbitrate between the British government and the Scottish Executive. All disputes ought to have been resolved by the time a Scottish bill is passed to the Queen for the royal assent.

Even so, a situation in which a bill has been allowed to go through all of its stages in the Scottish Parliament and is then declared to be unacceptable by the Secretary of State under section 35, is likely to arouse considerable animosity in Edinburgh. The hope must be, therefore, that intermediate political and administrative mechanisms such as the Joint Ministerial Committee (see p. 284) will resolve problems amicably before section 35 has to be brought into play.

*

The Government of Wales Act differs fundamentally from the Scotland Act in that it proposes a novel form of devolution, one hitherto untried in the United Kingdom. It confers executive but not primary legislative functions on a National Assembly for Wales—not a parliament as with Scotland. The assembly will have the power, transferred from ministers, primarily the Secretary of State for Wales, to make subordinate legislation in areas within its competence. The Government of Wales Act, by contrast with the Scotland Act, specifies, in schedule 2, fields in which the Secretary of State must consider whether functions are to be transferred. These include:

(*a*) Agriculture and fisheries.
(*b*) Culture.
(*c*) Economic development.
(*d*) Education and training.
(*e*) The environment.
(*f*) Health.
(*g*) Highways.
(*h*) Housing.
(*i*) Industry.
(*j*) Local government.
(*k*) Social services.
(*l*) Sport.
(*m*) Tourism.
(*n*) Town and country planning.
(*o*) Transport.

(*p*) Water.

(*q*) The Welsh language.

The courts have the power to determine whether the Assembly has acted within its powers, with the final court of appeal being the Judicial Committee of the Privy Council.

The National Assembly also has the power under section 27 to transfer to itself the functions of the health authorities in Wales, and then, if it so wishes, to abolish them. It may do the same, under section 28, with various Welsh nominated bodies specified in schedule 4. This comes near to giving the National Assembly legislative competence. Under section 113 (1) of the Act, the Assembly is required to prepare a scheme setting out how it proposes 'to sustain and promote local government in Wales'; and it is required also to establish a Partnership Council for Wales, with advisory powers, consisting of members of the Assembly and members of Welsh local authorities.

The Act provides for a National Assembly of sixty members, to be directly elected by the same system of proportional representation as the Scottish Parliament. Forty of the members are to be elected in the single-member parliamentary constituencies of Wales by first past the post, and the remaining twenty will be elected proportionally, four each from the five regional European parliamentary constituencies in Wales.

The Act requires the Assembly to elect a First Secretary and also to establish committees which must reflect the party balance in the Assembly. Section 56 of the Act requires the Assembly to establish an executive committee comprising the First Secretary and Assembly Secretaries. The model seems at first sight to be broadly of the local government committee type, with the executive committee corresponding to the Leader's Committee of a local authority, single party in nature, and the locus of political direction. This system was valued as a protection for minority parties. However, in the Commons, these minority parties urged a Cabinet system. Moreover, in its programme for the regeneration of local government, the government proposed that local authorities be allowed and indeed encouraged to adopt alternative models of internal management to remedy weaknesses in the traditional committee model which has dominated local government since the 1835 Municipal Corporations Act.[3] It would have been absurd if the government had declared that the committee model was unsuitable for local government, but required for the Welsh National Assembly. Therefore, the then Secretary of State for Wales, Ron Davies, tabled new clauses to the Government of Wales bill, giving the First Secretary rather than the subject committees the power to appoint Assembly Secretaries, and allowing the Assembly to delegate its functions. He indicated that he would not in fact approve any standing orders for the Assembly which did not allow for delegation of functions to the executive committee, and that a two-thirds vote would then be needed to alter the standing orders. Thus the Assembly will in practice operate a Cabinet-type system, with the executive committee being appointed by the First Secretary.

The Assembly will, by contrast with Westminster, but analogously to many local authorities, sit for a fixed four-year term, and, by contrast with Scotland, there is no possibility of early dissolution; moreover, and again by contrast with Scotland, the Assembly will have no revenue-raising powers.

Scotland and Wales are to retain their existing representation at Westminster. But section 86 of the Scotland Act amends the rule in the Parliamentary Constituencies Act of 1986 which provides that Scotland is to have no fewer than seventy-one parliamentary constituencies. It also provides for the Boundary Commission for Scotland, in the next full review of Scottish parliamentary constituencies, which will in fact not occur before 2003, to use an electoral quota for Scotland which is the same as the electoral quota for England, rather than, as now, an electoral quota for Scotland which is lower than the quota for England. Thus provision is made for Scottish over-representation to be ended, and for her to be represented in proportion to population on the same basis as England. That would mean, in practice, that instead of returning seventy-two members to Westminster, as at present, Scotland would return around fifty-nine MPs. There is no similar provision for Wales, it being thought, no doubt, that there is no case for a reduction because responsibility for primary legislation for Wales remains with Westminster.

There is to be no separate Scottish or Welsh civil service and the offices of Secretary of State for Scotland and for Wales are to remain. Their role, however, will be very different from what they have been in the past.

The Scottish Secretary will lose all of his departmental functions. He will survive solely as the link-man between the Scottish Parliament and the Cabinet. In the words of paragraph 4.12 of the White Paper, *Scotland's Parliament* (Cm. 3658, 1997):

Once the Scottish Parliament is in being, and the Scottish Executive established, the responsibilities of the Secretary of State for Scotland will change. The focus will be on promoting communication between the Scottish Parliament and Executive and between the UK Parliament and Government on matters of mutual interest; and on representing Scottish interests in reserved areas.

These, however, are the sorts of functions which between 1921 and 1972 were performed for Northern Ireland not by its own Secretary of State, but by the Home Secretary. For, so the Royal Commission on the Constitution believed, under such circumstances, 'there would in the ordinary course be little for a Secretary of State to do when devolution was working smoothly.' The Commission went on to say that:

Retention of the office of Secretary of State for Scotland with a separate department for Scottish affairs would then be difficult to justify. The principal spokesman for Scotland would be the head of the Scottish Government, and it would detract from his status if there were also to be a Secretary of State for Scotland in the United Kingdom Parliament.[4]

It will be difficult for the Scottish Secretary to speak at Westminster on domestic Scottish affairs when he no longer has statutory responsibility for them, and when policy is formulated and enacted by the Scottish Parliament. Under these circumstances, the power of the Scottish Secretary might well, as one critic of devolution forecast, 'be amputated, and an amputated limb is discarded and soon forgotten'.[5]

The Welsh Secretary will retain responsibility for primary legislation for Wales and a small team of civil servants, but powers of implementation will pass to the Assembly. The Secretary of State's task will be to represent government to the Assembly and the Assembly to government. As with the Scottish Secretary, however, problems may arise when the Secretary of State and the majority in the Assembly belong to different parties. There will then be disputes about who—the Secretary of State or the majority on the devolved body—is the real representative of Wales.

It must, moreover, remain open to question whether the Welsh Secretary retains sufficient responsibilities to justify a separate place in the Cabinet—without executive responsibilities or a budget, he might well come to be ignored; and also whether England will continue to tolerate territorial ministers for areas which have their own directly elected bodies. Significantly, the Conservatives, who secured no representation in either Scotland or Wales in the 1997 general election, did not appoint Shadow Secretaries for Scotland or Wales in the 1997 Parliament. It may be that the posts of Secretary of State for Scotland and for Wales will become merged with that of a minister for the regions so as to create a single territorial minister in the Cabinet. Such a figure would be more likely to be a senior figure in the government than the Secretaries of State for Scotland and Wales, and would, therefore, have greater weight in Cabinet discussions. An alternative would be to subsume the territorial responsibilities with those of the Home Secretary, who was responsible for Northern Ireland matters until 1972, and for Welsh matters between 1951 and 1957. A solution of this kind for the representation of areas with devolved bodies in the Cabinet was recommended by the Royal Commission on the Constitution.[6]

Government formation and dissolution

In Scotland, devolution seems, at first sight, to create a simulacrum of Westminster in Edinburgh. There are, however, two important dissimilarities, since, first, the provisions for the formation of the executive and the dissolution of Parliament differ from those at Westminster; and second, the electoral system is different.

In Northern Ireland, between 1921 and 1972, the sovereign's duties of choosing a government and agreeing to a request for the dissolution of parliament were carried out by the Governor, who acted as the sovereign's representative. Such a solution was thought unsuitable for Scotland, since a Governor would be a non-elected official who would seem to have little to do other than carry out a few ceremonial functions. Under the abortive Scotland Act of 1978, these functions would have been undertaken not by a Governor, but by the Secretary of State for Scotland. This provision gave rise to much criticism, since the Secretary of State is of course a member of the British government, and might well belong to a different party from that of the majority in the Scottish Parliament. It would have been difficult for him to act both as a party politician and also as a constitutional arbiter.

Under the Scotland Act of 1998, neither of these precedents has been followed. The Scottish Parliament and Executive will have their own direct relationships with the Crown, as occurred in Northern Ireland. The Secretary of State for Scotland will not be an intermediary, as he would have been under the provisions of the Scotland Act of 1978. Under the 1998 Act, the relationships between the Scottish Parliament and Executive and the Crown will be mediated by the Presiding Officer of the Scottish Parliament, an elected person, rather than by a Governor. It will be the Presiding Officer of the Scottish Parliament who carries out the sovereign's functions in Scotland. It will be he who, under section 46 (4), will recommend to the Queen the appointment of a particular First Minister after the Scottish Parliament has nominated one of its members to undertake that position; and it will be he, not the First Minister, who will, under the provisions of section 3, seek a dissolution, when the appropriate circumstances obtain. This is an entirely novel arrangement in Britain, and the role of the Presiding Officer in Scotland may well come to resemble that of the Speaker in Sweden, who has taken over the sovereign's constitutional prerogatives there since the time of the new Swedish Constitution, the Instrument of Government, in 1974. On the Continent indeed, the Speaker tends to be an active party member with direct involvement in the organization of parliamentary business, while the British and Commonwealth conceptions of the Speaker imply a strictly impartial presiding officer. It is this Continental conception which is being introduced in Scotland, and it is possible that if it is successful there, it will be used by some as an argument for the Westminster Speaker being given a similar role to that of the Presiding Officer in the exercise of the sovereign's prerogatives. However, the new functions proposed for the Presiding Officer in Scotland make it more rather than less necessary that he or she should be strictly impartial.

Relationships between the Scottish Parliament and the Scottish Executive will be quite different from those between Westminster and the United Kingdom government. For the processes of government-formation and the dissolution of parliament are bound to be more complex in a fixed-term parliament which is elected by proportional representation than in a parliament such as Westminster elected under the first-past-the-post system where a Prime Minister can normally obtain a dissolution at a moment of his own choosing.

It is difficult therefore to understand the rationale for the government's contention in para. 2.6 of the White Paper, *Scotland's Parliament*, Cm. 3658, that 'The relationship between the Scottish Executive and the Scottish Parliament will be similar to the relationship between the UK Government and the UK Parliament.' For one almost certain consequence of proportional representation is that no single party will enjoy a majority in the Scottish Parliament. The last popular majority in Scotland was achieved by the Conservatives in 1955, when they gained just over 50 per cent of the Scottish vote. Labour, by contrast, has never achieved a majority of the vote in Scotland. The last popular majority in the United Kingdom as a whole was achieved by the National government in 1935.

If, as is likely, there is no overall majority in the Scottish Parliament, it may not be immediately obvious after the election who should be the First Minister. Such a situation occurs rarely at Westminster, since the first-past-the-post system normally produces an overall majority for one party. On only three occasions since 1918 has it not done so—after the general elections of December 1923, 1929, and February 1974. When a hung parliament occurs, the sovereign invites someone, normally a party leader, to form a government. Thus, in the hung parliaments after the general elections of 1923 and 1929, George V asked Ramsay MacDonald to form a government, while in March 1974, Elizabeth II asked Harold Wilson to form a government. The sovereign may enjoy a genuine discretion in such situations. The Scotland Act, by contrast, makes the Queen's appointment of a First Minister purely formal, since it is the Scottish Parliament, not the sovereign, which chooses the First Minister, and, by sections 45 and 46 of the Act, Parliament's recommendation is conveyed to the Queen by the Presiding Officer.

In a parliament without a single-party majority, it is always possible for political alignments to change within the course of a parliament. Thus, the first Scottish Executive in 1999 might well be a coalition between Labour and a minority party in Scotland—either the Liberal Democrats or the SNP. That minority party might then decide to leave the coalition after, say, two years, on account of policy differences. The Labour First Minister might then be tempted to dissolve the Parliament for tactical reasons. In consequence, proportional representation combined with a First Minister's right of dissolution could lead to frequent and possibly destabilizing general elections. With a fixed-term parliament, by contrast, Labour, in the situation described above, would not be able to dissolve and would have to seek an alternative combination if it was to carry on governing in Scotland. The defect of a fixed-term parliament, however, is that it could lead to deadlock if it proves impossible to form a government able to command the confidence of parliament. The provisions in the Scotland Act seek to steer between the Scylla of frequent dissolutions and the Charybdis of deadlock. They comprise the second difference between Scottish Parliament–Executive relations and Westminster–UK government relations.

Westminster is a maximum-term parliament which can, under normal conditions, be dissolved by the Prime Minister at a moment of his choosing. It is only under very rare circumstances, as in 1924 or 1979, that a Prime Minister, commanding only a minority in the House of Commons, is forced to go to the country at a time not of his own choosing, following defeat in a vote of confidence. That is a consequence, in large part, of the first-past-the-post electoral system which converts a minority of the votes in the country into a majority in the House of Commons.

The Scottish Parliament, by contrast, will be not a maximum-term parliament, but a four-year fixed-term parliament. There are,

however, two circumstances in which there can be an early dissolution: when a two-thirds majority of the Parliament votes for it, or
when the Parliament fails, after twenty-eight days, to choose a First
Minister. This second provision is designed to avoid the deadlock
which could otherwise occur when a First Minister has lost the support of the Parliament, but there is no alternative government which
enjoys Parliament's confidence, and no two-thirds majority to dissolve. However, even when either of these contingencies occurs, it
is not, as in Westminster, the leader of the government, but the
Presiding Officer of the Parliament, who asks the Queen for a dissolution. The rationale behind this provision in the Scotland Act is
that it is Parliament and not the executive which decides that there
ought to be a dissolution and that the fixed-term rule should be
breached. It is for this reason that it is the chair of the Parliament,
acting, it is hoped, impartially, and not the head of the Executive,
the First Minister, who seeks the dissolution. Thus decisions on the
timing of the election are removed from the control of the leader of
the government. Moreover, the Presiding Officer seems to have no
discretion as to when to seek a dissolution. He can do so only under
very precisely formulated rules.

The requirement for dissolution is placed at two-thirds rather than
a majority of the Parliament so as to prevent a First Minister, in command of a majority, from stage-managing a dissolution at a moment
of his choosing by instructing his supporters to vote for it. But a First
Minister in command of a majority in the Scottish Parliament might
be able to stage-manage a dissolution in another way. For he could
instruct his followers who, *ex hypothesi*, are in the majority, to support a vote of no confidence; or simply resign. The majority can then
ensure that no alternative administration is chosen within the period
of twenty-eight days. In those circumstances, the Presiding Officer is
required to seek a dissolution from the Queen. It seems that, in this
way, a First Minister could *always* stage-manage a dissolution. It is
not clear whether such a situation was envisaged by those who
framed the Scotland Act. Nor is such stage-management a merely
theoretical possibility. It is precisely what Willy Brandt and Helmut
Kohl did under a similar provision in Germany in 1972 and 1983
respectively. On both occasions, the Chancellor sought to dissolve

the Bundestag at a favourable moment and therefore asked his supporters to ensure that a vote of no confidence was passed. In Scotland,
admittedly, by contrast with Germany, a dissolution, unless held within six months of the general election, does not obviate the need for the
ordinary general election which takes place at the end of the four-year
cycle; and this provision lessens the attraction of a stage-managed dissolution. Moreover, a stage-managed election would take place in the
full glare of publicity and would risk incurring the displeasure of the
electorate. Nevertheless, under the Westminster system, the sovereign
can prevent any abuse of the right to dissolution by refusing to grant
one. Under the provisions of the Scotland Act, it seems that she has
no such power. This could mean that one very real defence against an
abuse of the rights of parliament is lost.

*

The Welsh Assembly, by contrast with the Scottish Parliament, is to
be a fixed-term body with no provision for dissolution. The case for
this arrangement is that the Assembly, in its original form, would
have been like a local authority, based on the committee structure
and with no separate executive. But, as we have seen, the then
Secretary of State for Wales declared that he would not approve any
standing orders for the Assembly that do not provide for the delegation of powers from the committees to the Executive Committee, so
that the Assembly will operate under a *de facto* Cabinet system.

The danger of not providing for dissolution is that of a deadlock
in the Assembly. Like the Scottish Parliament, the Assembly will be
elected by proportional representation. It would be perfectly possible
for a change of political alignments in mid-term to deprive a particular administration in the Assembly of its majority, without any alternative administration being possible. Such a situation might have
arisen, even under the first-past-the-post electoral system, at
Westminster, after the election of February 1974, when, it could be
argued, it was only the possibility and the threat of a further dissolution which prevented a paralysis of government.

Moreover, the Welsh Assembly is not intended to be a mere local
authority. It is the National Assembly for Wales. As such, it needs
strong leadership. One criticism of the committee system in local

government, indeed, is that it does not yield such strong leadership. That, no doubt, is why the Secretary of State for Wales has proposed artificially to create a Cabinet system in Wales. But the executive committee may well be handicapped by its inability to dissolve. Indeed the fixed-term provision conflicts with the *raison d'être* of the National Assembly, and will make it more difficult for the Assembly to provide effective leadership in Wales.

The electoral system

The elections held in May 1999 for the Scottish Parliament and the Welsh National Assembly were the first to be held on the mainland by any proportional representation system since the abolition of the university seats in 1950. Until 1999, moreover, all proportional representation elections in the United Kingdom, with the exception of the election for the Northern Ireland Forum in 1996, where a list system was used, have been held by the single-transferable vote method of proportional representation. That, indeed, has been the method advocated by the Liberal Party, which supported proportional representation from 1922, and its successor party, the Liberal Democrats. It is also the method which was unanimously recommended by the Royal Commission on the Constitution for elections to any devolved bodies. Elections to the Scottish Parliament and Welsh National Assembly, however, are to be by an additional-member system, a system very similar to, although not exactly the same as, that used in Germany and in New Zealand since that country abandoned the first-past-the-post system in 1996.

In Scotland, the proposal for proportional representation derived, as we have seen, from the Scottish Constitutional Convention, from negotiations between Labour and the Liberal Democrats. Its effect, however, ironically, will be to benefit the parties which did not participate in the Convention—the Conservatives and the SNP.

Labour appreciated that proportional representation was the price which it had to pay for agreement with the Liberal Democrats. Nor was Labour unwilling to pay that price. The party was aware that one of the reasons why the Scotland Act of 1978 had failed to gain a sufficient majority in the 1979 referendum was the fear that, in a four-party system, Labour, representing just the central belt of Scotland, might gain an overall majority on just over 35 per cent of the vote; or, alternatively, that the SNP might gain an overall majority on just over 35 per cent of the vote and use that majority to claim that the Scottish people had given a mandate for independence. Under proportional representation, by contrast, the SNP would need to win 50 per cent of the vote to claim a mandate. Thus, while first past the post offered the prospect of a majority for Labour or the SNP, proportional representation offered the prospect of a majority for the union. But if Labour was prepared to accept proportional representation, it was not prepared to accept the single transferable-vote method. Labour has always been sceptical of this method, which involves intra-party competition, because it would publicly expose divisions within the party, both between Left and Right and between Old Labour and New. Moreover, Labour has traditionally been attached to the single-member constituency, an attachment that may well be shared by many Scottish voters. If, therefore, Labour would have to accept proportional representation to secure an agreement with the Liberal Democrats, the Liberal Democrats would, in turn, have to abandon their favoured system, the single transferable vote, to secure agreement with Labour. This they were prepared to do, and the additional-member system, therefore, became the compromise endorsed by the Convention.

In Wales, as in Scotland, the failure to adopt proportional representation may have been a contributory factor in the heavy defeat of devolution in 1979. For, under first past the post, the Assembly would, almost certainly, have been run by the Labour machine in south Wales. Proportional representation, on the other hand, offered some chance of overcoming the spatial and linguistic divide which had doomed prospects for devolution in Wales ever since the failure of *Cymru Fydd* in the 1890s.

The additional-member system, however, came about in a different way in Wales from Scotland, for there had been no cross-party Welsh Convention. This was so for two reasons. The first is that Labour has always been stronger and more self-confident in Wales than it has been in Scotland—between 1945 and 1970, indeed, it won over 50 per cent of the vote in Wales at every general election—and the separatist threat was much weaker. The second reason is that

Labour in Wales was more internally divided over devolution than Labour in Scotland. For in Wales many Labour MPs remained as sceptical about devolution as they had been in 1979. Thus, in Wales, by contrast with Scotland, policy on devolution was made by an internal party commission, which recommended retention of the first-past-the-post system. In 1995, the Welsh Labour Conference also declared for first past the post, contrary to the wishes of the Shadow Secretary of State for Wales, Ron Davies, and the party leader, Tony Blair. But Blair and Davies asked the Welsh party to think again, and in 1996 it duly did so, agreeing at last to accept proportional representation.

Under the additional-member system, each elector has two votes, one for a constituency member, the other for a party list. Constituency elections take place as under the first-past-the-post system. Votes for the party list are then used to elect additional members so as to secure a proportional outcome. Those who are to become additional members will be decided upon by the party concerned. If, say, three candidates are elected as additional members, then the top three candidates on the list are elected as additional members. Voters are not allowed to alter the order of the lists as determined by the parties.

The working of the additional-member system may be illustrated by the example shown in the table, taken from the notes on clauses to the Scotland bill, published by the Scottish Office in January 1998. The example is based on the North East of Scotland European parliamentary constituency. It is assumed that electors would cast their regional votes for the constituency candidate whom they voted for in the general election of 1997. Independent candidates and parties other than Labour, the Liberal Democrats, the SNP and the Conservatives are excluded.

The number of votes cast for each party list is first divided by the number of constituency members of the Scottish Parliament plus one. The use of this divisor is known as the d'Hondt method. There are also various alternative divisors. Under the d'Hondt method, however, Labour, which has won five constituency seats has its vote divided by 6. Then the party with the highest vote gains the first regional seat. In this case, it is the Conservatives. For the second to

Table 7.1 Voting in the North-East of Scotland European parliamentary constituency: the additional-member system

NE Scotland	Labour	Lib Dem	SNP	Conservative	Result
Party vote	113,021	69,164	95,493	82,079	-
Constituency members of the Scottish Parliament	**5**	**2**	**2**	**0**	-
1st additional member	18,837	23,055	31,831	82,079	Con.
2nd additional member	18,837	23,055	31,831	41,040	Con.
3rd additional member	18,837	23,055	31,831	27,360	SNP
4th additional member	18,837	23,055	23,873	27,360	Con.
5th additional member	18,837	23,055	23,873	20,520	SNP
6th additional member	18,837	23,055	19,099	20,520	LibDem
7th additional member	18,837	17,291	19,099	20,520	Con.
Additional members	**0**	**1**	**2**	**4**	
Total representation in NE Scotland	**5**	**3**	**4**	**4**	

the seventh seats, the same calculations are carried out, but party-list seats gained are included. Thus, on the second round, the Conservative figure is divided, not by 1 but by 2; and then, on the third round, after it has won two list seats, by 3. The final regional seat was won on 20,520 votes, which is around 5.7 per cent of the total vote.

That is the implicit threshold in this constituency, i.e. the hurdle which a party or indeed an independent candidate has to overcome to win a seat. Any party or independent candidate failing to win 5.7 per cent of the vote will not win a seat.

The working of the additional-member system in Scotland and Wales is slightly different from its working in Germany and New Zealand. In those countries, an equal number of members are elected from the list and from the constituencies. In Scotland and Wales, however, fewer members are elected from the list than from the constituencies. In Scotland, there will be 73 constituency members and 56 list members, a ratio of 57 to 43. In Wales, there will be 40 constituency members and 20 list members, a ratio of $66^2/_3$ to $33^1/_3$. The outcome in Scotland, therefore, is likely to be somewhat more proportional than in Wales, where the implicit threshold will be around 8 per cent. The Labour Party, however, is stronger in Wales than it is in Scotland, and so it would seem that Wales deserves more, not less, proportionality than Scotland. It is indeed not immediately apparent why the degree of proportionality should be different for elections to the two devolved bodies.

In Germany and New Zealand, proportionality is at *national* level, and subject to an explicit threshold. In Scotland and Wales, by contrast, there is no explicit threshold, but proportionality is at the level of the regional Euro-constituencies and not at the level of Scotland and Wales as a whole, and there will be no explicit threshold. The system as used in Scotland and Wales does, however, as we have seen, yield an implicit threshold.

The additional-member system is likely to increase the number of women elected to the Scottish Parliament and the Welsh Assembly. There is good evidence that it is more difficult for women to secure nomination in single-member constituencies, since constituency associations will tend to choose a 'safe' candidate who often turns out to be white, middle-aged, and male. Under the additional-member system, by contrast, a party would be wise to seek a more balanced ticket. Since the list will contain a large number of names, the absence of a due proportion of women will cause offence and narrow the appeal of the party. For, whereas under a single-member constituency system, it is the *presence* of a candidate who deviates from the male norm which is noticed, in a party-list system, it is the *absence* of a female candidate, the failure to present a balanced ticket, that would be noticed and made the subject of adverse comment. Under the German electoral system, as we have seen, 50 per cent of the candidates are elected by single-member constituencies and 50 per cent through party lists. Between 1949 and 1994, 790 women were elected to the Bundestag. Of these, no fewer than 605 were elected from the list, and only 185 from the constituencies.

The additional-member system has the further advantage that it enables the voter to indicate which coalition he or she favours. The voter can do this by, for example, supporting Labour on the constituency vote and, say, the Liberal Democrats on the list vote. This would indicate that the voter supported a Labour–Liberal Democrat coalition. A list vote for the SNP, by contrast, would indicate that the voter favoured a Labour–SNP coalition. In Germany, the Free Democrats, who have not won a constituency seat since 1957, once used as an election slogan: 'A FIRST-class decision; your SECOND vote for a THIRD force.' Signalling a coalition in this way limits the power of the party leaders. It prevents them from constructing, in proverbial smoke-filled rooms, coalitions which do not correspond with the wishes of voters. On the other hand, the additional-member system does not ensure such an outcome. For example, in the first New Zealand election held under this system, in 1996, the New Zealand First party held the balance of power between Labour and the National Party. The New Zealand First Party had seemed close to Labour, and the distribution of its constituency votes were more strongly Labour than National. Nevertheless, after eight weeks of negotiations, the New Zealand Party decided to ally itself with the National Party, and these two parties together formed the new government.

The additional-member system creates two kinds of MP—constituency members and list members. Before becoming a Welsh Office minister, the Labour MP Peter Hain had attacked the system on these grounds, saying that 'The Additional Member System (AMS) favoured by most PR advocates in the Labour Party would mean two classes of MP: some constituency-based, the others constituency free-loaders chosen from lists and without any constituency responsibilities.'[7] In 1993, the Plant Report, established by the Labour Party to consider various alternative electoral systems, argued:

It would be wrong to have two classes of members in the Commons—those who represent constituencies and those who do not. There would be a danger that the latter would still be less directly accountable; and there would be differences in workload with non-constituency members relieved of constituency casework. This could also mean the latter would be less in touch with the day-to-day concerns of the electors.[8]

The working party conceded, however, that there were compensating advantages to the system.

In Germany, there is no difference in status between the two kinds of MPs; once in the Bundestag they perform similar functions. But that is in large part due to the special circumstances of German federalism. For, in Germany, constituency work is the responsibility not of members of the Bundestag, but of local councillors and members of the Landtage—regional parliaments. Members of the Bundestag, unlike elected representatives in Britain, are not expected to involve themselves in constituency work. In Scotland and Wales, by contrast, the constituency representatives will presumably be expected to undertake such work. Therefore a difference in status between the two kinds of member might well arise. Moreover, if the figures for the 1997 election were to be replicated in the first elections to the Scottish Parliament, most of the additional members would be Conservatives who gained no seats despite winning 17.5 per cent of the vote; and Scottish Nationalists who gained only six of the seventy-two Scottish seats despite winning 22.1 per cent—over one-fifth—of the Scottish vote. In Wales, the extra seats would go to Conservatives, who won no seats despite winning 19.6 per cent of the vote; and to Liberal Democrats who won only two out of the forty Welsh seats despite winning 12.5 per cent—nearly one-eighth—of the Welsh vote. Thus the Labour members of the Scottish Parliament and the Welsh Assembly are likely to bear the brunt of the constituency work, while the other parties will be able to devote their time to scrutiny of legislation. The difference in function between the two types of member might come to be very marked. On the other hand, it is perfectly possible that the regional-list MPs come to take on constituency functions for those in the constituencies who voted for minority parties. This could lead to more effective representation since electors would be able to choose who to go to for constituency service, rather than, as now, being restricted to a single MP whose outlook may be alien to them.

In Scotland and Wales, as in Germany and New Zealand, the lists will be closed lists; the order will be decided by the party and the voter will not be able to alter it. This contrasts with the situation in many other west European countries, for example Belgium and Switzerland, where the voter can either alter or determine the order of the list. Under the closed list, party nomination to a high place on the list will normally prove sufficient to secure election. In the illustrative example above, all of the Conservatives seats in NE Scotland are from the list. The Conservative members of the Scottish Parliament from NE Scotland, therefore, will be chosen by the party apparatus, not by the voters. They will not have presented themselves to the voter, who will not be able to remove them. In the 1997 general election, the voters in Tatton *were* able to remove Neil Hamilton, even though he had been nominated as the Conservative candidate in what would normally be a safe Conservative seat. With a closed list, however, Hamilton, if put in a high enough position, would be irremovable by the voter.

The main virtue of the additional-member system is that it will secure a more proportional outcome than first past the post, although, in the form adopted in Scotland and Wales, not a wholly proportional outcome. Its central weakness is one that it shares with first past the post. It deprives the voter, except in marginal seats, of any choice of candidate. It is in danger of giving too much power to the party machine at the expense of the ordinary voter. This may have important consequences for devolution. Much of the work of the Scottish Parliament and the Welsh Assembly will involve negotiations with the United Kingdom government. These could well prove to be negotiations between different branches of the Labour Party machine, in London, Edinburgh, and Cardiff. Members of the Scottish Parliament and the Welsh Assembly might, as a result of the electoral system, be a little too eager to support the party leadership so that they can be renominated to a high position on the party list. Thus the electoral system will tend to the strengthening of the devolved executives at the expense of the legislatures. The additional-member system, especially when accompanied by a closed list, operates against the values of devolution and democratic accountability which require the transference of power away from Westminster to Edinburgh and Cardiff. It could easily lead to the recentralization of power through the party machines. If that happens, the ideal of devolution will come to be undermined by the realities of the modern political party machine.

The West Lothian Question

The West Lothian Question was named after Tam Dalyell, who was MP for West Lothian when devolution was debated at Westminster in the 1970s. The question asks whether it is justifiable for Scottish MPs, after devolution, to continue to be able to vote for English domestic affairs when non-Scottish MPs will no longer be able to vote on Scottish domestic affairs. Scottish MPs would be able to vote on the arts in Alnwick, but English MPs would not be able to vote on the arts in Armadale, West Lothian. Scottish MPs would be able to vote on local government reform in London, but English MPs would not be able to vote on local government reform in Linlithgow. Scottish MPs would be able to vote on schools in Sheffield, but English MPs would not be able to vote on schools in South Queensferry. In this situation, policy on English domestic affairs might be decided by the balance of Scottish MPs although English MPs had lost the practical opportunity of voting on Scottish domestic affairs. This situation would have occurred, for example, in 1964 or October 1974 when, without Scottish MPs, Labour would not have enjoyed a majority in the House of Commons.

Would it, moreover, be appropriate, after devolution, for a Scottish MP to become a minister in a British government exercising functions which, in Scotland, were the responsibility of the Scottish Parliament? On 16 February 1992, Robin Cook, as Shadow Secretary of State for Health, said in the BBC television programme *On the Record* that it would not. 'Once we have a Scottish parliament handling health affairs,' Cook added, 'it would not be possible for me to continue as Minister of Health, administering health in England.' Cook was, admittedly, disowned by the then Labour leader, Neil Kinnock. Nevertheless, during the years when Northern Ireland enjoyed devolution, no Northern Ireland MP occupied a Cabinet post involving responsibility for matters devolved to the Northern Ireland Parliament.

The West Lothian Question was pursued with much pertinacity by Tam Dalyell in the 1970s. Francis Pym, the Conservative spokesman on devolution, then called it 'the single most contentious problem to arise in our debates',9 while, in a speech on St Andrew's Day in 1995, Michael Forsyth referred to it as 'the Bermuda triangle of devolution'. During the committee stage of the first devolution bill, the Scotland and Wales Bill, in February 1977, Tam Dalyell declared: 'The point cannot be made too often.' To which the Minister of State at the Privy Council Office, John Smith, who was in charge of the bill, replied: 'Yes, it can.'10

The West Lothian Question draws attention to a constitutional and political imbalance arising from asymmetrical devolution in an otherwise unitary state. It asks: after devolution, how ought Scotland to be represented in the House of Commons? This is the same question which, as we have seen, baffled Gladstone in the nineteenth century. Indeed, one constitutional authority has written that only 'those with short memories called this the "West Lothian Question" '.11

There is only one logical answer to the West Lothian Question, but it is politically unrealistic: it is for Britain to implement legislative devolution all round, so becoming a thoroughgoing federal state. But there is no demand for legislative federalism in England. Even if English regional assemblies were eventually to come about—and that at the present time hardly seems likely—they would almost certainly not be given legislative powers. Their powers would be much more like those of the Welsh Assembly than those of the Scottish Parliament, and statutory responsibility for English legislation would, therefore, remain with Westminster.

It might perhaps prove possible for England to mitigate the effects of the West Lothian Question by adopting special parliamentary arrangements such as an English Grand Committee, composed only of English MPs, to consider English legislation. There is indeed a Standing Committee on Regional Affairs in the Commons, formed in 1975, in anticipation of devolution to Scotland and Wales. This Committee comprises all the MPs for English constituencies, together with five additional members. It met between 1975 and 1978 to debate various regional matters. It has not, however, met since 1978, and indeed, if all 529 English MPs were to attend, it would be a somewhat cumbrous body, hardly equipped for parliamentary committee work; but in any case it is the House of Commons, not the Grand Committee, which actually votes on legislation. Moreover, such special parliamentary arrangements for England would not overcome the problem which would arise when, as in 1964 or October 1974, the political majority in England differed from that in the United Kingdom as a whole. The West Lothian Question cannot, therefore, be answered by special parliamentary arrangements for one part of the country.[12]

The other proposed answers to the West Lothian Question are as inadequate today as they were over a hundred years ago when Gladstone first proposed them. It would obviously be absurd to exclude Scottish MPs altogether from Westminster while Parliament remains responsible for reserved matters. Under the Scotland Act, all taxation for Scotland, unless Scotland uses its very limited tax-varying power, continues to be imposed by Westminster. It would be unjust for Scotland to be taxed by Westminster without being represented there.

Two further answers to the West Lothian Question are to cut the powers of the Scottish members by allowing them to vote only on Scottish matters, or to cut the numbers.

Cutting the powers of the Scottish members would be to revert to the 'in and out' solution which Gladstone proposed in 1893 and then abandoned. The Ferrers amendment, section 66 of the 1978 Scotland Act, was also, as we have seen, an example of an 'in and out' clause. In Northern Ireland, as noted in Chapter 3, Harold Wilson, when the Labour government enjoyed a majority of only two in 1965, sought to deter MPs from the province from interfering in British domestic affairs. On that occasion, the Conservatives insisted that MPs from Northern Ireland should exercise the same rights as every other Member of Parliament. Peter Thorneycroft, the Conservative Shadow Home Secretary, spoke as follows:

The honourable Member for Manchester, Blackley [Paul Rose], argued that honourable Members representing Northern Ireland seats should not have the right to talk about very much in the House of Commons except Northern Ireland. We have heard some rather loose talk of that kind from some other quarters on the Government side from time to time. I hope that the Joint Under-Secretary will make it absolutely clear that that kind of nonsense does not form any part of the Government's thinking, that every Member of the House of Commons is equal with every other Member of the House of Commons, and that all of us will speak on all subjects, subject always to keeping within the bounds of order.[13]

An 'in and out' solution is almost certainly unworkable for two reasons. The first is that it puts the onus on the Speaker, who would have to decide on contentious bills whether or not they were purely Scottish bills. 'I am afraid', Gladstone told Lord Rosebery when the latter proposed the 'in and out' solution in 1886, 'that the Speakership would hardly bear the weight of your proposal.'[14] The difficulty would be all the greater now since, under the Barnett formula (see next section), an increase in expenditure on a domestic service, such as education in England, would have consequential effects on the total of Scotland's block grant, and therefore on the total of public expenditure in Scotland. In addition, of course, increases in expenditure on English domestic affairs would involve an increase in taxes throughout the United Kingdom. As the Royal Commission on the Constitution noticed:

Ability to vote could not depend simply on whether the matter at issue related to a reserved or transferred subject. Any issue in Westminster involving expenditure of public money is of concern to all parts of the United Kingdom since it may directly affect the level of taxation and indirectly influence the level of a region's own expenditure.[15]

It is questionable, therefore, whether there are any specifically 'English' domestic issues in the sense of issues which have no consequential effects in Scotland and Wales

The fundamental reason, however, why the 'in and out' solution is constitutionally impossible is that, when party majorities in Scotland

and the United Kingdom were different, as in 1964 or February 1974, it would bifurcate the executive. The government in London, Labour in each case, would lack a majority on English domestic affairs when the Scottish MPs withdrew. There would thus be a Labour government on foreign affairs and defence, but a Conservative government when the Scottish MPs were absent, on health and education. It is not easy to see how effective government could continue under such circumstances.

It has been suggested that such situations would be highly infrequent, since it has only been in the short parliaments of 1964–6 and March–October 1974 that a non-Conservative government has faced a Conservative majority of English MPs, and 'these short parliaments did not inflict major legislative changes on a bitterly hostile electorate'.[16]

The chances of such an outcome occurring again are, however, greater than this argument suggests. This is because the gap between the number of seats gained by Labour and by the Conservatives in Scotland has increased enormously in recent years. In 1950, the two parties won an equal number of seats in Scotland; but in 1987 Labour won forty more seats than the Conservatives, and in 1992 thirty-nine more. In 1997, Labour won fifty-six seats in Scotland and the Conservatives none. Thus the chances of a Conservative majority in England being outvoted by a Labour majority in Scotland must be much greater now than they have been in the past, unless there is a substantial reversal in political trends in Scotland.

The alternative approach, of cutting the number of Scottish MPs, still leaves open the possibility of a majority of Scottish MPs of a different colour from the majority in the rest of the United Kingdom determining the domestic affairs of England; but of course it lessens the likelihood of such an outcome actually occurring; and cutting the numbers can be justified on other grounds as a means of remedying the over-representation of Scotland at Westminster.[17]

Scotland's over-representation has been defended by Neil MacCormick on the basis of 'reasonable assurance for minority countries . . . Since a whole country [in 1707] was being incorporated into a larger, there was special reason to ensure that its interests could not be ignored or belittled. There was also concern about unfair discrimination against the interests of a minority with a long prior history of conflict with the new majority'.[18] The Royal Commission on the Constitution, similarly, put forward the argument that:

the maintenance of the representation of Scotland and Wales at their present levels would be justified by their separate national status. England already has a preponderance of representation in Parliament compared with the smaller nations. To base representation simply on the basis of counting heads is to ignore the important nationality factor. Moreover, there are ample precedents, for example, in international organisations and in the second chambers of many federal countries, for giving to smaller states a greater representation than would be justified by their populations.[19]

Yet Scotland has been over-represented, not since 1707, but only since 1922. Scottish over-representation is not, therefore, a result of the Treaty of Union, which did no more than guarantee Scotland forty-five seats in the House of Commons. The over-representation is rather a result of the successful use of bargaining power by the Scots and Welsh and it has no constitutional status at all.[20]

Moreover, the Royal Commission on the Constitution did not believe that Scottish over-representation would continue to be justified after legislative devolution. For, after all, the Scottish Parliament is likely to provide at least as good a 'reasonable assurance', to use MacCormick's words, that Scotland's interests will be respected, as over-representation at Westminster. The Royal Commission therefore recommended that any area of the country which enjoyed legislative devolution should have its representation at Westminster reduced. That is the approach which the government has adopted in the Scotland Act. It decided, however, not to reduce the representation of Wales, which will thus enjoy the twin benefits of over-representation and executive devolution. Over-representation may perhaps be seen by the Welsh as compensation for the absence of legislative devolution. To the English, however, it may seem over-compensation.

If the West Lothian Question cannot be answered, a second question poses itself. Is the imbalance of representation an acceptable anomaly or a fatal weakness in the attempt to institute asymmetrical devolution in an otherwise unitary state?

It is noticeable that, on the Continent, anomalies of the type represented by the West Lothian Question have in fact been accommodated without difficulty. In Denmark, the Faeroe Islands and Greenland both have their own parliaments and both are outside the European Union, of which Denmark remains a member state. In Portugal, the two island areas—Madeira and the Azores—enjoy devolution while mainland Portugal remains a unitary state. In France, Italy, and Spain, there has been devolution across the country as a whole but it has been asymmetric, with some regions enjoying greater powers than others. In France, Corsica and the overseas territories have special status. In Italy, there are fifteen ordinary regions with no exclusive legislative powers at all, but five special regions—Valle d'Aosta, Trentino–Alto–Adige, Fruili–Venezia–Giulia, Sardinia, and Sicily— with exclusive legislative powers in economic, social, and cultural matters. The five special regions, moreover, were set up in 1948, twenty-two years before the other regions were established. In Spain, seven of the seventeen 'autonomous communities'—Andalusia, the Canaries, Catalonia, Euskadi (the Basque country), Galicia, Navarre, and Valencia—have a greater degree of autonomy than other areas, with power over their own health and education services; some of them also run their own police forces. Yet there is no 'West Madeira Question' nor any 'West Sardinian Question', nor any 'West Catalonian Question', in these countries. In France and Portugal, this is because the consequences of asymmetry are minimal, the regions in Portugal being geographically isolated and containing only 5 per cent of the Portugese population. In Italy and Spain, however, the consequences of asymmetrical devolution are by no means minimal, and yet devolution has proved perfectly workable. There seems no reason why the same should not prove true in Britain also.

The West Lothian Question, moreover, would be less likely to come into play were there to be a change in the electoral system for the House of Commons to one of proportional representation. For Labour's strength in Scotland is in part a product of the first-past-the-post system.

The 1997 general election results in Scotland are shown in Table 7.2. Under a strictly proportional system, however, the seats would have been distributed quite differently (Table 7.3).

Table 7.2 General election results, Scotland, 1997

	Seats	% of vote
Labour	56	45.6
Conservative	0	17.5
Liberal Democrats	10	13.0
SNP	6	22.1
Others	0	1.9

Table 7.3 Distribution of seats under a proportional-representation system

	Seats
Labour	33
Conservative	13
Liberal Democrats	10
SNP	16

The chances of Scottish Labour MPs making the difference between a Conservative and a Labour government at Westminster would be much reduced, although not of course eliminated. If that is so, then non-Scottish MPs need not regret the loss of their power to discuss and scrutinize Scottish legislation; for, as we have seen, even under the pre-devolution arrangements, Scottish legislation was largely the province of Scottish members. Hardly any non-Scottish MPs took much interest in it, and any who did were likely to be regarded by Scottish MPs as intruders. Thus, English MPs have little interest in Scottish domestic affairs, while England's dominant position in the United Kingdom means that there are hardly any wholly 'English' domestic issues of no concern to MPs from Scotland and Wales. In a sense, then, the West Lothian Question is falsely posed.

Nevertheless, the question raises in an acute form the issue of whether it is possible to devolve to one part of an otherwise unitary state. The answer rests on a political judgement as to whether it is better to accept the risks of asymmetry in preference to the alternative risk of fuelling support for Scottish separatism by denying devolution. The unionists take their stand on a symmetrical constitution. The devolutionists can point to the long history of Britain's relations with Ireland as well as experience on the Continent in countries such as Italy and Spain, and they can argue that this experience yields the following answer to the West Lothian Question: where the will to conciliate is present, special treatment may, by containing centrifugal impulses, help to preserve the unity of a country when the urge to symmetry would destroy it. That at least must be the premiss on which the policy of devolution is based.

However, devolution will alter the role of Westminster very radically, by introducing the spirit of federalism into its deliberations. Before devolution, every Member of Parliament was responsible for scrutinizing both the domestic and the non-domestic affairs of every part of the United Kingdom. After devolution, by contrast, MPs will normally play no role at all in legislating for the domestic affairs of Northern Ireland or Scotland, nor in scrutinizing secondary legislation for Wales. Only with respect to England will MPs continue to enjoy the power which, until now, they have enjoyed for the whole of the United Kingdom. Westminster, from being a parliament for both the domestic and the non-domestic affairs of the whole of the United Kingdom, is transformed into a domestic parliament for England, part of a domestic parliament for Wales, and a federal parliament for Northern Ireland and Scotland. The West Lothian Question, then, draws attention to the fact that devolution will transform Westminster into the quasi-federal parliament of a quasi-federal state.

Financing devolution

Finance is the spinal cord of devolution, for it is the financial arrangements which will largely determine the degree of autonomy enjoyed by the devolved administrations; the financial settlement, therefore, will exert a dominant influence on whether the aims of devolution are sustained or frustrated.

Post-war experience has not augured well for supposing that the financing of devolution would necessarily be consistent with the policy aim of dispersing power away from Whitehall to Edinburgh and Cardiff. For, over the past fifty years, the allocation of functions to public authorities and the pattern of public finance have come increasingly to be divorced from each other. The result has been that finance has frequently frustrated, and rarely sustained, broader policy aims.

The 1980s saw a progressive weakening of local autonomy which went along with a weakening in the tax-base of local authorities. In 1979, under the rating system, local authorities raised around 40 per cent of their revenue locally. The Royal Commission on the Constitution declared in 1973, at a time when 60 per cent of local revenue came from the centre, that 'This degree of financial dependence on the centre is generally considered to be unhealthy.'[21] The council tax, however, accounts for an even smaller proportion of local government revenue—around 20 per cent in most authorities. Local autonomy has suffered because local revenue has been insufficiently buoyant to accommodate the expansion of public services. This has been of some comfort to central government, seeking to control the totality of public expenditure, and fearful that local authorities will refuse to comply with government requests for restraint. From this point of view, the revenue-raising power of local authorities may be seen as a loophole in the system for controlling public expenditure. Even so, governments have been hesitant about abolishing local tax-raising powers entirely, for fear, perhaps, of totally extinguishing local autonomy.

Two fundamental factors have been responsible for the increasing drift to the centre. The first is that distribution according to relative need is the cardinal feature of the UK system of allocating public expenditure. Resources are distributed not according to geography, but according to need. The danger, then, of any devolution of the taxing power is that it will enable the richer parts of the country to benefit at the expense of those less well favoured. According to Sir George Godber, a former Chief Medical Officer at the Department of Health and Social Security:

Anyone familiar with the pattern of development of local authority health services before 1948 ... knows well that the wealth of an authority has a direct bearing on the quality of the service provided. This was not the sole factor, but it was in my belief, the most important. A county like Surrey, for instance, was able to recruit doctors for its public health services in the 1930s much more easily than a county borough like, say, Bootle, for the simple reason that it offered £600 a year as compared with £500 a year, which was the minimum negotiated rate.[22]

It was indeed because they feared that devolution would lead to the allocation of public resources on the basis of geography and political clout, rather than need, that left-wing MPs such as Eric Heffer and Neil Kinnock were so opposed to devolution in the 1970s. They took the view that only central government could determine the relative degree of deprivation in different parts of the country, and that those living in Glasgow, for example, should not get a better deal than those living in Liverpool, simply because Glasgow was a part of the country with an elected assembly which could put political pressures upon Westminster and Whitehall.

In a debate on tax-raising powers for the Scottish and Welsh Assemblies in January 1978, Neil Kinnock declared in the Commons:

We shall be introducing into all political considerations an argument that has barely figured at all in British political dialogues and discussions. There has barely been a vote to be gained in this country, except among nationalist paranoiacs, throughout the time that we have had the modern pluralistic, parliamentary, elected democracy, on the basis of where a candidate comes from or the immediate interests he is trying to serve. We have had divisions on a class basis, but not on a geographic or nationalistic basis.[23]

The philosophy that the allocation of public expenditure should be determined on the basis of need and that only central government is in a position to be able to secure the equitable distribution of public resources on the basis of need, still exerts a powerful hold on politicians of both left and right, and also upon the civil service, and in particular the Treasury.

The second fundamental factor militating against the devolution of tax-raising powers is that central government's approach to finance must always be different from that of local authorities or devolved administrations. Local or devolved bodies need revenue to finance their expenditure plans; central government by contrast is responsible for stabilizing the economy, controlling borrowing and holding down the burden of taxation to sharpen incentives in the private sector. The Treasury's fear has always been that the dispersal of revenue-raising powers will make economic management more difficult. For the larger the amount of public expenditure which lies outside the direct control of the government, the greater the scope for evading measures of macroeconomic control. The governments of Margaret Thatcher and John Major, for example, found their attempts at public expenditure control hampered by left-wing local authorities which refused to comply with government requests, and instead of cutting expenditure, sought to raise extra revenue locally in order to finance a higher level of services than the government thought desirable. It was largely for this reason that Margaret Thatcher's government assumed, in the Rates Act of 1984, powers to cap the rates, i.e. impose maximum rate levels on local authorities. This principle of capping was continued with the community charge—the poll tax—and also the council tax which has replaced it. Capping was a constitutional innovation in that, for the first time, government was telling individual local authorities how much revenue they could raise locally. In opposition, Labour opposed rate-capping, but the Labour government elected in 1997 had not, by 1999, surrendered the bulk of its capping powers. How much more difficult it would be for governments to carry out their macroeconomic policies successfully if they were confronted, not only with recalcitrant local authorities, but also with powerful devolved bodies with their own revenue-raising powers, bodies with much more political weight than local authorities, and therefore better able to resist government requests for restraint.

British governments in the post-war period have believed that macroeconomic stabilization policy requires them to control not only the global totals of expenditure, but also the balance between public and private spending, which could of course be altered through decisions taken by the devolved bodies. It was for these reasons that

Labour governments, both in the 1970s and in the 1990s, decided not to devolve substantial tax-raising powers to Scotland or Wales.

The Welsh Assembly, as defined in the Government of Wales Act of 1998, is to have no revenue-raising powers at all, but the Scottish Parliament will have the power to vary the basic rate of income tax by 3p in the pound. This was first suggested by the Scottish Convention which was unable to be more radical because it feared giving the opponents of devolution and of Labour an opportunity to gain a propaganda victory with attacks on a new 'tartan tax'.

The tax-varying power is in fact minimal. It gives the Scottish Parliament control over £450m.—index-linked—out of a total Scottish Office budget of £14.6bn. It is difficult, however, to imagine this power being used except to *raise* taxes. For, if it is used to lower taxes, then expenditure on public services in Scotland would have to be cut. The British government would then reduce the overall level of resources passed to the Scottish Parliament in the block grant.[24] Tony Blair has promised that Labour, if it forms the Executive in Scotland, will not raise taxes during the first Scottish Parliament; as Lord Sewel, a Parliamentary Under-Secretary at the Scottish Office, declared during the devolution debates, 'there is a world of difference between having a power and exercising that power through a policy'.[25] Thus, for practical purposes, the Scottish Parliament will be entirely dependent on Westminster for its financing.

The Scottish Parliament and the Welsh National Assembly do, however, enjoy a hidden power to tax, by withholding finance from local government and keeping it for their own use. For the block funds which the devolved bodies receive include an element taking account of the need to provide revenue support grant to local authorities. Almost 40 per cent of Scotland's annual block of £14.6bn.—£5.2bn.—goes to finance local authority expenditure, with around £1.2bn. of Scottish local authority expenditure being financed from the council tax. But it is for the Scottish Parliament to decide, after consultation with local authorities, whether to distribute £5.2bn rather than a higher sum or a lower one. The Welsh Assembly has a similar power. That is part of the essential discretion of the devolved bodies to reorder priorities in devolved spending. But the result is that Scottish and Welsh local authorities will be seeking funds from the devolved bodies, which may well wish to earmark them for their own purposes. There is thus an inbuilt conflict of interest between local authorities and the devolved bodies, which will have their own views of the appropriate mix of local expenditure in Scotland and Wales, and will, no doubt, seek to ensure influence over how available moneys are spent. Were the devolved bodies to withhold finance from local authorities, the latter would of course need to raise the level of council tax very considerably to maintain services, given the high proportion of their income which derives from central grants.

Alternatively, or in addition, the Scottish Parliament, though not the Welsh Assembly, could return the levying of the uniform business rate to local government and reduce the amount which it gave to local authorities. Local authorities would have to raise either the council tax or the non-domestic rate to maintain services. Thus the Parliament would be able to secure revenue of its own while it would be local authorities which incurred the odium.

Another way in which the Scottish Parliament, but not the Welsh National Assembly, could enjoy a hidden power to tax would be by keeping for itself the income raised from the business rate. This is at present equalized in England and Scotland, although 10 per cent lower in Wales. Previous Conservative governments have pledged that these levels would remain. These pledges, however, cannot bind the Scottish Parliament, since local government finance is a devolved matter.

It may be argued that this hidden tax-raising power is not an innovation in that, before devolution, the Secretary of State could, if he so chose, withhold money from Scottish or Welsh local authorities. Responsibility for the determination of local government funding must, after all, be located somewhere. After devolution, this power will be located not with a member of the Cabinet, but in a body that is specifically accountable to the Scottish or Welsh people. This may be regarded as a democratic advance.

What is clear, however, is that the hidden tax-raising power is capable of securing far more revenue for the devolved bodies than raising income tax in Scotland by 3p in the pound. But if there were to be too rapid a rise in local authority expenditure, then the government would act. Paragraph 7.27 of the White Paper, *Scotland's Government*, Cm. 3658, declares:

Should self-financed expenditure [by Scottish local authorities] start to rise steeply, [and] . . . if growth relative to England were excessive and were such as to threaten targets of the United Kingdom economy . . . it would be open to the United Kingdom government to take the excess into account in considering the level of their support for expenditure in Scotland.

The justification for this would be that the financial policy of Scottish local authorities would be entrenching upon macroeconomic policy, which is a reserved and not a devolved matter.

Nevertheless, the arrangements for the financing of the Scottish Parliament and Welsh Assembly are hardly compatible with the dispersal of power that devolution is intended to achieve. If local authority autonomy is secured by the power to raise local taxation, however small a portion of local revenue is actually comprised by local taxation, it seems odd that bodies intended to represent the people of Scotland and Wales should not be given a similar power. The Welsh Assembly which is to have no revenue-raising powers at all is in a worse position than parish and community councils in England and Wales which can precept on councils, and raise revenue from fees and charges.

The central criticism of the financial arrangements is that they divorce the power to raise money from the power to spend it. That these two powers should be in the same hands has long been thought of as a fundamental tenet of responsible government. In its report to the Cabinet in 1912, the Committee on Irish Finance, the Primrose Committee, set up to consider the financial relationships between Britain and Ireland after Home Rule, claimed that it was:

a first principle of sound government that the same authority that has the spending of revenue should also have the burthen, and not infrequently the odium of raising that revenue. That one should have the unpopular duty of providing the same, and another the privilege of expending them, is a division of labour that leads to disaster.[26]

Over sixty years later, the Layfield Committee on Local Government Finance echoed this sentiment when it declared: 'whoever is responsible for spending money should also be responsible for raising it so that the amount of expenditure is subject to democratic control'.[27] In Scotland and Wales, with the responsibilities separated, the danger will always be that the Scottish and Welsh executives claim credit for improvements in services while blaming their problems upon the parsimony of London. As Lord Vaizey said in the debates on the 1978 Scotland Act: 'Nobody in his senses would say, "I am standing on the basis of switching expenditure from housing to hospital services." That is what the Government want him to say, but he will not say it. What he will say is that he will come to Westminster and say that he wants to change the formula.'[28]

The devolved administrations may thus take on the character of pressure groups focused on London rather than responsible political bodies. Moreover, the pressure-group relationship is bound to be an unstable one. For the demand for improved public services in Scotland and Wales is almost infinite. Whenever the standard of roads or hospitals or schools in Scotland or Wales is held to be inadequate, London will be blamed. Deficiencies in public services in Scotland and Wales will be attributed less to the devolved administrations in Scotland and Wales than to the niggardliness of London in refusing to adopt a more generous formula for distributing grant. The SNP and Plaid Cymru will benefit the most from this instability. For they alone will not be constrained by wider UK party loyalties in bidding for funds from London. A Labour administration in Edinburgh or Cardiff would be under some pressure from a Labour government in London not to damage national economic policy by overspending. Conservatives would not wish to appear profligate when one of the Conservative Party's main policies is tight control of public spending. The SNP and Plaid Cymru, however, will be continually seeking to prove that it is only the parsimony of the British government which is preventing them from improving services.

Moreover, the devolved administrations may have fewer incentives to economize when they are not raising their own funds. Devolved administrations would be much more likely to spend moneys which they receive from central government than moneys that they had to raise themselves. The only financial initiative, however, which the devolved administrations seem able to take is to suggest that the government alter the formula for distributing grant, and then blame London if it does not do so. Thus failure to devolve revenue-raising powers will fundamentally affect the working of the devolved administrations.

The arrangements for distributing grant to Scotland and Wales after devolution will continue to be based on the Barnett formula, developed in 1978, and named after Joel Barnett, then Chief Secretary of the Treasury. The formula has been in operation since 1980, but the principles behind it were not set out in public until December 1997 in a written answer by Alistair Darling, Chief Secretary to the Treasury.[29]

The formula is based on the population of the different territories comprising the United Kingdom. It is designed to deal with changes—whether increments or decrements—in comparable public expenditure. The formula was originally 85 : 10 : 5—that is, for every marginal £85 on comparable public expenditure on English services equivalent to those in the Scottish/Welsh block, the Scottish block automatically received £10, and the Welsh £5. The formula was extended to Northern Ireland, which received an extra £2.75 when comparable expenditure in Great Britain on services that in Northern Ireland were within the block increased by £100.

The Barnett formula has been much misunderstood. In the second reading debate in the Lords on the Government of Wales Bill, Lord Callaghan, the former Prime Minister, reminisced, declaring that the formula added 'something which was fairly rational onto something which was completely irrational'.[30] The rational element is the formula for marginal changes in public expenditure; what Lord Callaghan referred to as the irrational element is the base, the overall level of public expenditure. The Barnett formula, then, is *not* designed to deal with the overall level, which was inherited when the formula was introduced, reflecting past negotiations and historic, rough and ready estimates of the needs of the different parts of the United Kingdom.

The formula entails that public expenditure in Scotland, Wales, and Northern Ireland is driven by the level of public expenditure in England, since it is the change in the English level, agreed by English departmental ministers in Cabinet, which determines the sum available to other parts of the United Kingdom.

The formula originally gave Scotland 11.76 per cent of any change in English spending and Wales 5.88 per cent. It was, however, recalibrated in 1992, following the 1991 census, to reflect

Scotland's smaller share of the population. The new ratios were 85.7 : 9.14 : 5.16, and, on the new formula, Scotland gained just 10.66 per cent of changes in comparable English expenditure, while the Welsh share went up to 6.02 per cent. Northern Ireland's share went up to 2.87 per cent of changes in comparable expenditure in Great Britain.

The Barnett formula was developed in 1978 when devolution to Scotland appeared likely. Its purpose was to avoid an annual squabble for funds between the Treasury and the executive of the proposed Scottish assembly. In the eighteen years prior to 1979, Scotland and Wales seemed to have gained considerably in terms of relative public expenditure per head. The formula was intended to help secure territorial justice by preventing further relative gains on the part of Scotland and Wales, and indeed by producing convergence in levels of funding per head. Whether it would in fact produce convergence depended upon two factors: first, the rate of growth of comparable spending in England—the faster the rise in spending in England, the more rapid the convergence; and second, the relative stability of population relativities within the United Kingdom—were the Scottish population to decline relatively, as has in fact happened, that would tend to offset the convergence effect.

Scottish Office ministers were content to accept the Barnett formula in the late 1970s, perhaps because they foresaw that Britain was entering a period of financial retrenchment, when Scotland's position might come under threat. Scotland, as we have seen, has benefited considerably, since at least the time of Thomas Johnston, by having a minister of her own who could press for her needs to be recognized. That era, however, appeared to be coming to an end in the late 1970s.

In 1980, in the Select Committee on Scottish Affairs, Donald Dewar asked the then Conservative Secretary of State for Scotland, George Younger, whether the basis for the Scottish Office's acceptance of the Barnett formula was 'What we have we hold'. Younger's reply was: 'Yes'. A Scottish Office official elaborated on this: 'I think it was calculated that the arrangement was advantageous because public expenditure control was getting tighter and more complex and that the days of table-thumping were ceasing to have their effect. This was the consideration that was borne in mind in accepting this arrangement.'[31]

The Barnett formula, it has been suggested, 'introduces a quasi-federal funding arrangement, which guarantees to Scotland and Wales a fixed proportion of the spending allocated to England, while preserving any historical advantages'.[32] It provides, parallel to the Scottish, Welsh, and Northern Ireland Offices, a mechanism for the determination of expenditure on territorial rather than functional grounds. Had the formula not been in existence, the Conservative governments of the 1980s, whose electoral basis of support lay in southern England, might otherwise have shifted expenditure from Scotland and Wales to England. Moreover, the Barnett formula freed the Scottish and Welsh Secretaries of State from annual negotiations with the Treasury and gave them the freedom to switch expenditure between services. Once the block for Scotland and Wales had been determined, the Secretaries of State were free to adopt the spending mix they thought appropriate for their territories regardless of the approach adopted by English departmental ministers. They were allowed to adopt a territorial rather than a functional approach to public expenditure. This meant that when, for example, in the 1980s Sir Keith Joseph, as Education Secretary, refused to seek higher spending on education, George Younger and Malcolm Rifkind, as Scottish Secretaries, were able to switch money from other programmes into education to meet what they saw as Scotland's own particular needs.

The Barnett formula succeeded, to some extent, in protecting Scotland from expenditure cuts in the 1980s and 1990s, since, without it, cuts in the Scottish block might have been more severe, on account of alleged 'over-provision' in Scotland. But the formula does not seem to have achieved convergence between Scotland and England. The reason for this is that the two factors on which the operation of the formula depended have worked to prevent convergence. For there was retrenchment in public spending in the 1980s and 1990s, and the Scottish population declined.

Since the 1970s, the distribution of public spending between different parts of the United Kingdom has become much more explicit. This has led to criticism, primarily in England, suggesting that the higher share of per capita identifiable expenditure in Scotland is, of its very nature, unjust, and that it ought to be reduced or ended following devolution. Such expenditure would not, however, be unjust if it reflected Scotland's greater needs as compared with those of England; and it would in any case be quite wrong to exclude Scotland from the national needs-assessment process simply because she had voted for devolution. The question, however, is whether the higher share of per capita identifiable expenditure in Scotland does in fact wholly reflect Scotland's needs.

The difficulty in answering this question is that there is no scientific or objective way of determining needs. The Barnett formula never claimed to be anything more than a very rough and ready approach but it has so far proved politically acceptable to British governments, whether Conservative or Labour. The formula was designed to secure a convergence in expenditure ratios by ensuring that changes in expenditure were determined by the extant population ratios. The ratios are to be recalibrated regularly to take account of population changes, but not to take account of changing needs as one part of the United Kingdom becomes relatively richer or relatively poorer than another. It could, of course, be argued that because the formula has failed to lead to convergence between Scotland and England, it ought to be altered to England's advantage; on the other hand, it seems that the position of Wales has worsened since the formula was adopted, because Wales, in the words of a Welsh Office official, now

has the lowest level of GDP per head of any region in Great Britain, 18 per cent below England, the lowest level of personal disposable income of any region, 17 per cent below England; the level of economic activity in Wales is only above Merseyside and North East, average earnings in Wales second lowest in Great Britain, 11 per cent below England. Wales has the highest proportion of population with limited long-standing illness in the United Kingdom, and of those figures, GDP per head, average earnings, economic activity rates and household income proportionate to England have all actually gone backwards since the 1970s.[33]

As part of the preparation for devolution, the Treasury carried out a needs-assessment survey, which was published after the Scotland and Wales Acts were repealed in December 1979. It concluded that, using data for 1976-7, the relative amounts of expenditure per capita

Table 7.4 Relative expenditure per capita for devolved services (per capita public expenditure 1976–7 at 1978 survey prices, expressed as a percentage of expenditure in England)

	England	Scotland	Wales	Northern Ireland
A. Per capita public expenditure	100	122	106	135
B. Relative needs	100	116	109	131
Relation of expenditure to needs		+6	–3	+4

Source: HM Treasury, *Needs Assessment Study Report*, para. 6.5, HMSO, 1979

required to provide the same range and level of service as in England for devolved services were as indicated in Table 7.4.

The Barnett formula was not, however, adjusted to take account of this assessment. Nor has any similar needs assessment been carried out since 1979. Indeed, part of the reason for adopting and retaining the Barnett formula was to *avoid* highly contentious annual arguments in Cabinet concerning the 'true' needs of Scotland and Wales. The reason why no further needs assessment has been carried out is clear: if such an assessment were to suggest that the Barnett formula ought to be altered to Scotland's disadvantage, there would be a political outcry in Scotland; and it would be argued, perfectly correctly, that needs assessment cannot be a scientific activity. The Scots would suggest that there were special factors which the needs assessment had not taken into account, or to which it had given insufficient weight. Indeed, referring to the 1979 Needs Assessment exercise, George Younger, as Secretary of State for Scotland, told the Select Committee on Scottish Affairs in 1980: 'My opinion is that the bases upon which the study was made are unproven and therefore I regard it as an interesting document but not as a definitive document.'[34]

The Welsh, on the other hand, might well feel that a new needs assessment is imperative so as to allow the formula to be changed to their advantage. Indeed the House of Commons Welsh Affairs Committee in its First Report of 1997–8 on 'The Impact of the Government's Devolution Proposals on Economic Development and Local Government in Wales', argued that the needs assessment should be brought up to date. The Treasury Committee, a majority of whose members represented English constituencies, in its report on the Barnett Formula, agreed.[35] English Members of Parliament, many of whom are somewhat sceptical of devolution, could well face requests from their constituents, especially in the north-east and the north-west, to ensure that Scotland does not benefit at the expense of underprivileged regions in England. During the preparatory phase of campaigning for nomination as Labour candidate for mayor of London, Ken Livingstone, the former leader of the GLC, argued that territorial justice required some of Scotland's money to be diverted to London. On 15 April 1998, the *Scottish Mirror* replied, on its front page, 'You want £2bn. from Scotland? Get Lost! Fury over cash demand from man who would be Mayor of London'.[36] That may be just a foretaste of what is to come.

It was because of such possibilities that the Royal Commission on the Constitution argued against a formula approach, declaring that:

In view of the practice which has been built up for the detailed measurement of needs, service by service, it is very doubtful whether an arbitrary formula, resulting in a fixed grant for any five year period, would be acceptable or indeed workable. It would be necessary to construct a more flexible system which, whilst retaining the block grant idea, would include a fairly sensitive measurement of marginal needs, probably every year.[37]

The Barnett formula will be transformed, after devolution, 'from a mechanism *internal* to government to one used for regulating the transfer of money *between* tiers of government'.[38] In theory, it could be altered by ministerial discretion. In practice, it will be difficult to alter it to the disadvantage of the Scots or the Welsh. For it would be politically difficult if not impossible for central government, having decided to established devolved bodies in Scotland and Wales, to apply a more detailed needs assessment, such as the standard spending assessments which apply to local authority expenditure in England, to these bodies. This might give them *less* discretion than the Secretaries of State had enjoyed, and would hardly be compatible with a policy of devolution which implies a dispersal rather than a recentralization of power. Moreover, removing the excess in Scotland would yield England only a minuscule benefit. One authority has calculated that 'If the Treasury analysis [of the excess of Scottish public spending over needs in 1979] was precise (which it is not), it would imply *at most* a reduction in Scottish spending compared with the UK average of £800m. If this were made available to the English population, it would amount to around £17 per capita, a minimal impact.'[39] The problem of underprivileged English regions, then, might be seen as one for England to solve through altering the allocation of public expenditure to regions within England rather than by redistributing from Scotland to England.

The government has proposed, therefore, that, apart from annual recalibrations of the formula to meet changing population relativities, any changes to the formula would, in Alistair Darling's words, 'need to be preceded by an in-depth study of relative spending requirements and would be the subject of full consultation between the devolved administrations and the United Kingdom Government'.[40]

Although the devolved administrations will be *consulted*, changes could nevertheless, in theory at least, be made without their *consent*, since Westminster remains sovereign. Thus the devolved administrations will not enjoy a formal veto power over alterations in the formula. In practice, however, these bodies, representing the people of Scotland and Wales, may well have what amounts to a veto power, since it would take a brave government to face the outcry and loss of electoral support that would ensue as a result of changing the formula to the disadvantage of Scotland or Wales. This will especially be the case during the inaugural period of the devolved administrations, when altering the formula could easily be seen as an attempt to punish Scotland for having voted for devolution. Moreover, it can be argued that devolution was supported in the referendum on the understanding that the existing grant and formula arrangements would continue as outlined in the White Paper. To suggest that the Scottish Parliament should begin by cutting its services, an inevitable consequence of altering the formula to Scotland's disadvantage, would yield a propaganda gift to the SNP; and yet, the purpose of devolution was to contain separatism, not to encourage it. In practice, therefore, Westminster will probably decide on a quiet life and let sleeping dogs lie.

A further weakness of the formula approach, however, is that expenditure in Scotland and Wales comes to be determined by expenditure in England. The point was made in relation to the Goschen formula which, between 1888 and 1957, determined Scotland's public expenditure as eleven-eightieths of that of England, by R. Munro-Ferguson, a Liberal MP, who told the Commons in 1912: 'Scotland is simply tied to the tail of England, and she is denied all initiative. She becomes the dumping ground for some equivalent grant when expenditure is undertaken in England for some purpose that in Scotland is practically uncalled for.'[41]

Such a position is inevitable with a formula arrangement, given the discrepancy in population sizes between England and Scotland. With expenditure in Scotland driven by expenditure in England, an additional £85 in England yields an extra £10 in Scotland and £5 in Wales. With a formula driven by Scotland, however, extra Scottish expenditure of £10 would yield an extra £85 in England and £5 in Wales. The multipliers are 17.65 per cent and 900 per cent respectively. As one authority has commented: 'No UK Treasury could ever be unaware of this asymmetry: equivalent provision for Scotland involves a modest increment over the English cost, whereas equivalent provision for England would involve a huge budgetary cost.'[42] Thus it is expenditure in England which will determine the levels of Scottish and Welsh expenditure. In particular, the funds available to the devolved bodies will depend upon the skills of English spending ministers in such departments as education and health in protecting their budgets, both against the Treasury, and against ministries dealing with reserved matters such as foreign affairs and defence. Were a Conservative government in London, for example, sharply to raise the defence budget and cut the education budget in compensation, that would clearly entail a drastic cut by means of the Barnett formula in the moneys available to Scotland and Wales. The powers of the devolved bodies would in those circumstances be limited. All they could decide is where to make cuts. Or suppose that a future

Conservative government decided to introduce tax incentives for private health insurance, reduce spending on the NHS, and cut income tax. That would lead automatically, under the Barnett formula, to a cut in the additions to the block grant for Scotland and Wales. Yet the devolved bodies in Scotland and Wales might well not wish to follow Conservative policy by reducing NHS spending.[43]

The implication of devolution is that there can be a good justification for differences in public expenditure patterns between Scotland, Wales, and England. In Scotland there is already less middle-class exit from the National Health Service, and less use of private facilities than in England, while students stay at school for a shorter period and spend longer at university than students in England or Wales. The Scottish Executive might well wish to build on these divergences to develop distinctively Scottish policies in health and education. But the more expenditure patterns come to differ from those in England, the more arbitrary the formula may appear, and the more incentive there will be for the devolved administrations to press for alterations in the formula on the ground that the different pattern of expenditure justifies more money. Thus the formula approach seems to contradict the very purpose of devolution.

Labour governments, both in the 1970s and 1990s, in deciding not to devolve major revenue-raising powers to the devolved bodies, drew on the distinction which the Royal Commission on the Constitution had made between a revenue basis for financing the devolved institutions and an expenditure basis for financing them.

Under a revenue basis, a devolved government is given certain taxation powers and certain fixed sources of revenue and is obliged to finance services out of the income which these sources produce. Under such a system, the main determinant of the total amount spent by a devolved government is the taxation decisions which it takes. That, as we have seen, was the basis of finance in Northern Ireland under the Government of Ireland Act of 1920.

Under an expenditure basis, by contrast, the expenditure requirements of the devolved government are decided, and it is then provided with the income to meet its requirements. Under such a system, the main determinant of the total amount spent by a devolved government is the resources provided for it by the centre. The system of finance in Northern Ireland, as we have seen, began on a revenue basis but came in practice to operate on an expenditure basis.

The Royal Commission on the Constitution believed that an expenditure basis was preferable to a revenue basis on the ground that only an expenditure basis was compatible with the distribution of public resources on the basis of need. The case of Northern Ireland was also adduced to show that an expenditure basis was to be preferred.[44] A revenue basis would mean that the public expenditure of each devolved part of the country would, so the Commission argued, depend upon its resources, not upon its needs.

If that argument were correct, however, it would also be an argument against local authorities being given revenue-raising powers. Yet such powers are not thought to be incompatible with the equitable distribution of public expenditure, provided that they are supplemented by an equalization element. So also, it would be perfectly possible for the devolved administrations to be financed on a revenue basis, but for this to be supplemented by an equalization element. The failure, indeed, of the Northern Ireland system of finance derived not from its being established on a revenue basis, but from the absence of such an equalization element. The Northern Ireland government did not agitate for such an element, since, as we saw in Chapter 3, its central concern was to maintain parity with the rest of the United Kingdom, to follow expenditure patterns elsewhere rather than to diverge from them. The Scottish and Welsh administrations will be under no equivalent temptation.

The right approach towards financing the devolved administrations would have been to ensure that as much as possible of their revenue came from transferred taxes and from local shares of reserved taxes, together with an equalization element. Of course, there would be an inevitable element of subjectivity about the size of the equalization element, precisely because it is not possible to discover an objective criterion for Scottish or Welsh needs. Nevertheless, since the equalization element would be a far smaller element of Scottish revenue than the block grant which will finance the whole of the Scottish Parliament—with the minimal exception of the tax-varying power—and the Welsh Assembly, it would not be so controversial. The debate in Scotland and Wales would not then turn so continuously on the parsimony of London and on the question of which party in Edinburgh or Cardiff would be best able to squeeze more money out of the British government.

A second-best alternative would have been a system of assigned taxes such as that in operation in Germany. The vast majority of regional finance in Belgium, Portugal, and Spain also derives from assigned revenues. Such a system would not have yielded tax-raising powers to the devolved administrations, and would not have made them as accountable to their electorates as would a revenue-based system. But it would at least have given them an entitlement to revenues, in place of the relationship of dependence which the Scotland Act and the Government of Wales Act will create. In Germany, this entitlement is crucially dependent upon the part which the *Länder* are able to play in the process of determining how much they receive from the federal government through the participation of their governments in the upper house, the Bundesrat; and there is of course no equivalent to the Bundesrat in Britain. Even in Germany, however, the *Länder* are arguing that they should have their own tax-raising powers.

The devolved administrations in Britain will enjoy no constitutional protection similar to that of the *Länder* in Germany. In a unitary state, the Cabinet is the forum within which the territorial division of public expenditure is decided. There is, however, a definite need for some other forum at which territorial financial questions can be discussed and at which both the British government and the devolved administrations can be represented. The Royal Commission on the Constitution suggested that a nominated National Exchequer Board, on the model of the Exchequer Board for Northern Ireland under the 1920 Government of Ireland Act, also composed of nominated members, be established. But a nominated body could not be allowed to take *decisions* on the territorial distribution of public moneys. For, as we have seen, these decisions depend upon essentially political judgements. So an Exchequer Board, if one were to be established, should enjoy only advisory and not executive or arbitral functions; it should be a body which collects information and applies expertise, such as the Commonwealth Grants Commission in Australia, rather than a body enjoying the power of decision.

We may conclude, however, by reiterating that the financial provisions constitute the weakest element in the devolution legislation. Not only do they represent a centralist solution, but they may also give rise to instability and conflict in the relationships between the devolved administrations and Westminster. Paradoxically, a less centralist solution, devolving revenue-raising powers to the devolved bodies, would be more likely to bind them into the United Kingdom than a solution which denies the devolved bodies the financial responsibilities that should naturally accompany their powers. Nevertheless, if devolution is indeed to prove a process and not an event, it is reasonable to hope that the financial provisions mark the beginning and not the end of the debate on the financing of the devolved administrations. That debate will only have been concluded when financial arrangements are put in place which serve to sustain rather than to frustrate the fundamental purpose of devolution—the dispersal of power.

The Welsh model

The Government of Wales Act provides not legislative devolution but executive devolution, the devolution of secondary legislation and other executive powers. The rationale for this has never been wholly clear. The Royal Commission on the Constitution believed that, in both Scotland and Wales, there were large numbers 'who wish their distinctive national identities to be recognised in the system of government in some way short of separation', and that 'In these two countries the centralisation of politics and government in London is resented more than it is in England.'[45] From this, it would seem to follow that Scotland and Wales should receive common treatment on grounds of nationhood. It would be odd to suggest that the Scottish identity was that of a primary legislation nation, while the Welsh identity was only that of a secondary legislation nation. There were, as we have seen, only two members of the Commission—Professor Street and Mrs Trenaman—who favoured different treatment for Scotland and Wales, and Mrs Trenaman was later to withdraw her support for devolution entirely. Only four members of the Commission—Lord Foot and Sir James Steel, as well as the two signatories of the Memorandum of Dissent, Lord Crowther-Hunt and Professor Peacock—favoured executive devolution for Wales, but these four favoured executive devolution for Scotland also.

Labour governments in the 1970s and 1990s, however, were impressed, and perhaps over-impressed, as were Professor Street and Mrs Trenaman, by the case for special treatment for Scotland on the grounds of her separate legal system. Indeed, it seemed, in the 1990s, that Labour regarded only Scotland as a nation. The White Paper, *Scotland's Parliament*, Cm. 3658, 1997, begins with a resounding declaration by the Prime Minister, 'Scotland is a proud historic nation in the United Kingdom'. But the White Paper, *A Voice for Wales*, Cm. 3718, 1997, contains no such declaration. Instead, the foreword by the then Welsh Secretary, Ron Davies, declares that 'The referendum offers the people of Wales a new beginning, *alongside other successful economic regions* of Europe' (my italics). Scotland, then, is a nation, Wales a region. The model of devolution proposed for Wales is indeed more suitable for a region than a nation. The consequence, however, is that, of all the bodies represented in the British–Irish Council created by the Belfast Agreement—the Republic of Ireland, the United Kingdom, the Isle of Man and the Channel Islands, and the devolved bodies of Scotland, Wales, and Northern Ireland—only the Welsh Assembly will be without primary legislative powers.

Executive devolution may appear at first sight as merely a weaker variant of legislative devolution. The Welsh Assembly will have no power to pass primary legislation, but only secondary legislation, responsibility for primary legislation remaining with Westminster. Secondary legislation involves orders, rules, and regulations which fill in the details of the framework set out in the primary legislation, the Act of Parliament. Executive devolution, however, is not so much a weaker form of devolution than legislative, but a quite different one, which introduces into Britain a wholly new and as yet untried structure of governmental relationships. For, while the Scotland Act introduces a form of quasi-federalism into British government, the Government of Wales Act provides for a form of regionalism.

Legislative devolution involves a *transfer* of powers, executive devolution involves a *division* of powers at present united in the hands of ministers as well as a transfer of powers. It is possible broadly to ascertain the precise functions of a parliament such as the Scottish Parliament with legislative powers by inspecting the provisions of the relevant legislation, in this case the Scotland Act. With the Welsh National Assembly, by contrast, its functions depend not only on the provisions of the Government of Wales Act, but also upon the way in which legislation for Wales is drawn up by the government and the degree of discretion which central government thinks it right to confer upon the Assembly. For there is, in Britain at least, no clear dividing line between policy-making and administration, and thus no basis of principle for determining whether a particular matter falls under primary legislation, in which case it ought to be retained, or secondary legislation, in which case it ought to be devolved.

Legislative devolution involves a decision as to whether or not to transfer responsibility for a particular function, for example education. Executive devolution involves a second decision—*how much* decision-making power should be transferred. This requires an answer to the prior question of how primary legislation ought to be drafted. If it is drafted loosely, then there will be greater scope for the Welsh Assembly than if it is drafted more tightly. If, for example, an Act were to provide that 'Provision may be made for Wales by Order as the Assembly sees fit', that would yield considerable autonomy to the Assembly. If, however, it were to provide that 'Provision for Wales shall be by Order by the Assembly in like manner as for England in this Act', the Assembly would have very little autonomy. A Conservative government at Westminster, faced with a politically hostile Welsh Assembly, might well have been tempted to legislate in this manner on some controversial policy initiative of the 1980s such as, for example, the introduction of grant-maintained schools, the sale of council houses, or the poll tax, so as to prevent the Assembly from frustrating its policies.

It is often suggested that devolution would have spared Wales the poll tax. But the National Assembly would have had to introduce it since it was, of course, provided by primary legislation. Moreover, the bill, as drafted, allowed little scope for discretion in the secondary legislation. The most that the Welsh Assembly might have been able to achieve would have been the variation of the bands so that the tax approached a little more closely to a local income tax. Of course, it might be argued that, had the Assembly been in existence at that time, this would have induced a spirit of greater co-operation from central government. It is difficult, however, to imagine Margaret Thatcher's government allowing a Welsh Assembly to evade what she regarded as a vital part of her policy. Indeed, with a Welsh Assembly in existence, Margaret Thatcher might well have drawn up the poll-tax legislation not more loosely but more tightly, depriving the Assembly of the opportunity even of varying the bands. It is important, therefore, not to exaggerate what devolution can be expected to achieve.

Executive devolution involves dividing powers which have hitherto been united and creating a new layer of government to administer a portion of them. There is of course nothing novel in creating bodies with subordinate powers in Britain. Indeed, local authorities are such bodies. But there is no general guidance available on the appropriate division of powers between central government and a devolved body to which powers of ministers are to be transferred, and no general rule as to whether a particular function should or should not be transferred. Moreover, because there is no clear basis of distinction between policy-making and administration, then, to quote the Royal Commission on the Constitution, the division of functions: 'would not be capable of simple definition. . . . The division would be an arbitrary one in that the range of powers conferred on the assemblies would depend upon a political judgement of the extent of the control it was necessary to retain at the centre'.[46]

In Britain, legislative and executive powers have, until now, been so closely fused that, to quote again from the Royal Commission on the Constitution, 'the division between them is not a precise one, and under the present arrangements they are not clearly separated'.[47] In the past, legislation does not seem to have been guided by any clear principles. The dividing line seems rather to have been drawn for reasons of convenience. As the Permanent Secretary at the Welsh Office, Rachel Lomax, declared in a speech to the Institute of Welsh Affairs on 7 November 1997, 'The Secretary of State's present powers have accumulated piecemeal over a long period of time, and the

distinction between matters that are dealt with in primary and secondary legislation has reflected pragmatic considerations as much as
principle.'

The reason for this is that the distinction between primary and
secondary legislation was never intended to provide the basis for a
division of powers between different elected bodies. Instead, primary and secondary legislation have been regarded as part of a single
process. Therefore, with regard to existing legislation, the Welsh
Assembly could easily find that its powers were of uneven scope and
depth since there would be no reason why the division between primary and secondary legislation in one policy area, for example,
health, should match the division in another, for example, education.
If that were so, the initial powers of the Assembly would have no
clear rationale and an integrated approach to policy-making would
become impossible.

Powers are to be transferred to the National Assembly in two
ways. First, under section 22 of the Government of Wales Act, functions of a minister of the Crown can be transferred by Order in
Council, subject to an affirmative resolution in both Houses. The
Welsh Office has published a draft Transfer Order which give the
Assembly powers to make subordinate legislation. The government's
intention is that virtually all of the executive powers currently exercised by the Secretary of State should be so transferred.

Second, functions can be conferred directly on the Assembly by
primary legislation. Sections 27 and 28 of the Government of
Wales Act, for example, confer directly on the Assembly powers to
reform the Welsh health authorities and other Welsh public bodies.
This is of particular importance since one of the arguments for
Welsh devolution has been that too many governmental functions
are carried out by *ad hoc* bodies of various sorts—quangos.
Sections 27 and 28 provide for the amendment of primary legislation by means of secondary legislation—known as a Henry VIII
power—and, in effect, they give the Welsh Assembly a power of
primary legislation.

Once the existing functions of the Secretary of State have been
conferred upon the Assembly in the first Transfer Order, there are
two methods of giving the Assembly additional functions: first, by

further Transfer Orders, to effect transfers of existing executive powers exercised by other ministers *vis-à-vis* Wales; and, second, by
means of new primary legislation conferring new functions and powers on the Assembly directly. In paragraph 3.39 of the White Paper,
A Voice for Wales, Cm. 3718, 1997, it is said that: 'The Government
will consider, in drafting each Bill that it introduces into Parliament,
which of the new powers it contains should be exercised by the
Assembly. This could include giving the Assembly responsibility for
bringing the Bill's provisions into force in Wales.'

This means that future bills dealing with matters covered by the
fields within which the Assembly exercises responsibility will be,
in a sense, devolution bills in that they will set out the limits within which secondary legislation can take place; and, given the possibility of further transfers of powers from other ministers to the
National Assembly, devolution will, as the former Secretary of
State for Wales Ron Davies often insisted, be not an event but a
process.[48] Tax-varying powers, however, since these are not powers given to ministers, would require primary legislation. The powers of the Welsh National Assembly, then, might be very different
after, say, ten years from what they are when the Assembly begins
its work.

Thus executive devolution, devolution of a 'horizontal' type, is
not just a weaker form than legislative devolution, devolution of a
'vertical' type, but a wholly different kind of animal and it raises
problems which have not hitherto been confronted in the British
political system. If executive devolution is to prove effective, two
fundamental problems will need to be resolved.

First, primary legislation for Wales will have to be drawn up more
loosely than primary legislation for England, so as to give scope to
the Assembly, without giving too great a discretion to ministers in
charge of English departments. This means that future statutes will
have to be framed differently for England and for Wales. For, if they
were to be framed similarly, either they would be very loosely drawn
both for England and for Wales, in which case the Assembly would
have considerable scope but English ministers would be given too
wide a discretion; or, alternatively, if the legislative framework were
drawn up equally tightly for England and Wales, the Welsh Assembly

would find that its powers over secondary legislation did not amount to very much.

Second, principles must be devised to regulate the dividing line between primary and secondary legislation. Such principles have been developed in Germany, whose federal system is based primarily on the division of executive rather than legislative powers, although the *Länder* do have some legislative powers. In Germany there is a system of administrative law which 'displays a relatively high degree of coherence and homogeneity' so that 'it is possible . . . to achieve a consistency of principles . . . which is unattainable within the traditions of pragmatic positivism which have shaped both the common law and the statutory public law in Britain'.[49] Whereas in Britain, statutes generally confer duties on local authorities and other public bodies and controlling and supervising powers on ministers, in Germany they are normally drafted in general declaratory terms. They provide only the framework of policy, leaving a good deal of initiative to the *Länder* in implementation. But the discretionary powers of government have to be exercised in accordance with general constitutional principles or they will be challenged in the courts. An approach of this kind, however, would involve fundamental changes in our notions of public law and in such constitutional doctrines as the responsibility of ministers to Parliament.

Because this framework is so unfamiliar in Britain, it will be difficult to attain some basis of principle for the transfer of powers, a basis of principle which could be used to regulate future legislation for Wales. The ideal would be a convention or published concordat regulating what can be dealt with by primary legislation for Wales and what by secondary, so that primary legislation affecting Wales becomes more permissive, laying down only very broad general objectives instead of providing also the details.

Even if this is done, however, the Welsh Assembly would not be the final authority on the policies for which it is responsible, for Westminster still retains control of all primary legislation for Wales. Moreover, many devolved functions involve the supervision of services delivered by local authorities, and the Assembly is required to set up a Partnership Council with local government which will be empowered to make representations to the Assembly on matters affecting local government. No doubt this Council will have as one of its tasks the drawing-up of conventions governing the respective spheres of the Assembly and local authorities in the government of Wales. Nevertheless policies involving, for example, education or the social services will have to proceed through three layers of government—central government, the Welsh Assembly, and Welsh local authorities. This could lead to a confused system of government with no clear lines of demarcation between the different layers.

It may become more difficult, after devolution, for the government to draw up primary legislation for Wales, since it will have lost contact with Welsh local authorities actually delivering services, such contact being mediated by the Assembly. Deprived of this contact and of feedback, the Secretary of State for Wales may well find himself less well informed about the needs of Wales. His weight in Cabinet will also be less since he will have lost his executive powers, while officials preparing Welsh legislation will no longer be responsible for its implementation in Wales.

The Assembly will, of course, be in a better position to appreciate Welsh needs; but, because it has no primary legislative powers, it will have to rely upon close co-operation with the Secretary of State for Wales to promote legislation. In Germany, the *Länder* are in a much stronger position in this regard since their role is constitutionally guaranteed through the representation of their governments in the federal upper house, the Bundesrat. Matters affecting the rights of the *Länder* require the consent of the Bundesrat as well as the lower house, the Bundestag, and so the governments of the *Länder* can veto legislation if they believe that its consequences would be deleterious for them.

Under section 31 of the Government of Wales Act, the Secretary of State is required to consult with the Assembly on the government's programme, 'as appears to him to be appropriate'. But there is no requirement to consult on every bill. The Secretary of State may refuse to do so if he 'considers that there are considerations relating to the bill which make it inappropriate for him to do so'. Of course, the Secretary of State might well belong to a different party from that of the majority in the Assembly. Under those circumstances, there might be two contradictory voices speaking for Wales, the Secretary of State and the First Secretary of the Assembly. If there is conflict, it would prove difficult for the Assembly to gain influence over government legislation, but equally difficult for the government to enforce its policies for Wales over the head of a politically hostile National Assembly. What is certain is that consultation and co-operation cannot be taken for granted. Even so, under the pre-devolutionary dispensation, Welsh Office ministers and officials consulted with their colleagues in Whitehall and served on teams drawing up legislation when Welsh interests so demanded. It is not clear whether the Assembly will be able, similarly, to examine policy proposals which are in the process of formulation by ministers. For this to happen, the Secretary of State would have to be prepared to engage in a genuine dialogue with the Assembly, representing both the government to the Assembly and the Assembly to the government. He would have to be prepared, for example, to put forward amendments to draft government legislation to his colleagues even if he were not wholly convinced of their merits. All this implies a new and untried set of relationships in British government.

Nevertheless, the hope must be that, in the words of a Cabinet paper written in 1975 in preparation for the abortive Wales Act of 1978:

the Assembly's views will carry more weight than those of most other bodies. First, the Assembly will represent the people of Wales and will speak with a virtually unique political authority on matters affecting the Principality. Second, the Assembly will be responsible for the implementation of legislation on devolved matters in Wales; it will know the situation 'on the ground' and will speak with knowledge on proposals relating to that situation. In reality, therefore, the Assembly's *influence* on legislation could be substantial.[50]

The Assembly is likely to be a powerful pressure-group on primary legislation as it affects Wales. It is likely, under favourable circumstances, to be a more powerful pressure-group on government than the Secretary of State for Wales has been in the past. The Assembly will also yield more detailed scrutiny, openness, and public participation in the making of secondary legislation than occurs at Westminster. Moreover, it will be possible to amend secondary legislation for Wales in the Assembly, while at Westminster, by contrast, secondary legislation must be either accepted or rejected and no amendment is possible.

It is clear that the effectiveness of devolution in Wales, executive devolution, relies, even more than legislative devolution, upon co-operation between the Assembly and central government. Where instead of co-operation there is an adversarial relationship, as might have occurred during the period of John Redwood's Secretaryship of State between 1993 and 1995, had there been an Assembly in existence at that time, the Assembly would find itself in the invidious position of being required to implement legislation with which it fundamentally disagreed, and with which, *ex hypothesi*, the majority in Wales also disagreed. Such an adversarial relationship can by no means be excluded. Indeed, since 1868, apart from the war years, the political complexion of the government in power has been different from that of the majority in Wales for around two-thirds of the time.

In Germany, by contrast, the country from which the idea of executive devolution is derived, political relationships, even between members of opposing parties, are often co-operative and consensual rather than adversarial. Moreover, the division of powers in the federal system is buttressed by a constitutional court which ensures that the demarcation lines are observed. In Britain, there is, of course, no such constitutional court and there is no way in which Westminster could bind itself to observe those principles regulating the division between primary and secondary legislation which happened to be drawn up by a particular government at a particular time.

In order to meet this problem, the government has proposed that there be a series of non-statutory concordats defining the working relationship of officials with Whitehall departments. The concordats will be published and will create what Lord Falconer, as Solicitor-General, called 'a legitimate expectation of consultation'.[51] They will, however, not be enforceable in the courts, although if an individual is damaged by the breach of a concordat, it may be that the breach can be raised in court proceedings. The idea of the concordat is an innovation in British constitutional life, since it imposes a self-denying ordinance upon government, limiting its power to legislate.

Welsh devolution, if it is to succeed, will require a considerable alteration in our constitutional habits. Not only will it require governments to accept principles which limit their power; it will require government and the Welsh Assembly to share power, to co-operate, rather than indulge in adversarial relationships. It will require what the Royal Commission on the Constitution called 'a new style of thinking, positively favourable to devolution and based on co-operation rather than the exercise of central authority'.[52] It will require, in short, a very radical change in our whole political culture.

The English dimension

England is hardly mentioned in the devolution legislation, and yet England is, in many respects, the key to the success of devolution. This is because any devolution settlement has to be acceptable not just to the Scots and the Welsh but also to the English, who return 529 of the 659 Members of Parliament to Westminster and who constitute 85 per cent of the population of the United Kingdom. The success of devolution will depend in large part upon whether English opinion believes it to be a fair and equitable settlement.

There may, at first sight, seem to be no reason why devolution to Scotland and Wales should have any consequences for England at all. Devolution, after all, involves the transfer of power over only Scottish and Welsh domestic matters, and the legislation provides that the central instruments of economic management, together with all major economic and industrial powers, remain with Westminster. Moreover, the government will continue to be responsible for the nationwide allocation of resources throughout the United Kingdom on the basis of need. Devolution, then, seems restricted to those matters which primarily affect those living in Scotland and Wales, and which can be administered separately without deleterious consequences on those living in England. The Long Title of the Scotland Act refers to its providing for 'the establishment of a Scottish Parliament and Administration and other changes in the government of Scotland'; the Long Title of the Government of Wales Act refers to its purpose as being 'To establish and make provision about the National Assembly for Wales'. They make no reference to the fact that they are making very radical changes to the government of the United Kingdom as a whole. They therefore imply that the establishment of a Scottish Parliament and a Welsh Assembly will not prejudice the interests of England.

Devolution, however, will accentuate an already existing constitutional imbalance in favour of Scotland and Wales. They already have their own Secretaries of State pressing their case at Cabinet level; they are over-represented in the House of Commons by comparison with England; and there is a good case for arguing that Scotland at least benefits more from public spending than those English regions whose GDP per head is lower. After devolution, Scotland and Wales will have control over local government spending on devolved services; they will have freedom to establish their own expenditure priorities; they will enjoy an advantage through their powerful political status in bidding for industry, and very possibly a greater opportunity of putting their case directly to the European Union. Above all, they, but not the English regions, will be able to negotiate with the government on any revisions of the Barnett formula or the assessment of needs; and this may well give them what amounts to a veto on changes deleterious to their interests. The Scottish Parliament and the Welsh Assembly are thus likely to enjoy very considerable political power and influence.

Those living in the more underprivileged English regions, such as the north-east or the north-west, may already regard themselves as second-class because they have no territorial ministers able to argue their case in Cabinet. After devolution, they may come to believe that they are third-class, since they have no assemblies either. It is by no means clear that a constitutional imbalance which has been broadly acceptable until now will continue to be acceptable after devolution. It is misleading, then, to regard devolution simply as a process by which the Scots and the Welsh manage their own domestic affairs. The Scottish Parliament and the Welsh Assembly may well be able to use their influence to ensure that they achieve an even greater share of resources than they obtain at present. If that occurs, it is likely to be the less well-off regions of England which will suffer. It will be difficult for the English regions, lacking representation in the Cabinet and without assemblies of their own, to counter this influence. In this way, the *constitutional* imbalance accentuated by devolution could lead to a serious *economic* imbalance favourable to Scotland and Wales, but unfavourable to the less privileged English regions. One consequence of this imbalance might be the generation of powerful regional lobbies in England. Whether that happens or not, the consent, or at the very least the acquiescence, of England is essential to the success of devolution.

In his poem 'The Secret People' G. K. Chesterton wrote, 'Smile at us, pay us, pass us, but do not quite forget; for we are the people of England that never have spoken yet.' England has not yet spoken because, constitutionally, England does not exist. 'England', it has been said, 'is a state of mind, not a consciously organised political institution'.[53] There has been no English parliament since 1536. There is no English Office comparable to the Scottish, Welsh, or Northern Ireland Offices, the 'English' ministers being so only because their non-English functions have been hived off to the territorial departments. The 'English' legal system comprises both England and Wales. The Treaty of Union which the Scots claim to have agreed with the 'English' in 1707 was in fact agreed with the English state, which then comprised both the English and the Welsh people.

England has long been the stumbling-block for supporters of devolution. For England, since the time of the union with Scotland in 1707, has resisted integration, while remaining unsympathetic to federalism. It is the supposedly unified and homogeneous nature of England which has in large part been responsible for the preservation of the unitary state. It is largely for this reason that England has not until now sought devolution. Until she does, governments have taken the view that she ought not to have devolution thrust upon her. In 1977, when the Scotland and Wales bill was under consideration by Parliament, Michael Foot declared that 'The Government do not propose to initiate any major constitutional change in England until there is evidence of much more extensive support for it.' [54] That remains the position of the Labour government elected in 1997. There could be no justification for requiring England to accept devolution against her wishes just because there has been devolution to Scotland and Wales. To force devolution upon England, far from assuaging resentment against Scotland and Wales, could well intensify it.

In February 1998, however, the Conservative leader, William Hague, called for changes to be made in the government of England, following devolution to Scotland and Wales. He put forward as suggestions an English Grand Committee or an English parliament. There is in fact, as we have seen, provision in the standing orders of the House of Commons for a Standing Committee on Regional Affairs, a kind of English Grand Committee. But that Committee has not met since 1978 for the very good reason that it proved to be nothing more than a cumbrous talking-shop.

In January 1998, the Eurosceptic Conservative back-bencher Teresa Gorman moved a private member's bill calling for a referendum on Hague's other proposal, an English parliament. The main purpose of such a parliament would be to resolve the West Lothian Question. Yet it would be pointless to 'resolve' it by a massive upheaval in England unless that were also desired for other reasons, and unless it served to make government more effective. An English parliament, however, would yield a form of 'Home Rule All Round' which would be highly unbalanced in population terms. Indeed, an English parliament could hardly avoid becoming a real rival to Westminster. As the Royal Commission on the Constitution warned,

A federation consisting of four units—England, Scotland, Wales, and Northern Ireland—would be so unbalanced as to be unworkable. It would be dominated by the overwhelming political importance and wealth of England. The English Parliament would rival the United Kingdom federal Parliament; and in the federal Parliament itself the representation of England could hardly be scaled down in such a way as to enable it to be outvoted by Scotland, Wales and Northern Ireland, together representing less than one-fifth of the population. A United Kingdom federation of four countries, with a federal Parliament and provincial Parliaments in the four national capitals, is therefore not a realistic proposition.[55]

Moreover, an English parliament would do nothing to remove the problems of over-centralization and lack of democratic accountability which comprise the dynamic behind devolution. Were an English parliament to be set up, there would still be a need to disperse power within England. So an English parliament, while it might resolve the West Lothian Question, would not resolve the problem to which devolution is the answer. Devolution in England, therefore, if it is to serve the same ends as devolution in Scotland and Wales, must be devolution to the English regions, not to an English parliament. It is no doubt for this reason that, in the preface to the White Paper, *Scotland's Parliament*, Cm. 3658, Tony Blair indicates that his government's 'comprehensive programme of constitutional reform' involves as well as 'a Scottish Parliament and a Welsh Assembly' 'more accountability in the regions of England'. 'The Union', the document goes on to say, 'will be strengthened by recognising the claims of Scotland, Wales and the regions with strong identities of their own'.

There are, however, no ministers for the English regions as there are ministers for Scotland and Wales and, by contrast with the Scottish and Welsh Offices, the regions are not directly represented in the Cabinet. The Labour government elected in 1997, however, established a new Department of the Environment, Transport and the Regions; and, since 1994, there have been Government Offices for the Regions, which bring together the regional offices of the Departments of the Environment, Transport, and the Regions, Trade and Industry, and the Training, Enterprise and Education Directorate of the Department for Education and Employment. These Offices administer or advise on programmes such as housing, urban regeneration projects, and training and education budgets. They provide a single point of contact with central government for local businesses and councils whose bids for money for economic development and urban regeneration are submitted via the Government Offices, as are bids for industrial aid and moneys from the European Union regional and social funds.

The establishment of these Offices in the regions involved a further change of great importance for the debate on devolution, in that it marked a step towards the establishment of common regional boundaries in place of the previous unsystematic arrangements. When John Gummer, the Conservative Environment Secretary, commended the

Government Offices for the Regions to the House of Commons, he declared: 'For the first time, there will be coterminous regions for the Departments, and that is the vital change. It has always seemed ridiculous to me that different departments had different regions. That made any sort of planning almost impossible.'[56]

Admittedly, there is still considerable variation between the boundaries of the Government Offices, and those of agencies, established under the 'Next Steps' programme, and non-departmental public bodies, even those run by the departments brought together in the Government Offices for the Regions. Major executive agencies within departments participating in the Government Offices, for example the Highways Agency, have an established regional structure with boundaries differing quite markedly from those of the Regional Offices. In addition, the regional boundaries of the NHS also differ from those of the Government Offices. Moreover, by no means all of the regional functions of government are carried out through the Offices. Regional functions in health and education as well as the regional functions of the Home Office, for example, do not operate through the Government Offices. One authority has discovered nearly a hundred different regional structures ranging from the six regional crime squads covering England and Wales to the nine Bee Health Inspection regions of the Ministry of Agriculture, Fisheries and Food.[57]

It would be wrong to regard these regional institutions as comprising a regional layer of government. Many of them are regional outposts of central government, a structure still primarily determined in England by functional rather than territorial considerations and one whose features are influenced as much by administrative convenience and historical accident as by any deliberate policy of regionalism. Regional institutions are highly fragmented, comprising as they do a jumble of heterogeneous bodies with quite varying functions and no clear pattern. Nor do most regional institutions enjoy policy-making functions, being primarily concerned with the administration of policy decided in Whitehall and the casework flowing from it. They administer nationally determined policies, which are not necessarily suitable for regional devolution. It is a fallacy, therefore, to suppose that because a function is carried out in a region, it is a function suitable for regional devolution.

Moreover, unlike local authorities, regional institutions do not in the main provide services, but rather distribute resources and grants to local authorities and other bodies. Thus, if the functions of the Government Offices for the Regions were to be transferred to directly elected regional assemblies, the powers of these assemblies would be largely concerned with the distribution of resources to local government. They would then be very tempted to establish tighter supervision over local government. If that happened, devolution would centralize government, not decentralize it. The existence of regional institutions cannot, therefore, be used as a conclusive argument for regional devolution in England.

Moreover, regional devolution in England would almost certainly require further reorganization of local government. England, unlike Scotland or Wales, still has a predominantly two-tier structure of local government outside London. Devolution was made easier in Scotland and Wales because local authorities had already been reorganized and unitary authorities established there. In England, by contrast, there was no legislation providing for reorganization; instead a Local Government Commission was set up to consult with local opinion. This Commission failed to discover any consensus for reorganization and, in consequence, thirty-four of the thirty-nine shire counties in England retain a two-tier system of local government. There is indeed no standard region with wholly unitary local government outside London. To impose regional assemblies on a two-tier system of local government is hardly feasible. 'One thing we are clear about in England,' Jack Straw declared as Shadow Home Secretary in 1995; 'you cannot establish regional assemblies as well as having shire counties and districts underneath them'.[58] Regional assemblies, then, would mean the end of county government in England, and the regions would replace the counties. Thus regional government in England would require a further reorganization of local government which practically no one wants. Reorganization, moreover, would probably mean that some of the functions of the upper tier of local government, the counties, would be transferred, not to the lower tier of local government, the districts, but to the regions. It would be natural to propose a new division of functions such that personal services—education and social services, for example—remained with local authorities, while strategic services, such as planning, transport, economic development, and European liaison, were transferred upwards to regional level. That would be seen as a threat by local government and as contrary to the purpose of devolution, which is to disperse power.

The fundamental difficulty with devolution to the English regions, however, is that there is so little demand for it. It is for this reason that English regionalism has been called 'the dog that never barked'.59 Devolution in England has to confront the problem that the regions are in large degree simply ghosts. For regional institutions to be effective, there would need to be a much stronger sense of regional awareness, similar to the sense of Scottish or Welsh awareness. At present, a sense of regional awareness does exist in those regions most distant from London, the north-east and the north-west, and perhaps also in the south-west, where geographical remoteness from Westminster co-exists with a feeling of economic disadvantage. It is possible that regional institutions could increase that sense of regional awareness, just as the Welsh Office seems to have increased Welsh awareness, but it cannot yet be said that there is a regional consciousness sufficiently strong to sustain directly elected regional institutions with powers devolved from central government.

In the 1970s, proposals for devolution to Scotland and Wales did, it is true, stimulate regional feeling in England, especially in the north of England. But that feeling was primarily directed at preventing devolution. There was little spontaneous demand for regional assemblies, and indeed the demand for such assemblies would probably not have been put forward at all had the Labour government not proposed devolution for Scotland and Wales. With devolution a *fait accompli*, however, it may be that the strategy of those who feel that their interests have been deleteriously affected will alter, and they might seek to establish regional assemblies in England in order to counter the greater political weight of Scotland and Wales. In November 1997, in what may prove a portent, a Declaration for the North appeared, calling for a regional assembly. It was signed by the majority of Labour MPs in the north-east, the region's four MEPs, and by much of the Labour establishment in the region. Pressure for a northern assembly may well increase once the Scottish Parliament is in operation.

Developments in Europe may also contribute to regional awareness, although, as the next section shows, the significance of these
developments should not be overestimated. The European Union is
very far from being a Europe of the Regions, and it would require
radical changes in the policies of the member states to create it.
Nevertheless, in order to improve their position in bidding for
European Union funds, local authorities have begun to organize
themselves on a regional level. The whole of England is now covered
by regional associations of local authorities, and there is thus an
embryonic bottom-up regionalism, to match the top-down regionalism of the Government Offices. The 1999 European Parliament elections in Britain may also serve to strengthen regional feeling, for they
are to be conducted by proportional representation based on regional lists. Thus the regions, for the first time, might become political
units in their own right.

The Labour government elected in 1997 faced the same problem
as its predecessor in the 1970s. It was instinctively sympathetic to
regional devolution in England, but felt unable to proceed in the
absence of clear indicators of support for it. The government therefore decided to adopt an evolutionary approach. In 1997 it issued a
White Paper, *Building Partnerships for Prosperity*, Cm. 3814, which
proposed the establishment of regional development agencies, and
also indirectly elected regional chambers chosen primarily from
local authorities. These chambers, according to para. 1.7 of the White
Paper, 'may be a first step towards greater devolution in England'. In
the House of Commons, John Prescott, the Secretary of State for the
Environment, Transport and the Regions, declared: 'We are committed to moving, with the consent of local people, to directly elected
regional government in England. That complements devolution in
Scotland and Wales and the creation of a Greater London Assembly.
Demand for directly elected regional government varies across
England, and it would be wrong to envisage a uniform approach at
this stage'.[60] The White Paper expresses the hope, however, that the
creation of regional development agencies 'will help to foster a sense
of regional identity and develop a regional capability. In time, this
may lead to further transfers of functions and responsibilities to
regional structures' (p. 52). Nevertheless, devolution to the regions

is unlikely in the 1997 Parliament. Richard Caborn, the Minister for Regions, Regeneration and Planning, told the Environment, Transport and Regional Affairs Committee of the House of Commons, that people in the regions would 'be given the opportunity . . . to make them [the chambers] directly elected at a time after the next general election'.[61]

The essence of the programme for devolution in England is that it will be granted to any region which seeks it; at the same time a region which does not seek devolution will not be able to prevent any other region from embracing it. Devolution in England, however, is to be subject to a threefold test to ensure that there is real popular demand for it. First, there must be a plan for devolution drawn up and approved by the regional chamber, indicating that it is supported by the majority of local authorities in the region. Second, the plan must be approved by Parliament, with the Secretary of State being required to consult the opposition parties before giving it his own approval. Third, there must be clear evidence of popular support, probably including a referendum. Thus, in contrast to the 1970s, when Labour, despite having promised regional government in opposition, delivered nothing, in the 1990s the party proposes a staged approach which perhaps offers a greater chance of success.

This staged approach, or rolling devolution as it is often called, is similar to that adopted in Spain after the death of Franco in 1975 and the return to democratic government. In Spain, a distinction was made between the so-called historic communities—Catalonia and the Basque country—corresponding perhaps to Scotland and Wales, and the other regions where the demand for devolution seemed less pressing. The new democratic government legislated immediately for devolution to Catalonia and the Basque country, and waited until a popular demand for devolution was expressed elsewhere. Thus, as with the United Kingdom, devolution was not introduced at the same time for every region of the country, but only if and when there was a demand for it. The hope was that the success of devolution in the historic communities would lead to a demand for devolution elsewhere; and that, indeed, was what occurred. Moreover, and again there is a parallel in the United Kingdom, devolution was asymmetrical, with Catalonia, the Basque country, and five other regions being given greater responsibilities than the remaining ten regions. The principle of rolling devolution adopted by the Labour government offers the best hope of constructing a practical devolution policy for the whole of the United Kingdom, one which addresses the fact that the different nations and regions of the country seek devolution, if at all, with very different degrees of intensity.

In one part of England, however, London, a quite different route has been taken. For, instead of a regional authority in London, there is to be a directly elected mayor and a city-wide local authority. Whereas the leaders of the Scottish and Welsh devolved bodies are to be chosen by the devolved bodies themselves, the mayor of London is to be directly elected. This gives him or her a powerful popular mandate, but he or she will enjoy comparatively few powers. Indeed, there is to be no devolution of central government powers to London at all, not even powers over secondary legislation. The mayor will have no health, training, further education, or economic regeneration functions and, by contrast with the Welsh Assembly, he or she will have no powers over land-use or development control. It is the Secretary of State for the Environment, Transport and the Regions, not the mayor, who will remain the final appeal on planning matters; and the mayor, unlike the Welsh Assembly, will have no block grant from Whitehall. Although the London authority will be the largest local authority in the country, the mayor will have to rely, like a county council, on precepting the lower tier of local government, and also upon predominantly fixed grants from central government. Most government funds will in fact still be channelled through the London boroughs. Nor will the mayor have the power of the Welsh Assembly to place various public bodies—quangos— under his or her authority, or even to abolish them if he or she so wishes. All he or she will be able to do is to make appointments to them. The role of the authority will be primarily one of scrutiny.

Thus the London mayor and authority will be part of a weak upper tier of local government rather than an embryonic regional authority. The mayor's lack of powers, by contrast with those of the Welsh Assembly, will make it more likely that he or she will interfere with the service-delivery responsibilities of other local authorities, just as the GLC, enjoying only a few functional responsibilities, sought to encroach on the powers of the London boroughs. In providing for a mayor and an authority in London, therefore, the government took a conscious decision against devolution. The concept of a directly elected mayor is quite opposed to that of power-sharing executives in Scotland and Wales, chosen by bodies elected by proportional representation.

The government's proposals for the regeneration of local government, moreover, envisage mayors in other large cities where there is demand. Such mayors would constitute a powerful institutional force against devolution to the regions since regional assemblies would be likely to detract from their authority. Moreover, mayors might claim that it is they who are the true spokespersons for their regions. A mayor of Newcastle, for example, might well claim to be the spokesperson for the north-east, while a mayor of Liverpool might claim a similar role in the north-west. The new assertiveness of the cities would make it more difficult to implement the programme for regional assemblies. Thus the proposals for local government reform, like the policies adopted for London, cut across those for regionalism. Perhaps they will prove a substitute for it.

The development of regional government in England, therefore, remains highly problematic. Were it ever to occur, however, it could have profound effects upon the political system. For the fundamental purpose of elected regional authorities would be to allow for divergences of policy. There would be no point in creating regional assemblies simply to replicate national policies at regional level. Regionalism, therefore, would make for much greater policy diversity. This could well serve to loosen and diversify party structures, so that locality would come to act as a counterweight to the disciplines of the national political parties. Policy would no longer be wholly determined at Westminster by a centralized and disciplined party, but would come to have a much greater local and regional input. Were there to be a fragmentation of the party system along these lines, this could reinforce regional diversity, and territory might once again come to be a crucial factor in politics as it was in the years before 1914. Moreover, while regional devolution would not resolve the West Lothian Question, except in the unlikely event of regional authorities being given legislative powers, it might help to reduce its political salience. For if Scottish MPs were to continue to legislate in detail on the domestic affairs of, for example, the north-east of England, that would only be because the north-east of England had chosen not to take advantage of an offer of devolution, less devolution than that granted to Scotland, but substantial all the same.

Were regional devolution in England to occur, we would have embarked on a process of rolling devolution which could turn Britain into a quasi-federal state, still asymmetrical, but with a rough balance of power between Scotland, Wales, and the English regions. Perhaps the government's proposals for the regions will lead the country in the direction, slowly, almost by stealth, step by step towards a quasi-federal Britain. If this occurred, it would be characteristic of constitutional reform in Britain in that it develops not through any explicit acceptance of a new principle, but by means of piecemeal reforms to meet concrete needs. If a quasi-federal Britain comes about in this way, it will be, perhaps, an excellent illustration of the Hegelian notion of the Cunning of Reason.

The European dimension

The European Union is based in part on the premiss that the nation state is no longer necessarily the best unit for carrying out certain functions of government, which may be better conducted at supranational level. It would be natural, then, to believe that some of the functions of the state are best carried out at *subnational* level. Europe involves power-sharing with other member states, devolution the sharing of power within a single member state. Europe and devolution, therefore, represent twin challenges to the traditional role of the state.[62] For this reason, in many of the member states of the European Union, there is an alliance between Europhiles and decentralizers. That is certainly the case in Britain where many, although by no means all, of those who support closer European integration also support devolution. Conversely, many Eurosceptics are also hostile to devolution, believing as they do that power should remain with the nation state.

Two developments in the Maastricht Treaty of 1991 seemed to give the devolutionist cause added strength. The first was the creation, under Article 198a–c of the Treaty, of the Committee of the Regions. The second was the introduction of the doctrine of subsidiarity under Article 3b. These developments, however, are unlikely to have more than a symbolic effect on relations in Britain between Westminster and the devolved bodies.

The Committee of the Regions is a body with purely consultative powers, but it does institutionalize the role of the regions implying as it does that the construction of European Union requires the contribution of subnational as well as national governments. The Committee indeed seeks to organize the participation of subnational bodies in the decision-making processes of the European Community. These bodies are likely to press the case for the regions at European level. Indeed, the German *Länder* wanted the Committee to be a second chamber of the European Parliament and the leader of the government of the Catalan autonomous region in Spain, Jordi Pujol, has echoed this call. Such a transformation, however, if it ever occurs, lies a very long way in the future.

The significance of the Committee of the Regions should not be exaggerated. Its establishment is very far from bringing about a Europe of the Regions. For the Committee comprises representatives of local authorities as well as regions. The British representatives are entirely local councillors appointed by the government, although in future the devolved bodies are likely to be represented on it. Only Austria, Germany, Italy, and Spain send a majority of representatives from the regions, as opposed to local authorities, to the Committee. Were England to have a regional layer of government, no doubt regional representatives would be included on the Committee. Yet, precisely because the Committee is composed of representatives from bodies whose constitutional status differs widely, it is difficult to envisage it enjoying, for the foreseeable future, more than consultative powers.

The principle of subsidiarity in the Maastricht Treaty requires that decisions should, as far as possible, be taken at the lowest level of government. This principle applies, however, only to relationships between member states and the European Union. It does not apply to relationships between governments and subnational governments. Indeed, the European Union has no jurisdiction over such relationships, and it would probably be regarded as an intrusion if it did. For the freedom of each member state to decide upon the division of powers which it thinks appropriate might well be considered part of the very meaning of subsidiarity.

European regional policy has, since 1988, brought the regions directly into the European Union decision-making process, in the bidding for regional funds. But this does not in practice seem to have increased the political power of the regions. Although the regions do, it is true, establish bilateral relationships through the regional directorate-general of the European Commission, it is nevertheless the member states which lay down the guidelines for regional policy. In Britain, the exigencies of negotiating in and with the European institutions have served to strengthen rather than weaken the lead role of the Department of Trade and Industry.

This is because the institutions of the European Union, far from transcending member states, work through them.[63] The Union is primarily an arena within which the member states bargain, rather than an arrangement for superseding them. Thus, whatever the internal political arrangements of a country, whether it is federal or unitary, the European Union holds member states liable for their obligations under European Community law. Europe has, therefore, despite the subsidiarity principle, undoubtedly exercised a centralizing effect both on relationships between central and local government and on relationships between central government and subnational layers.

The Committee of the Regions and the principle of subsidiarity do not alter this basic constitutional position, that the conduct of relations with the European Union remains the responsibility of member states. Precisely because it is the governments of member states which are liable for European Union obligations, it must remain for these governments to determine their nature and extent. Moreover, each member state, in negotiations within the Council of Ministers, must put forward a common negotiating position and that position must be put forward by a united delegation. There can be no question of a regional unit negotiating independently with Brussels or acting in opposition to its national government, whether that region lies in a federal relationship with its government or is merely devolved.

It is important all the same for regional and subnational voices to be heard in Brussels. If they are unstructured, as is the case in Britain, then regional interests may not be given the weight they deserve. In Britain, the regions are at a disadvantage as compared with the *Länder* in Germany, where there is a constitutionally defined means of determining regional priorities.

Before devolution, the interests of Scotland and Wales were represented by the Secretaries of State for Scotland and Wales, and the Secretary of State for Scotland was specifically charged with ensuring that policy-making in the European Union took account of the special features of the Scottish legal system. After devolution, however, responsibility for a number of areas of European Community legislation, and in particular agriculture and fisheries, will be in the hands of the devolved bodies. In theory, the Scottish Executive will have full responsibility for agriculture and fisheries, while the Welsh Executive will have partial responsibility for them. Policy in these areas, however, is determined primarily in Brussels. Yet there is no statutory requirement that the devolved bodies be involved in negotiation with Brussels. Thus, while the Scottish ministers who will be responsible to the Scottish Parliament for agriculture and fisheries will have no statutory right to be part of the negotiating process and can be overruled by ministers in the British government, ministers in the British government who are responsible for negotiating will not be responsible to the Scottish Parliament. There is thus a disjunction between the constitutional position of the devolved bodies and their actual powers, which could cause disillusionment in Scotland and Wales when it comes to be appreciated that there is a countervailing force to devolution in the form of the European Union.

In this area, as in so many others, devolution will work successfully only if there is close and effective liaison between the government and the devolved executives. The government proposes that ministers and secretaries of the devolved bodies should be involved, as part of the British negotiating team, when matters of Scottish or Welsh concern are being considered. Ministers from the devolved executives might even be able to speak, with the agreement of the lead minister, for the United Kingdom in the Council of Ministers. Scotland and Wales would then become the only subnational units in the European Union with individual access to the Council of

Ministers, since subnational access in Austria, Belgium, and Germany is by common representatives putting forward collective subnational positions. Access to the Council of Ministers by subnational units has become possible in virtue of the revised Article 146 of the Treaty of European Union, agreed at Maastricht, which declares that 'The Council [of Ministers] shall consist of a representative of each member state at Ministerial level, authorized to commit the government of that member state'. This Article was put in to persuade the governments of the German *Länder*, represented in the Bundesrat, to accept the Maastricht Treaty. In fact, however, Article 146 does not offer subnational governments much, merely the right to be a mouthpiece for the position of a member state which they may have played but a small role in formulating. Moreover, since the votes of a member state in the Council of Ministers cannot be split, subnational units must agree a common position with the government of their member state. Thus the devolved executives might, by agreement, speak for the United Kingdom, but they would be doing so as representatives of the UK government, not as representatives of Scotland or Wales.

Involvement by the devolved executives, then, will be subject to their accepting the agreed United Kingdom position which they may or may not have helped to formulate. The devolved executives will not be able to put forward a specifically Scottish or Welsh position which is not also the position of the British government; and it is because the United Kingdom must put forward an agreed position to the Council, which is that of the British government, and because Britain is not becoming a federal state, that Scottish and Welsh executives cannot have a *right* of representation at the Council. They will be invited only if they are prepared to accept the agreed negotiating position of the government. In the words of the White Paper, *Scotland's Parliament*, Cm. 3658, 1997, para. 5.12, 'Provided the Scottish Executive is willing to work in that spirit of collaboration and trust, there will be an integrated process which builds upon the benefits of the current role of the Scottish Office within government.'

The devolved executives will, moreover, be bound by the conventions of confidentiality and collective responsibility which apply to the Cabinet, 'without which', to quote the White Paper again, 'it would be impossible to maintain such close working relationships' (para. 5.4). Thus the devolved bodies do not even enjoy a right of consultation. They will be consulted only if they are prepared to accept the conventions which go with consultation. Moreover, the devolved bodies will also be bound by the confidentiality of meetings of the Council of Ministers.

Thus, whatever role the devolved executives play, they will still be bound by government decisions. Formally, then, devolution will not increase the powers of Scotland and Wales nor alter their constitutional status *vis-à-vis* Europe. Subnational units of government can only be separately represented in Brussels on the Council for a matter for which they enjoy exclusive competence; these, except for language in Belgium, and education in Germany, are generally of a minor kind. But, given that, in Britain, Parliament remains constitutionally supreme, there is *no* matter on which the Scottish Parliament or Welsh Assembly will enjoy exclusive competence.

This, of course, could give rise to problems for Scottish and Welsh interests in Europe. The danger is that Scotland and Wales come to be excluded from the negotiations and the forums in which the vital decisions are made; and that, even when they are admitted, this will be only on sufferance. It is, moreover, difficult to influence a process when one is not part of the give and take of Cabinet discussion. A dispute between, for example, the interests of agriculture in Scotland and East Anglia might be arbitrated, not in negotiations between government and the Scottish Executive, but in Cabinet, a forum in which Scottish interests will be weaker, because the Secretary of State for Scotland no longer enjoys executive functions. If the Scottish or Welsh executives were tempted to publicize their disagreements with the British government, the penalty could be exclusion from the negotiating and decision-making process entirely.

It was to avoid problems of this kind that in Germany the Bundesrat insisted, as a condition of accepting the Maastricht Treaty, on a new Article 23 in the Basic Law, the German constitution, to protect the rights of the *Länder*. This article guarantees the *Länder*, acting collectively through the Bundesrat, involvement in any European Union matters affecting them. A nominated representative from the Bundesrat, moreover, has the right of representation in the German delegation in the Council when a matter of exclusive competence to the *Länder* is being considered, such as culture or the arts. But, even so, there must still be an agreed member-state position in the Council, since the representative of the *Länder* is committing the German government, not just the *Länder*. It is, however, easier for the German *Länder* to secure involvement in the governmental decision-making process than it would be in Britain, for two reasons. First, there are sixteen *Länder* of equal constitutional status covering the whole country, rather than asymmetrical devolution with bodies of very different constitutional status covering just a small part of the country; and second, there is so much more compromise and consensus between the German parties, and the system of government is coalitional at both federal and land level. This makes it possible for there to be members of opposing parties in the German national delegation so that representatives of the *Länder* can become in effect national representatives. It is by no means so clear that such a congenial result could occur in Britain. It is not easy to envisage an SNP executive in Edinburgh, for example, working happily as part of a national delegation with a Labour or Conservative government in London; nor to envisage a Labour administration in Edinburgh working successfully with a Conservative government in London.[64]

It may seem, then, that the position of Scotland and Wales could well be weakened after devolution, and that they will be cut off from the process of decision-making in London, and therefore find that their influence on the process of deciding the United Kingdom position in the Council of Ministers is reduced. Such a judgement, however, may overestimate the influence of the Scottish and Welsh Offices on the pre-devolution decision-making process. On European matters, these Offices have not often taken independent initiatives. Moreover, the Scottish and Welsh Secretaries of State are not frequent attenders at the Council of Ministers. In the years between 1992 and 1996, for example, Scottish Office ministers attended very few meetings:

1992: attended 8 meetings out of 125.
1993: 8 out of 125.
1994: 6 out of 125.
1995: 7 out of 83.
1996: 15 out of 84.[65]

It can be argued, then, that Scotland and Wales will gain rather than lose, since the devolved bodies could prove to be powerful pressure groups influencing both Whitehall and Brussels. They will, in particular, be able to influence the European Commission, which in practice sets the agenda for the European Union. In addition, the devolved administrations will almost certainly open offices in Brussels, which will enable them to bang on doors and lobby more effectively. It is possible that Scotland and Wales will gain more through this pressure-group activity than they will lose through having their European interests represented by the Scottish and Welsh Secretaries. As in so many other areas, devolution is a trade-off and it will not be possible for many years to come to see whether it works for or against Scottish and Welsh interests.

*

Devolution is a transfer of powers. It seems to imply the removal of powers from a superior layer of government to a lower layer of government. It seems to create new independent layers of government. Yet, in reality, it creates not independent but new interdependent layers. As with Europe, so with the financial settlement: devolution will work successfully only if there are interlocking arrangements between central government and the devolved administrations. Such arrangements would also be helpful in ensuring that primary legislation relating to Wales is confined to broad and major questions of policy so that the scope of the Welsh Assembly is not unnecessarily diminished. The Welsh model of devolution, even more obviously than the Scottish, creates interdependence between two layers of government. Indeed, in the modern world, it is hardly possible in any democracy to maintain a rigid line of demarcation between different levels of government. That is why, in most modern federal states, 'dual federalism', of two layers of government each with its own carefully defined sphere of action, has been replaced by 'co-operative federalism', marked by an interdependent relationship between the federal government and the provinces. Devolution, too, if it works successfully will establish not independent, but interdependent bodies in Scotland and Wales, and it will require co-operation and reciprocity between the devolved executives and central government.

Interlocking arrangements generally play an important role in federal systems of government. In Canada, for example, the interlocking principle is given effect through interministerial conferences between representatives of the federal government and the provinces. In Germany, there are regular intergovernmental meetings between ministers and officials of the federal and land governments. In addition, of course, the Bundesrat is itself a powerful instrument of coordination.

In the 1978 devolution legislation, no provision was made for such interlocking institutions; nor was any provision made in the actual legislation in 1997. During the House of Lords debates on the Scotland bill, however, a government minister, Baroness Ramsay of Cartvale, made an important announcement:

The Government intend that there should be standing arrangements for the devolved administrations to be involved by the UK Government at ministerial level when they consider reserved matters which impinge on devolved responsibilities. It is envisaged that this would be achieved through the establishment of a joint ministerial committee of which the UK Government and the devolved administrations would be members. The joint ministerial committee will be an entirely consultative body, supported by a committee of officials and a joint secretariat. . . . Where there is agreement between the parties that it should do so, the JMC could also discuss the treatment of devolved matters in the different parts of the UK.[66]

The proposed joint ministerial committee provides institutional recognition of the fact that devolution creates a situation of interdependence rather than a separation of powers. Germany, however, has developed the interlocking principle much further through her second chamber, by means of which the *Länder*, through the representation of their governments in the Bundesrat, are enabled to participate, as of right, in national policy-making. The Bundesrat also provides a countervailing pressure to the natural processes of centralization which affect all governments, whether of the Left or of the Right. As we have seen, the Bundesrat played an important role during the negotiations for the Maastricht Treaty in ensuring that the centralizing tendencies of the European Union were counteracted by the forces of subnational governments. In Britain, co-operation is likely to be greater when the same parties are in office in London,

Edinburgh, and Cardiff, than where there is party conflict. Germany, with its coalitional system, is less troubled with this problem, and there has never been a time when all *Länder* governments have been headed by the same party or parties, although the Bundesrat has on occasion had a different majority from the lower house.

Pressures from subnational government for formal representation at the centre are likely to increase following devolution. Already, in March 1998, the Scottish TUC called for a Scottish seat on the Bank of England's monetary policy committee. This led the Conservatives, no doubt mischievously, to propose an amendment to the Scotland Bill, which was passed in the Lords, but rejected by the Commons, giving the Scottish First Minister power to nominate a representative to this committee.

The most valuable way of creating a forum for subnational interests, however, would be to follow the German model by giving the devolved governments formal access to the legislative process in a reformed second chamber. With reform of the House of Lords currently under consideration, it would be natural to suggest the creation of a second chamber similar to the Bundesrat to replace the present upper house of hereditary and nominated peers. That would be one way of ensuring that the second chamber in Britain gained democratic legitimacy while at the same time basing it on a principle of representation different from that of the Commons.

All such interlocking arrangements, however, raise difficult problems of political accountability which have nowhere been fully resolved. Interlocking means that more decisions are reached through bargaining, at one remove from the electorate, who will find it difficult to pinpoint responsibility. This makes it easier to pass the buck and avoid accountability for unpopular decisions. In the German federal system, there is so much sharing and overlapping of functions that it is difficult for the voter to determine who is responsible for what. Where power is interdependent, to whom is it accountable?

The structure of government in Scotland and Wales, and indeed in the United Kingdom as a whole, is bound to become more complex after devolution. If devolution is to be successful, it will require the construction of new political relationships of tact and harmony between those working in different levels of government, and from different political parties. Devolution requires, and may conceivably help create, new relationships of consensus and co-operation. It will have very profound consequences not only for the government of Scotland and Wales, but for the whole of the United Kingdom.

Conclusion
Federal Devolution

> A federal state is a political contrivance intended to reconcile national unity
> and power with the maintenance of 'state rights'.
>
> (A. V. Dicey, The Law of the Constitution)

I

When the Scottish parliament voted for union with England, so dissolving itself, the Scottish Lord Chancellor, the Earl of Seafield, wryly declared, 'There's ane end of ane auld sang.' The setting-up of the Scottish Parliament and the Welsh Assembly mark the start of a new song. They seem to imply that the United Kingdom is becoming a union of nations, each with its own identity and institutions, rather than as the English have often seen it, according to the Royal Commission on the Constitution, 'one nation representing different kinds of people'.[1]

Constitutionally, devolution is a mere delegation of power from a superior political body to an inferior. Politically, however, devolution places a powerful weapon in the hands of the Scots and the Welsh; and, just as one cannot be sure that a weapon will always be used only for the specified purposes for which it may have been intended, so also one cannot predict the use which the Scots and the Welsh will make of devolution. For the devolved bodies will represent areas of the United Kingdom with long histories of national identity and pride. It will be the reaction of these attitudes upon the new institutions which will determine their path of development. The impact of the Scottish Parliament and the Welsh Assembly will thus depend far more on political and indeed psychological factors than on constitutional ones. To form an estimate of the consequences of devolution, therefore, we must peer beyond the formal arrangements in order to penetrate the realities which lie beneath.

The White Paper, *Scotland's Parliament*, Cm. 3648, states the

constitutional position after devolution. It retains, however, a traditional constitutional vocabulary, proclaiming in stern Diceyan tones
in paragraph 42 that 'The United Kingdom Parliament is and will
remain sovereign in all matters', while section 28 (7) of the Scotland
Act announces that 'This section', which provides for the Scottish
Parliament to make laws, 'does not affect the power of the
Parliament of the United Kingdom to make laws for Scotland.' So
also the 1978 Scotland Bill contained as its first clause an assertion
that it did not affect Parliament's 'supreme authority to make laws
for the United Kingdom or any part of it'. MPs, however, threw out
the clause and it did not form part of the Scotland Act. Were they not
displaying a better grasp of the political realities than the government? For what can it mean to reiterate the traditional vocabulary of
the Constitution and assert supremacy when such wide legislative
powers are being devolved to another directly elected body?

Constitutionally, the Scottish Parliament will clearly be subordinate. Politically, however, it will be anything but subordinate. For the
Scotland Act creates a new locus of political power. Its most important power will be one not mentioned in the Act at all, that of representing the people of Scotland. The basic premiss of devolution, after
all, is that there is a separate political will in Scotland. The First
Minister in Scotland will be seen as an executant of that political
will, backed as he or she will be by a popular majority in Scotland.
It will be the First Minister who will claim the right to speak for
Scotland, and claim that he or she has more right to do so than
Westminster MPs or the Secretary of State who will have been
denuded of his powers, and who, in any case, may represent a party
unable to command a majority in Scotland. In practice, therefore, the
First Minister in Scotland is likely to be seen as the real leader of
Scottish opinion; he or she is likely to be seen as the Prime Minister
of Scotland.

It will thus not be easy to bring into play the constitutional
restraints in the Scotland Act. For it would be difficult to imagine an
issue more likely to unite Scottish opinion than a conflict between
the Scottish Parliament and a remote, London-based government.
Even if London were to get its way in the end, this would probably
be at the cost of considerable political disaffection and loss of sup-

port. In practice, therefore, Westminster will find it extremely difficult to exercise its much-vaunted supremacy.

Section 75 of the 1920 Government of Ireland Act offered a far more ringing declaration of supremacy than is to be found in the 1998 Scotland Act: 'Notwithstanding the establishment of the Parliament of Northern Ireland—or anything contained in this Act, the supreme authority of the Parliament of the United Kingdom shall remain unaffected and undiminished over all persons, matters and things in Northern Ireland and every part thereof.'

Yet we have seen in Chapter 3 how difficult it was for Westminster to exercise its supremacy over Northern Ireland. Indeed, on one of the only two occasions when the Lord Lieutenant seriously considered exercising his reserve powers to withhold assent to proposed legislation from Northern Ireland, abolishing proportional representation in local government in the province, he was met by a threat of resignation from the government of Northern Ireland and was compelled to give way. If Westminster found itself incapable of exercising its supremacy over the Northern Ireland Parliament, how much more difficult its task will be *vis-à-vis* Scotland. For Northern Ireland did not see herself as a separate nation within the United Kingdom, nor had she sought devolution. Therefore she had every incentive to avoid conflict with the British government. The Scottish Parliament will have no such incentive. It will speak, moreover, not for an artificially created province in danger of being extruded from the United Kingdom against its wishes, but, as the Scots conceive themselves to be, a nation. For Scotland has, as we have seen, a history of statehood and a national tradition embodied in concrete and ever-present institutional form. Independence is therefore a very real option for her, which it never was for Northern Ireland.

We have seen that the White Paper *Scotland's Parliament* insisted that supremacy remained with Westminster. Many Scots, however, and by no means only those who vote for the SNP, take the view that if Scotland is a nation, it enjoys an inherent right to self-determination. That indeed was the position of the *Claim of Right*, the foundation document of the Scottish Constitutional Convention. The *Claim of Right* was, as Neil MacCormick has noticed, as categorical as the White Paper, 'but in an opposite sense'.[2] It declared: 'We, gathered as the Scottish Constitutional Convention, do hereby acknowledge the sovereign right of the Scottish people to determine the form of Government suited to their needs'. Sovereignty, on this view, lies with the Scottish people not with Westminster, a claim perhaps implicitly accepted by Labour, which, both in 1979 and 1997, restricted the vote in the devolution referendum to electors registered in Scotland.

In the Government of Ireland Act of 1920, the supremacy of Parliament was preserved not only by section 75, but also by section 6 and section 12 of the Act, allowing the Governor to withhold assent to Northern Ireland legislation. This led K. C. Wheare in his classic text *Federal Government*[3] to deny that Northern Ireland lay in a federal relationship with Westminster. In practice, however, as we have seen, the Government of Ireland Act did create a quasi-federal relationship between the parliament of Northern Ireland and Westminster, and the canons of interpretation adopted by the courts when dealing with the legislative competence of the Northern Ireland Parliament came to be very similar to those applied in federal systems. In the leading case *Gallagher* v. *Lynn*, for example, Lord Atkin declared (emphasis added):

These questions affecting limitation on the legislative powers of subordinate parliaments *or the distribution of powers between parliaments in a federal system* are now familiar, and I do not propose to cite the whole range of authority which has largely arisen in discussion of the powers of Canadian Parliaments.[4]

The relationship between Scotland and Westminster, like that between Northern Ireland and Westminster, will also come to be quasi-federal. Wheare in *Federal Government* finds the distinguishing mark of federalism to lie in a constitutionally guaranteed division of powers between co-ordinate and independent levels of government. Clearly neither the Scottish Parliament nor the Welsh Assembly will enjoy such a constitutional guarantee. But the division of powers in Scotland, and to some extent Wales, will be guaranteed in a different way, by the support of their people against any attempt by Westminster to vindicate its supremacy.

If the new arrangements work as intended, the Scottish Parliament will be the supreme authority over Scottish domestic affairs. 'As happened in Northern Ireland', Lord Sewel, a Scottish Office minister, told Parliament, ' . . . we would expect a convention to be established that Westminster would not normally legislate with regard to devolved matters in Scotland without the consent of the Scottish Parliament.'5 The normal convention will be that Westminster ceases to legislate for Scotland, or to intervene in her domestic affairs. The devolution of powers to the Scottish Parliament is likely to be accompanied, as it was with Northern Ireland, by the removal of ministerial responsibility for Scottish domestic affairs from Westminster. No doubt the convention will be adopted as it was in Northern Ireland that questions about Scottish domestic affairs can no longer be asked at Westminster since there is no minister responsible for them. If so, then it will hardly be possible for Westminster to continue to legislate for Scottish domestic affairs when there cannot be that continuous scrutiny and calling to account of ministers which is the hallmark of ministerial responsibility. It is difficult to see how Westminster could continue to legislate for the domestic affairs of Scotland when it will no longer be debating them and no longer holding ministers to account for them.

It is then in constitutional theory alone that full legislative power remains with Westminster. It is in constitutional theory alone that the supremacy of Parliament is preserved. For power devolved, far from being power retained, will be power transferred; and it will not be possible to recover that power except under pathological circumstances, such as those of Northern Ireland after 1968. Thus the relationship between Westminster and Edinburgh will be quasi-federal in normal times and unitary only in crisis times. For the formal assertion of parliamentary supremacy will become empty when it is no longer accompanied by a real political supremacy.

In Scotland then, the supremacy of Parliament will bear a very different and attenuated meaning after the setting-up of her parliament. It will certainly not mean the supremacy over 'all persons, matters and things' of the 1920 Government of Ireland Act. For Westminster, instead of enjoying a regular and continuous exercise of supremacy, will possess merely a nebulous right of supervision over this parliament. Political authority, however, depends upon its regular and continuous exercise; it is not the mere incursion of legislative authority once every ten, fifteen, or twenty years. In these circumstances, the assertion of supremacy becomes, in Enoch Powell's words, 'so empty that it could eventually be given effect only by what would in reality be a revolutionary act'.[6] Thus Westminster's supremacy in Scotland, which was once a real power to make laws affecting Scotland's domestic affairs, will become merely the power to supervise *another* legislative body which will make laws over a wide area of public policy.

In relation to the Scottish Parliament the supremacy of Westminster is thus likely to bear a highly attenuated meaning. It will probably mean no more than:

(*a*) The more or less theoretical right to legislate on Scotland's domestic affairs against the wishes of the Scottish Parliament, something never done in Northern Ireland; and

(*b*) The right to abolish the Scottish Parliament. It is, however, by contrast with the experience of Northern Ireland, difficult to see this happening against the wishes of the Scottish Parliament and people, especially as the Scottish Parliament, unlike the Northern Ireland Parliament established by the Government of Ireland Act in 1920, has been validated by a referendum. It would be difficult to abolish it without another referendum in Scotland.

It will not even be easy for Westminster unilaterally to alter the devolution settlement to Scotland's disadvantage. There is perhaps a case, as was argued in Chapter 7, for revising the needs assessment determining the size of the block fund going to Scotland, which, so it is alleged, is unduly favourable to Scotland. It will, however, be much more difficult to do this, with a Scottish Parliament in existence, than it was before. For, although the provisions of the Scotland Act can in theory be altered by a simple Act of Parliament at Westminster, it would in practice be very difficult to do so on a matter which the Scots regard as affecting their interests without the consent of the Scottish Parliament. Thus, in practice, the supreme body with the power to alter the provisions of the Scotland Act will be not Westminster alone, but Westminster together with the Scottish Parliament. In so far as any major amendment of the Scotland Act is concerned, Westminster will have lost its supremacy.

Dicey declared that one of the characteristics of the sovereignty of

Parliament was that there was no distinction between fundamental and ordinary laws. The Scotland Act, however, might come to enjoy just such a fundamental character. For it will not in practice be alterable in the same way as other legislation.

Thus the Scotland Act, although nominally an Act providing, as its Long Title declares, for 'changes in the government of Scotland', creates in reality a new Constitution for Britain as a whole. This is because it does more than devolve powers. It *divides* the power to legislate for Scotland between Westminster and Edinburgh, creating a quasi-federal relationship between the two parliaments. Moreover, as in a federal system, the operation of the Scotland Act will continually raise questions about the limits of authority of both Edinburgh and Westminster. A constitution which divides powers requires therefore a court to police the division. The Scotland Act provides for this also in that the division of powers will be adjudicated by the Judicial Committee of the Privy Council, which will come to assume the role of a constitutional court on devolution matters.

Of course, the Judicial Committee will be able to pronounce only on Scottish and not on Westminster legislation. It will be able to declare that a Scottish statute is repugnant to the constitution, i.e. that it contravenes the Scotland Act, but not that an Act of the Westminster Parliament is repugnant to it, since the supremacy of Parliament is in theory preserved. Nevertheless, if the Judicial Committee decides a dispute in Scotland's favour, it would be difficult for Westminster to legislate for Scotland on that matter when the Judicial Committee had ruled that it lay within the scope of Scotland's transferred powers. The decisions of the Judicial Committee, therefore, may well have the consequence that the prerogatives of Westminster are diminished. If that happens, Westminster will lose yet another of the characteristics of a supreme parliament, the right to make any laws it wishes. For both Westminster and the Scottish Parliament will have come to depend upon the Judicial Committee for the protection of their sphere of action, a condition characteristic of federal systems of government.

It is, moreover, worth noticing that the whole concept of the supremacy of Parliament is shakier now than it was when the

Government of Ireland Act was passed in 1920. This is because Britain is now a member of the European Union and Westminster seems, in consequence, voluntarily to have abrogated its sovereignty. Indeed, the *Factortame* cases have shown that judges will refuse to apply UK legislation which contravenes European Community law.7 Although of course the transfer of legislative powers to Scotland is quite different from the transfer of powers to the European Union, because Community law has direct effect in the United Kingdom, nevertheless it is not impossible to imagine a future phase of judicial activism whereby judges would refuse to allow provisions of the Scotland Act, which they might come to regard as fundamental constitutional legislation, to be impliedly repealed by Westminster. What is certain is that parliamentary supremacy no longer possesses the clarity and firmness which it enjoyed when the Government of Ireland Act was passed in 1920.

In his *Introduction to the Study of the Law of the Constitution*, Dicey detected 'three leading characteristics of completely developed federalism—the supremacy of the constitution—the distribution among bodies with limited and co-ordinate authority of the different powers of government—the authority of the courts to act as interpreters of the constitution.'8 The Scotland Act not only in effect distributes powers. It also introduces a judicial element into the determination of that distribution. It provides therefore for an enacted constitution establishing a quasi-federal system of government and in effect a constitutional court to interpret the distribution of powers. Moreover, the Scotland Act will in effect supersede the supremacy of Parliament, since Parliament will not in practice be able to alter its provisions without the consent of the Scottish Parliament. It would be difficult to imagine a more profound constitutional revolution in the government of the United Kingdom.

II

Dicey believed that a federal system, in order to be successful, requires 'a very peculiar state of sentiment among the inhabitants of the countries which it is proposed to unite. They must desire union, and must not desire unity. If there be no desire to unite, there is clearly no basis for federalism.'9 This 'peculiar state of sentiment' will also be needed if the quasi-federal arrangement established by the Scotland Act is to prove workable. The sense of common feeling will have to prevail over the sentiment of states' rights. Indeed, because it creates governmental relationships of some complexity, quasi-federalism probably requires a *greater* sense of loyalty to the whole, to the United Kingdom, than is necessary in a unitary state.

Will the new constitutional settlement preserve the unity of the United Kingdom; or will it prove a springboard for separatism? In the debate on the White Paper on Wales in the House of Commons, a senior Welsh Labour back-bencher, Donald Anderson, declared that devolution was the beginning of a 'mystery tour' whose final destination was unclear. 'I recall', Anderson went on, 'the fine story of a Welsh mystery tour by bus from Cwmrhydyceirw in my constituency. There was a sweep about where the tour would end, and it is said that the driver won. The people of Wales are driving this mystery tour. They will decide the pace and the direction'.10 The same is true in Scotland. It will be the people of Scotland who will decide whether devolution yields a stable settlement, or whether it proves but a staging-post on the way either to federalism or separatism.

Some of the demands which have fuelled support for devolution in Scotland and Wales have been economic in nature. Resentment against London stems from a feeling that Westminster and Whitehall have ignored Scotland's economic problems. Yet few economic powers are being devolved. This could lead to disillusion when the exaggerated claims made by supporters of devolution are contrasted with the realities. Critics would then argue that devolution had given Scotland the power to deal with matters on which there was comparatively little discontent, while denying them the power to deal with matters on which there was a great deal of discontent. If there is no rapid improvement in public services in Scotland, the Scottish Parliament could become a focus for discontent. Then, devolution would weaken the Union. The contrast between the powerful electoral base and legitimacy of the Scottish

Parliament and its comparatively limited powers could thus fuel separatism.

Devolution to Scotland, where nationalism is stronger than it is in Wales, may thus, by providing legitimacy for Scottish national claims, stimulate the demand for independence. It is sometimes, however, suggested that devolution will, in these circumstances, have *caused* separatism—the slippery-slope argument—but that is misleading. For it implies that the Scots will somehow find themselves independent without having sought to be so.

The constitutional hurdle to be overcome before Scotland becomes independent remains the same after devolution as it was before. Independence requires that the Scots return a majority of SNP MPs to Westminster. Parliament would not, as it did with the Irish, resist the wish of the Scottish people for independence, but it would ensure that independence was in fact Scotland's settled demand by holding a referendum. Separation, therefore, could come about with minimal disturbance, but it would hardly be possible for it to occur through inadvertence on the part of the Scottish people. It is unlikely to happen by accident.

It may seem, from the argument in the preceding chapter, that an independent Scotland would be worse off economically than it is today. Indeed, Ian Lang, the then Secretary of State for Scotland, declared in 1995 that an independent Scotland would have to raise income tax by 19p in the pound to maintain public services at their current level.[11] Yet a country seeking independence tends to find that it is economically feasible. Nations struggling to be free have rarely been deterred by the constraints of economics.

It does not follow, however, that devolution will in fact lead to break-up. A more benign scenario is possible. In Spain, Belgium, Italy, and France, devolution has led not to break-up but to power-sharing. In Catalonia, it has weakened the demand for independence, not strengthened it, and the main nationalist party there no longer seeks independence, its leader Jordi Pujol declaring that he is a non-secessionist nationalist. Devolution in Britain could well have the same effect, defusing the demand for independence, isolating extremists, and strengthening rather than weakening those powerful forces holding the United Kingdom together. The leitmotif of the twentieth century has, admittedly, been nationalism. But that of the twenty-first century could well prove to be power-sharing.

III

Separatism, then, is by no means the necessary or even the most likely outcome of devolution to Scotland. The nationalist parties may find that they have achieved not independence, but rather a dispersal of power to Scotland and Wales, the greatest reversal of the trend to centralization in government for many years. Many of the supporters of the nationalist parties indeed have sought not sep-aration, but the humanization of the state through a reduction in the scale of government. If they succeed, then the economic and tech-nological developments whose tendency has been to make men and women more and more alike will have found themselves checked by political pressures—the search for identity and the urge to par-ticipate. It was Rousseau who was the first to understand that these emotional needs demand satisfaction if men and women are to lead truly fulfilling lives. 'Mankind has lost its home,' Franz Kafka told his friend Gustav Janouch. 'Men always strive for what they do not have. The technical advances which are common to all nations strip them more and more of their national characteristics. Therefore they become nationalist. Modern nationalism is a defensive move-ment against the crude encroachments of civilisation.'[12] The demand that government be made more responsive and less remote, that its scale be smaller, may be seen as the reassertion of a human imper-ative against the dominant economic and technological forces of the age.

If there are these powerful centrifugal forces at work in Britain today, it might well be that the best way to strengthen national unity is to give way to them a little, the better to disarm them. Then those deep underlying causes which make for unity can be allowed to oper-ate without arousing antagonism or disenchantment.

Political science has been much concerned with the key question of how political societies are held together. To that question, the tra-ditional British answer has been to concentrate responsibility and political authority in one undivided central parliament. But the case that centralization makes for national unity is something that needs to be argued for and not simply asserted. This book has attempted to show that an alternative answer is possible—that a society may be held together through what Gladstone called a 'recognition of the distinctive qualities of the separate parts of great countries'.[13] If that answer is correct, then devolution will strengthen the United Kingdom, not weaken it.

Notes

Chapter 1. The Making of the United Kingdom

[1] L. J. Sharpe, 'The United Kingdom: The Disjointed Meso', in L. J. Sharpe (ed.), *The Rise of Meso Government in Europe* (Sage, 1993), 290.

[2] Richard Rose, *Understanding the United Kingdom* (Longman, 1982), 37.

[3] James Campbell, 'Observations on English Government from the Tenth to the Twelfth Century', *Transactions of the Royal Historical Society*, 25 (1975), 52.

[4] Conrad Russell, 'Composite Monarchies in Early Modern Europe: The British and Irish Examples', in Alexander Grant and Keith Stringer (eds.), *Uniting the Kingdom: The Making of British History* (Routledge, 1995), 146.

[5] Cited by Bernard Crick, 'The English and the British', in Crick (ed.), *National Identities: The Constitution of the United Kingdom* (Blackwell, 1991), 100.

[6] John Davies, *A History of Wales* (Penguin, 1993), 232.

[7] Edmund Burke, speech on conciliation with the colonies, 22 Mar. 1775, in Burke, *Speeches and Letters on American Affairs* (Everyman edn., 1961), 115.

[8] Cited in H. R. Trevor-Roper, *From Counter-Reformation to Glorious Revolution* (Secker and Warburg, 1992), 289.

[9] W. S. McKechnie, 'The Constitutional Necessity for the Union of 1707', *Scottish Historical Review*, 5 (1908), 55.

[10] J. D. Mackie, *A History of Scotland* (Penguin, 1969), 8–9.

[11] G. S. Pryde, *The Treaty of Union* (Nelson, 1950), 21.

[12] R. S. Rait, *The Parliaments of Scotland* (MacLehose and Jackson, 1924), 9.

[13] Pryde, *The Treaty of Union*, 37.

[14] William Ferguson, 'The Making of the Treaty of Union, 1707', *Scottish Historical Review*, 43 (1964), 110.

[15] T. C. Smout, 'The Road to Union', in G. Holmes (ed.), *Britain after the Glorious Revolution* (Macmillan, 1969), 191.

[16] Pryde, *The Treaty of Union*, 48–9.

[17] Cited in Sir R. Coupland, *Welsh and Scottish Nationalism: A Study* (Collins, 1954), 109.

[18] McKechnie, 'The Constitutional Necessity for the Union of 1707', 60.

[19] For a detailed analysis, see Colin Munro, 'The Union of 1707 and the British Constitution', 87–109, in P. S. Hodge (ed.), *Scotland and the Union* (Edinburgh University Press, 1998).

[20] Ibid. 97 –8.

[21] A. V. Dicey and R. S. Rait, *Thoughts on the Union between England and Scotland* (Macmillan, 1920), 253.

22 Stein Rokkan and Derek Urwin, 'Introduction: Centres and Peripheries in Western Europe', in Rokkan and Urwin (eds.), *The Politics of Territorial Identity: Studies in European Regionalism* (Sage, 1982), 11.

23 G. C. Bolton, *The Passing of the Irish Act of Union: A Study in Parliamentary Politics* (Oxford University Press, 1966), remains the best account.

24 A. V. Dicey, *England's Case against Home Rule (1886)* (Richmond Publishing Co., 1973), 191.

25 House of Commons Debates, 4th series, vol. 7, col. 215, 9 Aug. 1892.

Chapter 2. Irish Home Rule

1 Gladstone Papers: May 1886, BL Add. MS 44772, f. 82.

2 John Redmond, 'Historical and Political Addresses, 1883–1897', Dublin, 1898, cited in Grenfell Morton, *Home Rule and the Irish Question* (Longman, 1980), 87–8.

3 Gladstone Papers: BL Add. MS 44631.

4 A. G. Gardiner, *Life of Sir William Harcourt* (Constable, 1923), i. 497.

5 Gladstone Papers: BL Add. MS 44772, ff. 58–60 and House of Commons Debates, 3rd series, vol. 304, col. 1043, 8 Apr. 1886.

6 Ibid; BL Add. MS 44672, f. 95.

7 House of Commons Debates, 3rd series, vol. 304, col. 1082, 8 Apr. 1886.

8 A. W. Hutton and H. J. Cohen (eds.), *The Speeches and Public Addresses of the Right Hon. W. E. Gladstone, M.P.* (Methuen,1894), ix, 1886–8. Speech on Welsh and Irish Nationality at Swansea, 4 June 1887, p. 226.

9 Gladstone, *Special Aspects of the Irish Question* (John Murray, 1892), 133.

10 House of Commons Debates, 3rd series, vol. 304, col. 1081.

11 Ibid., cols. 1544–5, 13 Apr. 1886.

12 Speech on American Taxation in *Speeches and Letters on American Affairs* (Everyman edn., 1961), 59–60.

13 Gladstone Papers, Notes for Speeches, 8 Apr. 1886, BL Add. MS. 44672, f. 21.

14 *Special Aspects of the Irish Question*, 218–19.

15 House of Commons Debates, 3rd series, vol. 304, col. 585, 10 May 1886.

16 Gladstone Papers, BL Add. MS 44772, ff. 131–2.

17 *Special Aspects of the Irish Question*, 47.

18 Memorandum to the Queen, Mar. 1886: Gladstone Papers, BL Add. MS 44772, ff. 64–5.

19 *Special Aspects of the Irish Question*, 47, 49.

20 Gladstone to Peel, 17 Oct. 1841, BL Add. MS 40469, f. 20.

21 Gladstone Papers, BL Add. MS 44672, f. 122.

22 Lord Thring, 'Home Rule and Imperial Unity', in *Contemporary Review*, 51 (1887), 315. Lord Thring was chief parliamentary draftsman on the 1886 bill.

23 Gladstone Papers, BL Add. MS 44772, f. 51.

24 Ibid., f. 103.

25 Gladstone to the Queen, 2 Apr. 1886, PRO CAB 41/20/13.

26 Gladstone Papers, BL Add. MS 44255, f. 178.

27 L. P. Curtis, jun., *Anglo-Saxons and Celts: A Study of Anti-Irish Prejudice in Victorian England* (New York University Press, 1968), 103.

[28] Quoted in A. B. Cooke and J. R. Vincent, *The Governing Passion* (Harvester Press, 1974), 419.

[29] Gladstone Papers, Notes for Speech, 8 Apr. 1886, BL Add. MS 44672, f. 27.

[30] House of Commons Debates, 3rd series, vol. 304, col. 1055, 8 Apr. 1886.

[31] Ibid., col. 1056.

[32] Gladstone Papers, 8 Apr. 1886. Add. MS 44672, f. 27

[33] Ibid., MS 44772, ff. 47—8.

[34] Granville to Hartington, 20 Dec. 1885, cited in Lord Edmond Fitzmaurice, *Life of Earl Granville* (Longmans Green, 1905), ii. 468.

[35] Speech at Newcastle, 22 Apr. 1886, quoted in A. V. Dicey, *A Leap in the Dark* (John Murray, 1893), 43.

[36] Gladstone Papers, 8 Apr. 1886, BL Add. MS 44672, f. 28.

[37] Ibid., 5 May 1886, MS 44772, ff. 103–4.

[38] Lord Thring, 'Ireland's Alternative', in James Bryce (ed.), *A Handbook of Home Rule* (Macmillan, 1887), 204.

[39] Gladstone Papers, MS 44772, f. 101.

[40] Ibid., MS 44771, f. 81.

[41] W. R. Anson, 'The Government of Ireland Bill and the Sovereignty of Parliament', *Law Quarterly Review*, 2 (1886), 442.

[42] Quoted in F. S. L. Lyons, *Charles Stewart Parnell* (Collins,1977), 449.

[43] Ibid. 451.

[44] Memorandum by the Committee of the Irish Parliamentary Party on the Contribution by Ireland to Imperial Charges, 13 Jan. 1893, p. 9. PRO CAB 37/33. no. 7.

[45] Report of Committee on Irish Finance (Primrose Committee), Cd. 6153, 1912, p. 11.

[46] E. W. Hamilton, Finance brief. 17 July 1893, Harcourt MS Bodleian Library, Box 160, f. 277.

[47] Hamilton Diary, 14 Jan. 1893, BL Add. MS 48659, f. 81, and 20 Mar. 1893, 48660, f. 19.

[48] Childers to Gladstone, 18 Mar. 1886, Gladstone Papers, BL Add. MS 44132, f. 227.

[49] Dicey, *A Leap in the Dark*, 107.

[50] Memorandum by the Chancellor of the Exchequer on the financial arrangements proposed in the Government of Ireland Bill, 16 Jan. 1893, p. 4. PRO CAB 37/33, no. 4, f. 4.

[51] Harcourt to Ripon, 19 Jan. 1893, quoted in D. R. Brooks, 'Gladstone's Fourth Ministry, 1892–94. Policies and Personalities', Ph.D. thesis (Cambridge University, 1975), 99.

[52] PRO CAB 37/108, no. 132, p. 18.

[53] Harcourt to Gladstone, 15 Feb. 1893, BL Add. MS 44203 f. 52.

[54] Harcourt MS, Box 160 f. 97.

[55] Primrose Committee, Cd. 6153, 1912, p. 26.

[56] House of Commons Debates, 4th series, vol. 16, cols. 1504–7, 30 Aug. 1893.

[57] Cited in H. Montgomery Hyde, *Carson* (Constable, 1974), 116.

[58] House of Commons Debates, 4th series, vol. 10, col. 1629, 6 Apr. 1893.

[59] Cd. 6153, 1912, p. 22.

[60] Quoted in J. E. Kendle, 'The Round Table Movement and "Home Rule All Round" ', *Historical Journal*, 11 (1968), 338.

[61] House of Commons Debates, 5th series, vol. 116, col. 1930, 3 June 1919.

[62] Ibid., col. 1898.

63 Patricia Jalland, 'United Kingdom Devolution 1910–14: Political Panacea or Tactical Diversion?', *English Historical Review*, 94 (1979), 765–7; House of Commons Debates, 5th series, vol. 36, col. 1043, 11 Apr. 1912.

64 W. F. Monypenny and G. E. Buckle, *The Life of Benjamin Disraeli, Earl of Beaconsfield* (John Murray, 1920), vi. 510.

65 House of Commons Debates, 3rd series, vol. 36, col. 1205, 8 Apr. 1886.

66 House of Commons Debates, 3rd series, vol. 36, col. 1143, 7 June 1886.

67 Cited in John D. Fair, *British Interparty Conferences: A Study of the Procedure of Conciliation in British Politics, 1867–1921* (Oxford University Press, 1980), 229.

68 Report of a Joint Deputation from the Houses of Parliament to the Prime Minister on Federal Devolution, 26 June 1918, cited in Fair, *British Interparty Conferences*, 229.

69 Cited in R. J. Lawrence, *The Government of Northern Ireland* (Oxford University Press, 1965), 188.

70 A. V. Dicey, *England's Case Against Home Rule*, (Richmond Publishing Co. Ltd., 1973), 178.

71 A. V. Dicey, *Letters on Unionist Delusions* (Macmillan, 1889), 34–5.

72 Viscount Ullswater, *A Speaker's Commentaries* (Edward Arnold, 1925), ii. 269–70.

73 Conference on Devolution: Letter from Mr Speaker to the Prime Minister, Cmd. 692, p. 6.

74 Cited in John Kendle, *Ireland and the Federal Solution: The Debate over the United Kingdom Constitution, 1870–1921* (McGill, Queen's University, Kingston, Ontario, 1989), 222.

75 Letter from Mr Speaker, 38.

76 House of Lords Debates, vol. 33, col. 526, 5 Mar. 1919.

77 Ullswater, *A Speaker's Commentaries*, ii. 271.

78 Salisbury to Rev. M. MacColl, 12 Apr. 1889 in G. W. E. Russell (ed.), *Malcolm MacColl: Memoirs and Correspondence* (Smith, Elder, 1914), 137.

79 J. E. Cairnes, 'Fragments on Ireland', in *Political Essays* (Macmillan, 1873), 198.

80 Nicholas Mansergh, *The Government of Northern Ireland: A Study in Devolution* (Allen and Unwin, 1936) 16.

81 BL Add. MS 44772, f. 74.

82 House of Commons Debates, 3rd series, vol. 36, col. 1240, 7 June 1886.

83 Paul Bew, *C. S. Parnell* (Gill and Macmillan, 1980), 70.

84 Cited in H. C. G. Matthew, *Gladstone Diaries* (Oxford University Press, 1994), xiii. 126.

85 Kenneth Rose, *King George V* (Weidenfeld and Nicolson, 1983), 242.

Chapter 3. Northern Ireland

1 John Morrill, 'The British Problem c1534–1707', in Brendan Bradshaw and John Morrill (eds.), *The British Problem, c1534—1707: State Formation in the Atlantic Archipelago*, (Macmillan, 1996), 10

2 Oliver MacDonagh, *States of Mind: A Study of Anglo-Irish Conflict 1780—1980* (Allen and Unwin, 1983), 19–20.

3 House of Commons Debates, 3rd series, vol. 34, col. 1200, 8 Apr. 1886.

4 House of Commons Debates, 3rd series, vol. 15, col. 259. 6 Feb. 1833.

5 Lewis Harcourt Diary, Harcourt Mss, Bodleian Library, Box 378, f46, 29 Mar. 1886.

6 Mansergh, *The Government of Northern Ireland*, 93.

7 Cited in Michael Laffan, *The Partition of Ireland, 1911–1925* (Dundalgan Press, 1983), 33.

8 Ibid. 36.

9 House of Commons Debates, 5th series, vol. 39, col. 773, 11 June 1912.

10 House of Commons Debates, 5th series, vol. 59, col. 934, 9 Mar. 1914.

11 Letter from Lloyd George to Bonar Law, 2 Nov. 1918, Lloyd George papers, House of Lords Record Office, F/68/1.

12 House of Commons Debates, 5th series, vol. 123, col. 1198, 22 Dec. 1919.

13 Eamon Dyas, *Federalism, Northern Ireland and the 1920 Government of Ireland Act* (Institute for Representative Government, Belfast, 1920), 25.

14 Cabinet Committee on Ireland, 1919–20, 1st Report, 4 Nov. 1919, p. 5. PRO CAB 27/68.

15 Cited in St John Ervine, *Craigavon: Ulsterman* (Allen and Unwin, 1949), 444.

16 Cited in John Kendle, *Walter Long, Ireland and the Union, 1905–1920* (McGill, Queen's University Press, Montreal, 1992), 183. Emphasis added.

17 House of Commons Debates, 5th series, vol. 127, cols. 928–9, 29 Mar. 1920.

18 Cited in Nicholas Mansergh, 'The Influence of the Past', in David Watt (ed.), *The Constitution of Northern Ireland: Problems and Prospects* (Heinemann, 1981), 12.

19 Thomas Jones, *Whitehall Diary*, iii. *1918–25* (Oxford University Press, 1971), 128, 130.

20 Quoted in Ronan Fanning, 'Britain, Ireland and the end of the Union', in Lord Blake (ed.), *Ireland after the Union* (Oxford University Press, 1989), 116.

21 House of Commons Debates, 5th series, vol. 127, cols. 990–1, 29 Mar. 1920.

22 Jones, *Whitehall Diary*, iii. 131.

23 Ibid. iii. 161.

24 H. H. Asquith, *Memories and Reflections, 1852–1927* (Cassell, 1928), ii. 192.

25 House of Commons Debates, 5th series, vol. 129, cols. 1279–80, 18 May 1920.

26 Ibid., cols 1289 90.

27 *Correspondence between His Majesty's Government and the Prime Minister of Northern Ireland*, letter from Sir James Craig to Lloyd George, 11 Nov. 1921, p. 5.

28 Mansergh, *The Government of Northern Ireland*, 236–7.

29 House of Commons Debates, 5th series, vol. 127, cols. 989–90, 29 Mar. 1920.

30 R. J. Lawrence, *The Government of Northern Ireland: Public Finance and Public Services* (Oxford University Press, 1965), 181.

31 House of Commons Debates, 5th series, vol. 711, cols. 1560–2, 6 May 1965.

32 F. H. Newark, 'The Law and the Constitution', in Thomas Wilson (ed.), *Ulster Under Home Rule* (Oxford University Press, 1955), 31.

33 See e.g. the 5th edn. (London University Press, 1959), 157.

34 House of Commons Debates, 5th series, vol. 63, cols. 1624–5, 3 May 1923.

35 House of Commons Debates, 5th series, vol. 707, cols. 79–80, 22 Feb. 1965.

36 House of Commons Debates, 5th series, vol. 698, col. 1151, 14 July 1964.

37 House of Commons Debates, 5th series, vol. 718, cols. 45–6, 58, 26 Oct. 1965.

38 Paul Rose, *Backbencher's Dilemma* (Frederick Muller, 1981), 179.

39 House of Commons Debates, 5th series, vol. 751, col. 1686, 25 Oct. 1967.

40 Standing Advisory Committee on Human Rights, *The Protection of Human Rights in Northern Ireland* (HMSO, 1977), para. 2:11.

[41] Tom Hadden and Paddy Hillyard, *Justice in Northern Ireland: A Study in Social Confidence* (The Cobden Trust, 1973), 11.

[42] Jonathan Bardon, *A History of Ulster* (Blackstaff Press, 1992), 499.

[43] Meeting of the British co-signatories of the Irish Treaty, 7 Sept. 1922, PRO CAB 43/1.

[44] Quoted in Paul Arthur, 'Devolution as Administrative Convenience: A Case Study of Northern Ireland', *Parliamentary Affairs*, 30 (1977), 98. See, more generally, Patrick Buckland, *The Factory of Grievances: Devolved Government in Northern Ireland, 1921–39* (Gill and Macmillan, 1979), 268–75. This book, based largely on Northern Ireland government archives, presents a powerful case against the devolution experiment in the province; also P. Buckland, 'Who Governed Northern Ireland? The Royal Assent and the Local Government Bill, 1922', *Irish Jurist*, 15 (1980).

[45] Brigid Hadfield, *The Constitution of Northern Ireland* (SLS, Belfast, 1989), 36.

[46] Harry Calvert, *Constitutional Law in Northern Ireland: A Study in Regional Government* (Stevens, 1968), 87–9. This book contains the best account of the constitutional relationships between Westminster and Belfast before the troubles.

[47] Disturbances in Northern Ireland, Report of the Cameron Commission, Cmnd. 532, Belfast, paras. 229, 138, and 139.

[48] Quoted in Laffan, *The Partition of Ireland*, 114.

[49] Quoted in Buckland, *The Factory of Grievances*, 236.

[50] Mansergh, *The Government of Northern Ireland*, 138.

[51] Cornelius O'Leary, 'Northern Ireland, 1921–1929: A Failed Consociational Experiment', in Dennis Kavanagh (ed.), *Electoral Politics* (Oxford University Press, 1992), 254, 253.

[52] Mansergh, *The Government of Northern Ireland*, 143.

[53] Thomas Hennessey, *A History of Northern Ireland, 1920–1996* (Macmillan 1997), 54–5.

[54] Bardon, *A History of Ulster*, 511.

[55] Cameron Report, Cmnd. 532, Belfast, para. 229(a)(6).

[56] Colin Coulter, 'Direct Rule and the Ulster Middle Classes', in Richard English and Graham S. Walker, *Unionism in Modern Ireland* (Macmillan, 1996), 169–70.

[57] James Loughlin, *Ulster Unionism and British National Identity since 1885* (Pinter, 1995), 173.

[58] James Callaghan, *A House Divided: The Dilemma of Northern Ireland* (Collins, 1973), 1. See also Kenneth O. Morgan, *Callaghan: A Life* (Oxford University Press, 1997), 347.

[59] Terence O'Neill, *The Autobiography of Terence O'Neill* (Faber, 1972), 146.

[60] PRO CAB 24/137. CP 4081.

[61] Quoted in R. J. Lawrence, 'Devolution Reconsidered', *Political Studies*, 4 (1956), 8 n.

[62] Ibid.

[63] House of Commons Debates, 5th series, vol. 335, cols. 1708–9, 12 May 1938.

[64] Lawrence, *The Government of Northern Ireland*, 70.

[65] Cmnd. 5460, para. 1304.

[66] *The Autobiography of Terence O'Neill*, 39.

[67] Cmnd 5460, para. 1307.

[68] *Minutes of Evidence*, (HMSO, 1971), iii, para. 19.

[69] Martin Wallace, 'Home Rule in Northern Ireland: Anomalies of Devolution', *Northern Ireland Legal Quarterly*, 18 (1967), 161.

70 Richard Crossman, *Diaries of a Cabinet Minister* (Hamish Hamilton and Jonathan Cape, 1977), iii. 187.

71 *Minutes of Evidence*, (HMSO, 1971), iii. 176.

72 Lawrence, *The Government of Northern Ireland*, 143.

73 F. H. Newark, 'Some Developments in Northern Ireland Since 1921', *Northern Ireland Legal Quarterly*, 23 (1972), 96.

74 *Minutes of Evidence*, iii, para. 245.

75 Ibid.

76 Garret FitzGerald, *Towards a New Ireland* (Charles Knight, 1972), 77.

77 Terence O'Neill, *Ulster at the Crossroads* (Faber, 1969), 81.

78 Cited in Derek Birrell and Alan Murie, *Policy and Government in Northern Ireland: Lessons of Devolution* (Gill and Macmillan, 1980), 148, 380. This book offers a fine, albeit critical, analysis of the Stormont regime.

79 *Minutes of Evidence* (HMSO, 1971), iii, para. 27.

80 Cmnd. 5460, para. 1256.

81 Ibid., paras. 150, 151.

82 *Minutes of Evidence*, iii, 71.

83 Lawrence, *The Government of Northern Ireland*, 75.

84 D. P. Barritt and Charles Carter, *The Northern Ireland Problem: A Study in Group Relations* (2nd edn., Oxford University Press, 1972), 112.

85 Quoted in Martin Wallace, *Northern Ireland: 50 Years of Self-Government* (David and Charles, 1971), 52.

86 See M. N. Hayes, 'Some Aspects of Local Government in Northern Ireland', in Edwin Rhodes (ed.), *Public Administration in Northern Ireland* (Magee University College, Londonderry, 1967), esp. 88–97.

87 Callaghan, *A House Divided*, 66.

88 The structure of government at the beginning of direct rule is described by Lord Windlesham, one of the first Ministers of State for Northern Ireland, in 'Ministers in Ulster: The Machinery of Direct Rule', *Public Administration*, 51 (1973), 261–72, reprinted in his book, *Politics in Practice* (Jonathan Cape, 1975), ch. 5.

89 Cmnd. 7110, 1978.

90 James Prior, *A Question of Balance* (Hamish Hamilton, 1986), 191.

91 House of Commons Debates, 6th series, vol. 23, col. 479, 10 May 1982.

92 Prior, *A Question of Balance*, 182.

93 Quoted in David Blomfield and Maeve Lankford, 'From Whitewash to Mayhem: The State of the Secretary in Northern Ireland', in Peter Catterall and Sean McDougall (eds.), *The Northern Ireland Question in British Politics* (Macmillan, 1996), 148.

94 Prior, *A Question of Balance*, 194.

95 Letter from Professor J. H. Whyte to Clerk Assistant of the Northern Ireland Assembly, 19 Sept. 1984, in Northern Ireland Assembly, Second Report from the Devolution Report Committee (HMSO, 1985), vol. ii, NIA 182–II.

96 Cornelius O'Leary, Sydney Elliott, and R. A. Wilford, *The Northern Ireland Assembly 1982–1986: A Constitutional Experiment* (C. Hurst, London, 1988).

97 Ibid., p. v.

98 The Belfast Agreement: An Agreement Reached at the Multi-Party Talks on Northern Ireland, Cm. 3883, 1998.

99 Dail Debates, 21 Apr. 1998, col. 1028.

[100] This analysis of the Belfast Agreement owes a great deal to Brendan O'Leary, *The British–Irish Agreement: Power-Sharing Plus* (Constitution Unit, London), 1998.

Chapter 4. Scotland

[1] Hardwicke to Kames, 17 Oct. 1754, quoted in Philip C. Yorke, *Life and Correspondence of Philip Yorke, Earl of Hardwicke, Lord High Chancellor of Great Britain* (Cambridge University Press, 1913), i. 623.

[2] Quoted in Arthur Midwinter, Michael Keating, and James Mitchell, *Politics and Public Policy in Scotland* (Macmillan, 1991), 52.

[3] House of Commons Debates, 3rd series, vol. 304, col. 252, 13 Apr. 1886.

[4] H. J. Hanham, 'The Creation of the Scottish Office, 1881–87', *Juridical Review* (1965), 229.

[5] Report of Royal Commission on Scottish Affairs, Cmd. 9212, 1954, para. 13.

[6] Lord Morrison of Lambeth, *Herbert Morrison: An Autobiography* (Odhams, 1960), 199.

[7] J. M. Ross, *The Secretary of State for Scotland and the Scottish Office* (Studies in Public Policy, 87; Centre for Studies in Public Policy, Strathclyde University, 1981), 9.

[8] William Miller, *The End of British Politics? Scots and English Political Behaviour in the Seventies* (Oxford University Press, 1981), 10.

[9] Crossman, *Diaries of a Cabinet Minister*, iii. 48

[10] House of Commons Debates, 6th series, 29 Nov. 1995, vol. 267, col. 1234.

[11] Lord Kilbrandon, 'A Background to Constitutional Reform', Presidential Address to Holdsworth Club, University of Birmingham, 1975, 19.

[12] Scottish Home Rule Association, 'Statement of Scotland's Claim for Home Rule' (Edinburgh, 1888), 5, 10–11.

[13] In one Belgian election, the *Front Democratic des Francophones*, a party representing the French-speaking population of Brussels, gained a higher percentage of the vote in Brussels.

[14] Peter G. J. Pulzer, *Political Representation and Elections in Britain* (Allen and Unwin, 1967), 98.

[15] David Butler and Donald Stokes, *Political Change in Britain* (Penguin edition,1971), 189.

[16] Ian Budge and D. W. Urwin, *Scottish Political Behaviour* (Longmans, 1966), 134.

[17] William L. Miller with Bo Särlvik, Ivor Crewe, and Jim Alt, 'The Connection between SNP Voting and the Demand for Scottish Self-Government', *European Journal of Political Research*, 5 (1977), 99.

[18] W. Miller, J. Brand, and M. Jordan, *Oil and the Scottish Voter*, SSRC, North Sea Oil Panel Occasional Paper, No. 2 (London, 1980), 5.

[19] John Vincent, 'What Kind of Third Party?', *New Society*, 26 Jan. 1967.

[20] John Vincent, *The Formation of the Liberal Party, 1857–1868* (Constable, 1966).

[21] James Kellas, *The Scottish Political System* (2nd edn., Cambridge University Press, 1975), 210 n.

[22] Vincent, 'What Kind of Third Party?'. See also Ken Young, 'Orpington and the Liberal Revival', in Chris Cook and John Ramsden (eds.), *By-elections in British Politics* (UCL Press, 1997).

[23] R. Coupland, *Welsh and Scottish Nationalism* (Collins, 1954), 246.

[24] J. G. Lockhart, *Life of Sir Walter Scott* (C. A. & W. Galignani & Co., 1838), i. 299.

25 Crossman, *Diaries of a Cabinet Minister*, ii. 1976, 550–1.

26 *Scotland's Government*, The Report of the Scottish Constitutional Committee (Edinburgh, 1970), 62.

27 *Scotland's Government*, preface, p. v.

28 Ibid. 65, 41.

29 Quoted in J. P. Mackintosh, 'The Report of the Royal Commission on the Constitution, 1969–73', *Political Quarterly* (1974), 116.

30 Margaret Thatcher, *The Path to Power* (Collins, 1995), 322.

31 K. O. Morgan, *Wales in British Politics* (University of Wales Press, revised edn., 1970), 199.

32 Tom Johnston, *Memories* (Collins, 1952), 69.

33 Quoted in Michael J. Keating, 'Nationalism in the Scottish Labour Movement, 1914–74', unpublished paper prepared for the Political Studies Association Conference, Aberystwyth, 1977, p. 17.

34 Quoted in William Ferguson, *Scotland from 1689 to the Present* (Oliver and Boyd, 1968), 388.

35 Cited in Miller, *The End of British Politics?*, 21.

36 R. Rhodes James (ed.), *Winston S. Churchill: His Complete Speeches, 1897–1963*, viii. *1950–63* (Chelsea House, New York, 1974), 7936–7, election address, 14 Feb. 1950.

37 George Pottinger, *The Secretary of State for Scotland 1926–1976: Fifty Years of the Scottish Office* (Scottish Academic Press, 1979), 106, 102.

38 Royal Commission on the Constitution, *Minutes of Evidence*, iv (HMSO, Edinburgh, 1971), paras. 70, 126.

39 Crossman, *Diaries of a Cabinet Minister*, iii. 106.

40 H. M. Drucker, *Breakaway: The Scottish Labour Party* (Edinburgh University Students Publications Bureau, 1978), 28.

41 Tam Dalyell, *Devolution: The End of Britain?* (Jonathan Cape, 1977), 106.

42 Drucker, *Breakaway*, 29.

Chapter 5. Wales

1 Quoted in Coupland, *Welsh and Scottish Nationalism*, 48.

2 Quoted in Kenneth O. Morgan, *Wales in British Politics* (revised edn., University of Wales Press, 1970), 65.

3 Tom Nairn, 'Scotland and Wales: Notes on Nationalist Pre-History', *Planet*, 34 (Nov. 1976), 8.

4 Engels, *The Magyar Struggle* (1849), quoted by Harvie, *Scotland and Nationalism*, 26.

5 Henry Pelling, *The Social Geography of British Elections, 1885–1910* (Macmillan, 1967), 369, 415–16.

6 J. Vyrnwy Morgan, *The Philosophy of Welsh History* (John Lane, 1914), 154.

7 W. Llewelyn Williams, *Young Wales Movement: Cymru Fydd: Its Aims and Objects* (Roberts Bros., 1894), 3.

8 Morgan, *Wales in British Politics*, 164.

9 Quoted in J. Graham Jones, 'Michael Davitt, Lloyd George, and T. E. Ellis: The Welsh Experience, 1886', *Welsh History Review*, 18 (1997), 481.

[10] The quotations in this and the preceding para. are from Morgan, *Wales in British Politics*, 107, 231.

[11] Quoted in Neville Masterman, *The Forerunner: The Dilemma of Tom Ellis* (C. Davies, 1973), 256. See also, for this episode, Emyr W. Williams, 'Liberalism in Wales and the Politics of Welsh Home Rule, 1886–1910', *Bulletin of the Board of Celtic Studies*, 37 (1990).

[12] K. O. Morgan, 'The Welsh in English Politics, 1868–1982', in R. R. Davies *et. al.* (eds.), *Welsh Society and Nationhood* (University of Wales Press, 1984), 239.

[13] Coupland, *Welsh and Scottish Nationalism*, 199.

[14] Morgan, *Wales in British Politics*, 306–7.

[15] K. O. Morgan, 'Introduction' to *Lloyd George: Family Letters, 1885–1936* (University of Wales Press and Oxford University Press, 1973), 8.

[16] Henry Pelling, *Popular Politics and Society in Late Victorian Britain* (Macmillan, 1968), 112–13.

[17] Quoted in Ioan Bowen Rees, *The Welsh Political Tradition* (Plaid Cymru, 1975), 14.

[18] Royal Commission on the Constitution, Report, para. 349.

[19] House of Commons Debates, 5th series, vol. 403, col. 2312, 10 Oct. 1944.

[20] House of Commons Debates, 5th series, vol. 428, col. 405, 28 Oct. 1946.

[21] Kenneth O. Morgan, *Rebirth of a Nation, Wales 1880–1980* (University of Wales Press and Oxford University Press, 1981), 376.

[22] Alan Butt Philip, *The Welsh Question* (University of Wales Press, 1975), 316.

[23] Reprinted as 'The Fate of the Language', *Planet*, 4 (Feb.–Mar. 1971), 26–7.

[24] Gwynfor Evans, *Plaid Cymru and Wales* (Llyfrau'r Dryw, 1950), 17.

[25] Quoted in Butt Philip, *The Welsh Question*, 186.

[26] Philip N. Rawkins, 'Minority Nationalism and the Advanced Industrial State: A Case-Study of Contemporary Wales', Ph. D. thesis (Toronto University, 1975), 368.

[27] Gwynfor Evans, *Wales Can Win* (C. Davies, 1973), 124.

[28] David McKie, *Guardian*, 20 July 1968.

[29] P. J. Randall, 'The Development of Administrative Decentralisation in Wales, from the establishment of the Welsh Department of Education in 1907 to the creation of the post of Secretary of State for Wales in October 1964', M.Sc. Econ. thesis (University of Wales, 1969), 58.

[30] Notes for the President of the Board of Education, 'What the Welsh Department has done for Wales since its creation, 29 November 1909', quoted in Randall, 'The Development of Administrative Decentralisation', 51.

[31] W. J. Braithwaite, *Lloyd George's Ambulance Wagon* (Methuen, 1957), 222.

[32] Randall, 'The Development of Administrative Decentralisation', 72.

[33] Sir Henry Bunbury, 'Introduction' to Braithwaite, *Lloyd George's Ambulance Wagon*, 31.

[34] Quoted in Randall, 'The Development of Administrative Decentralisation', 101.

[35] James Griffiths, *Pages from Memory* (Dent, 1969), 161.

[36] Morgan, *Rebirth of a Nation*, 379.

[37] House of Commons Debates, 5th series, vol. 702, cols. 624, 627, 19 Nov. 1964.

[38] House of Commons Debates, 5th series, vol. 697, col. 755, 25 June 1964.

[39] Royal Commission on the Constitution, *Minutes of Evidence* (HMSO, 1971), i, para. 14.

40 Crossman, *Diaries of a Cabinet Minister*, ii. 344.
41 *Western Mail*, 19 Jan. 1968.
42 Crossman, *Diaries of a Cabinet Minister*, ii. 771.
43 *Western Mail*, 24 Mar. 1972.
44 'How Local Government?' *Planet*, 31 (Mar. 1976), 8.
45 House of Commons, Standing Committee D, 1971–2, vol. v, cols. 2914, 2890, 16 Mar. 1972.
46 Quoted in John Osmond, *Creative Conflict: The Politics of Welsh Devolution* (Routledge and Kegan Paul, 1977), 142, 143.
47 Osmond, *Creative Conflict*, 149.

Chapter 6. Devolution: Challenge, Defeat, and Renewal

1 Ross McKibbin, *The Evolution of the Labour Party, 1910–1924*, (Oxford University Press, 1974), 241–2.
2 Kenneth O. Morgan, *Labour People: Hardie to Kinnock* (Oxford University Press, revised edn., 1992), 32.
3 Hugh Seton-Watson, *Nations and States* (Methuen, 1977), 445.
4 House of Commons Debates, 5th series, vol. 885, col. 1031, 3 Feb. 1975.
5 House of Commons Debates, 5th series, vol. 922, col. 1369, 13 Dec. 1976.
6 Ibid.
7 Michael Steed, 'The Core-Periphery Dimension of British Politics', *Political Geography Quarterly*, 5 (1986), pp. S91–S103; and Vernon Bogdanor and William Field, 'Lessons of History: Core and Periphery in British Electoral Behaviour: 1910–1992', *Electoral Studies*, 12 (1993), 203–24.
8 Cmnd. 5460–1, para. 1.
9 Cmnd. 5460, para. 13.
10 Jenifer Hart, 'Some Reflections on the Report of the Royal Commission on the Police', *Public Law* (1963), 303.
11 Cmnd. 5460, paras. 498, 539.
12 Ibid., para. 1123.
13 Ibid., paras. 1108, 1123, 1189, and 1192.
14 Cmnd. 4360–1, para. 129, p. x and para. 126.
15 In *The Times*, 8 Oct. 1976.
16 Cmnd. 5460, paras. 1123, 1182, 1186.
17 Ibid., para. 1217.
18 Ibid., para. 1111.
19 House of Commons Debates, 5th series, vol. 936, col. 316, 26 July 1977.
20 House of Commons Debates, 5th series, vol. 870, col. 84, 12 Mar. 1974, emphasis added.
21 Edmund Dell, *A Hard Pounding: Politics and Economic Crisis, 1974–76* (Oxford University Press, 1991), 51.
22 Barbara Castle, *The Castle Diaries, 1974–76* (Weidenfeld and Nicolson, 1980), 179, 497.
23 House of Commons Debates, 5th series, vol. 924, col. 221, 18 Jan. 1977.
24 House of Commons Debates, 5th series, vol. 922, col. 992, 13 Dec. 1976.
25 Sir David Lidderdale (ed.), *Erskine May's Treatise on the Law, Privileges, Proceedings and Usage of Parliament* (19th edn., Butterworth & Co., 1976), 523.

[26] House of Commons Debates, 5th series, vol. 925, cols. 1715–16, 10 Feb. 1977.

[27] House of Commons Debates, 5th series, vol. 926, col. 1273, 22 Feb. 1977.

[28] House of Commons Debates, 5th series, vol. 936, col. 313, 26 July 1977.

[29] The Government's Devolution Plans: A Note of Dissent from the United Kingdom Liberal Party's Machinery of Government Policy Panel, Autumn 1977.

[30] *Guardian*, 14 Nov. 1977.

[31] S. E. Finer (ed.), *Adversary Politics and Electoral Reform* (Anthony Wigram, 1975), 18.

[32] Brigid Hadfield, 'Scotland's Parliament: A Northern Ireland Perspective on the White Paper', *Public Law* (1997), 668 n.

[33] House of Commons Debates, 5th series, vol. 942, col. 1462, 25 Jan. 1978.

[34] Letter from the late Ian Mikardo, MP, to the author, 15 Sept. 1979.

[35] George Cunningham, 'The Case for the 40 per cent Test', *Scotsman*, 1 Feb. 1978.

[36] J. S. Gardner, Electoral Registration Officer, Lothian Region, Letter to the *Scotsman*, 'Purpose of the Electoral Register', 26 Feb. 1979.

[37] This calculation represents the author's view of the maximum possible number of deductions. It is based on the research of David Butler and Colm O'Muircheartaigh, reported in *The Economist* on 19 Feb. 1979, and an article, 'The Two Registers', in the *Scotsman* on 12 Feb. 1979. The argument for the calculation is given in Vernon Bogdanor, 'The 40 per cent Rule' in *Parliamentary Affairs* (1980), 249–63, reprinted in Vernon Bogdanor, *Politics and the Constitution, Essays on British Government* (Dartmouth, 1996), 227–41.

[38] Harold Wilson, *Final Term* (Weidenfeld and Nicolson and Michael Joseph, 1979), 213 n.

[39] David Foulkes, J. Barry Jones, and R. A. Wilford (eds.), *The Welsh Veto: The Wales Act 1978 and the Referendum* (University of Wales Press, 1983), 125.

[40] Ibid. 134.

[41] The *Scotsman*, 15 Feb. 1979, and William L. Miller, *The End of British Politics? Scots and English Political Behaviour in the Seventies* (Oxford University Press, 1981), 249.

[42] Margaret Thatcher, *The Downing Street Years* (HarperCollins, 1993), 624, 619.

[43] Jim Bulpitt, *Territory and Power in the United Kingdom: An Interpretation* (Manchester University Press, 1983), 235.

[44] David Butler, Andrew Adonis, and Tony Travers, *Failure in British Government: The Politics of the Poll Tax* (Oxford University Press, 1994), 195.

[45] Kenyon Wright, *The People Say Yes: The Making of Scotland's Parliament* (Argyll Publishing, 1997), is an account of the genesis of the Convention and of its work by one of its two co-chairmen.

[46] I owe this point to Patrick Wormald.

Chapter 7. Legislating for Devolution: The Constitutional Problems

[1] Scottish Affairs Committee, 1 July 1998, HC 460–II, Qu. 328.

[2] Ibid., Qu. 325.

[3] See the White Paper, *Modern Local Government: In Touch with the People*, Cm. 4014, 1998, ch. 3, 'New Political Structures'.

4 Cmnd. 5460, 1973, para. 819.

5 George Pottinger, *The Secretaries of State for Scotland 1926–76: Fifty Years of the Scottish Office* (Scottish Academic Press, 1979), 197.

6 Cmnd. 5460, para. 820.

7 Peter Hain, 'Selling the System: The Alternative Vote', in Gareth Smyth (ed.), *Refreshing the Parts* (Lawrence and Wishart, 1992), 47.

8 *Report on the Electoral System* (Labour Party, 1993), 23.

9 House of Commons Debates, 5th series, vol. 936, col. 316, 26 July 1977.

10 House of Commons Debates, 5th series, vol. 925, col. 262, 1 Feb. 1977.

11 Brigid Hadfield, *The Constitution of Northern Ireland*, (SLS, Belfast, 1989), 89.

12 See R. L. Borthwick, 'When the Short Cut may be a Blind Alley: The Standing Committee on Regional Affairs', *Parliamentary Affairs*, 38 (1978), 201–9.

13 House of Commons Debates, 5th series, vol. 178, cols. 96–7, 26 Oct. 1965.

14 H. C. G. Matthew, *The Gladstone Diaries* (Oxford University Press, 1990), xi. 542, entry for 28 Apr. 1886.

15 Cmnd. 5460, para. 813.

16 Professor William Miller, in a letter to the *Scotsman*, 23 Jan. 1995, cited in *Scotland's Parliament: Fundamentals for a New Scotland Act* (Constitution Unit, 1996), 109.

17 See Iain McLean, 'The Representation of Scotland and Wales in the House of Commons', *Political Quarterly*, 66 (1995), 250–8.

18 Neil MacCormick, 'The English Constitution, the British State and the Scottish Assembly', *Scottish Affairs: Understanding Constitutional Change* (1998), 131.

19 Cmnd. 5460, para. 815.

20 See McLean, 'The Representation of Scotland and Wales', 250-8.

21 Cmnd. 5460, 1973, para. 659.

22 Sir George Godber, 'Regional Devolution and the National Health Service', in Edward Craven (ed.), *Regional Devolution and Social Policy* (Macmillan, 1975), 77.

23 House of Commons Debates, 5th series, vol. 941, col. 1540, 10 Jan. 1978.

24 See the remarks of Lord Sewel, a Parliamentary Under-Secretary at the Scottish Office, in House of Lords Debates, vol. 581, col. 150, 1 July 1997.

25 Ibid.

26 PRO CAB 27/108. No. 132, 36.

27 Committee on Local Government Finance, Cmnd. 6453, 1976, ch. 15, p. 283, para. 2.

28 House of Lords Debates, vol. 391, col. 330, 3 May 1978.

29 House of Commons Debates, sixth series, vol. 302, Written Answers, cols. 510–13, 9 Dec. 1997.

30 House of Lords Debates , vol. 588, col. 1055, 21 Apr. 1998.

31 Select Committee on Scottish Affairs, *Minutes of Evidence*, 7 July 1980, HC 689, 1979–80, Qu. 50.

32 James Kellas, 'The Scottish and Welsh Offices as Territorial Managers', *Regional and Federal Studies*, 8 (1998), 96.

33 David Richards, Principal Finance Officer, Welsh Office, giving evidence to the House of Commons, Treasury Committee, on *The Barnett Formula*, HC 341, 1997, Qu. 198.

34 Select Committee on Scottish Affairs, *Minutes of Evidence*, Qu. 32.

35 HC 329, 1997–8, para. 90; HC 341, 1997–8, para. 11.

36 I owe this reference to David Heald.

37 Cmnd. 5460, para. 669.
38 David Heald and Neil Geaughan, 'The Fiscal Arrangements for Devolution', to be published in J. McCarthy and D. Newlands (eds.), *Devolution in the United Kingdom* (Gower, 1999).
39 Treasury Committee, *The Barnett Formula*, HC 341, Memorandum by Arthur Midwinter, 31.
40 House of Commons Debates, sixth series, vol. 302, Written Answers, col. 513, 9 Dec. 1997.
41 Cited by David Heald, 'Formula-Based Territorial Public Expenditure in the United Kingdom', *Aberdeen Papers in Accountancy, Finance and Management* (1992), 57. Munro-Ferguson was later, as Lord Novar, to become, between 1922 and 1924, Conservative Secretary for Scotland.
42 Ibid.
43 Robert Hazell and Paul Jervis, *Devolution and Health* (Nuffield Trust Series, No. 3, 1998), 68.
44 Cmnd. 5460, paras. 649–56 and 1314. The Memorandum of Dissent, on the other hand, came out in favour of devolved taxes. See paras. 262–76 and appendices A and B of Cmnd. 5460–1.
45 Cmnd. 5460, para. 1100.
46 Ibid., para. 829.
47 Ibid., para. 828.
48 See e.g. House of Commons Debates, 6th series, vol. 302, col. 677, 8 Dec. 1997.
49 Royal Commission on the Constitution: Research Papers, Nevil Johnson, 'Federalism and Decentralisation in Germany', para. 6.
50 Extract from a Cabinet paper written in 1975, entitled 'The Role of the Welsh Assembly in Primary Legislation', quoted in John Osmond, *Creative Conflict* (Routledge and Kegan Paul, 1977), 153.
51 House of Lords Debates, vol. 588, col. 1132, 21 Apr. 1998.
52 Cmnd. 5460, para. 282.
53 Richard Rose, *Understanding the United Kingdom*, 29.
54 House of Commons, 5th series, vol. 939, Written Answers, col. 108, 15 Nov. 1977.
55 Cmnd. 5460, para. 531.
56 House of Commons Debates, 6th series, vol. 231, col. 524, 4 Nov. 1993.
57 Brian Hogwood, *Mapping the Regions: Boundaries, Coordination and Government*, Report to the Joseph Rowntree Foundation (1996).
58 Quoted in John Mawson, 'The English Regional Debate: Towards Regional Governance or Government?', in Jonathan Bradbury and John Mawson (eds.), *British Regionalism and Devolution: The Challenges of State Reform and European Integration* (Jessica Kingsley, 1997), 186.
59 Christopher Harvie, 'English Regionalism: The Dog that Never Barked', in Bernard Crick (ed.), *National Identities: The Constitution of the United Kingdom* (Blackwell, 1991), 105.
60 House of Commons Debates, 6th series, vol. 302, col. 359, 3 Dec. 1997.
61 Environment, Transport and Regional Affairs Committee, Regional Development Agencies, HC 415, 1997–8, Qu. 561.
62 Michael Keating, 'The Continental Meso: Regions in the European Community', in Sharpe (ed.), *The Rise of Meso Government in Europe*, 296.
63 Ibid. 306.
64 There is a valuable account of the role of the *Länder* by Hans-Georg Gerstenlauer

in his chapter 'German Laender and the European Community', in Barry Jones and Michael Keating (eds.), *The European Union and the Regions* (Oxford University Press, 1995).

65 Figures cited by Alex Salmond, leader of the SNP, House of Commons Debates, 6th series, vol. 304, col. 63, 12 Jan. 1998.

66 House of Lords Debates, vol. 592, col. 1488, 28 July 1998.

Chapter 8. Conclusion: Federal Devolution

1 Cmnd. 5460, para. 331.

2 Neil MacCormick, 'The English Constitution, the British State and the Scottish Anomaly', *Scottish Affairs* (1998), 142.

3 K. C. Wheare, *Federal Government* (4th edn., Oxford University Press, 1963).

4 [1937] AC 863. Emphasis added.

5 House of Lords Debates, 21 July 1998, col. 791.

6 House of Commons Debates, 5th series, vol. 924, col. 458, 19 Jan. 1977.

7 *R* v. *Secretary of State for Transport ex parte Factortame Ltd.* [1990] 2 AC 85; *R* v. *Secretary of State for Transport ex parte Factortame Ltd. (No. 2)* [1991] 1 AC 603; and *R* v. *Secretary of State for Transport ex parte Factortame Ltd. (No. 3)* [1991] 2 Lloyd's Rep 648.

8 *The Law of the Constitution*, 144.

9 Ibid.

10 House of Commons Debates, 6th series, vol. 298, col. 1164, 25 July 1997.

11 David Heald, Neil Geaughan, and David Robb, 'Financial Arrangements for UK Devolution', *Regional and Federal Studies*, 8 (1998), 35.

12 Gustav Janouch, *Conversations with Kafka* (2nd edn., André Deutsch, 1971), 175.

13 Speech at Swansea, 4 June 1887, in A. W. Hutton and H. J. Cohen (eds.), *The Speeches and Public Addresses of the Right Hon. W. E. Gladstone*, ix. *1886–1888* (Methuen, 1894), 225.

Suggestions for Further Reading

These suggestions make no pretence at being comprehensive. They comprise only those books and articles which proved most useful in preparing *Devolution in the United Kingdom*.

The Making of the United Kingdom

Aylmer, G. E., 'The Peculiarities of the British State', *Journal of Historical Sociology*, 3 (1990).

Bolton, G. C., *The Passing of the Irish Act of Union: A Study in Parliamentary Politics* (Oxford University Press, 1966).

Bradshaw, Brendan, and Morrill, John (eds.), *The British Problem c1534–1707: State Formation in the Atlantic Archipelago* (Macmillan, 1996).

—— and Roberts, Peter (eds.), *British Consciousness and Identity: The Making of Britain, 1533–1707* (Cambridge University Press, 1998).

Campbell, James, Observations on English Government from the Tenth to the Twelfth Century, *Transactions of the Royal Historical Society*, 25 (1975).

—— John, Eric, Wormald, Patrick, and Addyman, P. V. (eds.), *The Anglo-Saxons* (Phaidon, 1982).

Coupland, Sir R., *Welsh and Scottish Nationalism: A Study* (Collins, 1954).

Evans, Neil (ed.), *National Identity in the British Isles* (Coleg Harlech, 1989).

Grant, Alexander, and Stringer, Keith (eds.), *Uniting the Kingdom? The Making of British History* (Routledge, 1995).

Hodge, P. S. (ed.), *Scotland and the Union* (Edinburgh University Press, 1998).

Loyn, H. R., *The Making of the English Nation from the Anglo-Saxons to Edward I* (Thames and Hudson, 1991).

Mason, Roger (ed.), *Scotland and England 1286–1815* (John Donald, Edinburgh, 1987).

Robertson, John (ed.), *A Union for Empire: Political Thought and the British Union of 1707* (Cambridge University Press, 1995).

Russell, Conrad, 'John Bull's Other Nations', *Times Literary Supplement*, 12 March 1993.

Stafford, Pauline, *Unification and Conquest: A Political History of England in the Tenth and Eleventh Centuries* (Edward Arnold, 1989).

Thomas, Keith, 'The United Kingdom', in Raymond Grew (ed.), *Crises of Political Development in Europe and the US* (Princeton University Press, 1978).

Urwin, Derek, 'Territorial Structures and Political Development: The United Kingdom', in Stein Rokkan and Derek W. Urwin (eds.), *The Politics of Territorial Identity: Studies in European Regionalism* (Sage, 1982).

Williams, Glanmor, *Recovery, Reorientation and Reformation: Wales c.1415–1642* (Oxford University Press, 1987).

Wormald, Patrick, 'Engla Lond: The Making of an Allegiance', *Journal of Historical Sociology*, 7 (1994).

—— 'On Second Thoughts: The Making of England', *History Today*, 44 (1994).

Irish Home Rule

Dicey, A. V., *England's Case against Home Rule* (1886) (Richmond Publishing Co. Ltd., 1973).

—— *Letters on Unionist Delusions* (Macmillan, 1889).

—— *A Leap in the Dark* (John Murray, 1893).

—— *A Fool's Paradise* (John Murray, 1912).

Gladstone, W. E., *Special Aspects of the Irish Question* (John Murray, 1892).

Hammond, J. L., *Gladstone and the Irish Nation* (revised edn., Cass, 1964).

Jalland, Patricia, 'United Kingdom Devolution 1910–14: Political Panacea or Tactical Diversion?', *English Historical Review*, 94 (1979).

Loughlin, James, *Gladstone, Home Rule and the Ulster Question, 1882–93* (Gill and Macmillan, 1986).

Mansergh, Nicholas, *The Irish Question, 1840–1921* (George Allen and Unwin, 1965).

Northern Ireland

Bardon, Jonathan, *A History of Ulster* (Blackstaff Press, 1992).

Birrell, Derek, and Murie, Alan, *Policy and Government in Northern Ireland: Lessons of Devolution* (Gill and Macmillan, 1980).

Bogdanor, Vernon, 'The British-Irish Council and Devolution', *Government and Opposition* (1999).

Buckland, Patrick, *Ulster Unionism and the Origins of Northern Ireland, 1886–1922* (Gill and Macmillan, 1973).

——*The Factory of Grievances: Devolved Government in Northern Ireland, 1921–39* (Gill and Macmillan, 1979).

Calvert, Harry, *Constitutional Law in Northern Ireland: A Study in Regional Government* (Stevens, 1968).

Dyas, Eamon, *Federalism, Northern Ireland and the 1920 Government of Ireland Act* (Institute for Representative Government, Belfast, 1988).

Hadfield, Brigid, *The Constitution of Northern Ireland* (SLS, Belfast, 1989).

Hennessey, Thomas, *A History of Northern Ireland, 1920–1996* (Macmillan, 1997).

Laffan, Michael, *The Partition of Ireland, 1911–1925* (Dundalgan Press, 1983).

Lawrence, R. J., *The Government of Northern Ireland: Public Finance and Public Services 1921–1964* (Oxford University Press, 1965).

Mansergh, Nicholas, *The Government of Northern Ireland: A Study in Devolution* (George Allen and Unwin, 1936).

—— *The Unresolved Question*: *The Anglo-Irish Settlement and its Undoing* (Yale University Press, 1991).

—— *Nationalism and Independence*: *Selected Irish Papers* (Cork University Press, 1997).

Morgan, Austen, *The Belfast Agreement: A Practical Legal Analysis* (Belfast Press, London, 2001).

O'Leary, Brendan, *The British–Irish Agreement*: *Power-Sharing Plus* (Constitution Unit, London, 1998).

The Belfast Agreement: An Agreement Reached at the Multi-Party Talks on Northern Ireland, Cm. 3883, 1998.

Scotland

Bochel, John, Denver, David, and Macartney, Alan (eds.), *The Referendum Experience*: *Scotland 1979* (Aberdeen University Press, 1981).

Devine, T. M., and Finlay, R. J. (eds.), *Scotland in the Twentieth Century* (Edinburgh University Press, 1996).

Dicey, A. V., and Rait, R. S., *Thoughts on the Union Between England and Scotland* (Macmillan, 1920).

Finlay, Richard J., *A Partnership for Good? Scottish Politics and the Union since 1880* (John Donald, 1997).

Harvie, Christopher, *Scotland and Nationalism* (2nd edn., Routledge, 1994).

—— *No Gods and Precious Few Heroes*: *Twentieth-Century Scotland* (Edinburgh University Press, 3rd edn., 1998).

Levack, Brian P., *The Formation of the British State*: *England, Scotland, and the Union 1603–1707* (Oxford University Press, 1987).

McKechnie, W. S., 'The Constitutional Necessity for the Union of 1707', *Scottish Historical Review*, 5 (1908).

Miller, W., Brand, J., and Jordan, M., *Oil and the Scottish Voter* (SSRC, North Sea Oil Panel Occasional Paper No. 2, 1980).

James Mitchell, *Conservatives and the Union*: *A Study of Conservative Party Attitudes to Scotland* (Edinburgh University Press, 1990).

James Mitchell, *Strategies for Self-Government: The Campaigns for a Scottish Parliament* (Polygon, Eden, 1996).

Wright, Kenyon, *The People Say Yes: The Making of Scotland's Parliament* (Argyll Publishing, 1997).

Wales

Butt Philip, A., *The Welsh Question: Nationalism in Welsh Politics, 1945–1970* (University of Wales Press, 1975).

Davies, John, *A History of Wales* (Penguin, 1993).

Foulkes, David, Jones, Barry J., and Wilford, R. A. (eds.), *The Welsh Veto: The Wales Act 1978 and the Referendum* (University of Wales Press, 1983).

Morgan, Kenneth O., *Wales in British Politics 1868–1922* (University of Wales Press, revised edn., 1970).

—— *Rebirth of a Nation, Wales 1880–1980* (Oxford University Press and University of Wales Press, 1981).

Osmond, John, *Creative Conflict: The Politics of Welsh Devolution* (Routledge and Kegan Paul, 1977).

Williams, Emyr W., 'Liberalism in Wales and the Politics of Welsh Home Rule, 1886–1910', *Bulletin of the Board of Celtic Studies*, 37 (1990).

The contemporary debate

Official documents

Royal Commission on the Constitution, Cmnd. 5460, and Memorandum of Dissent, Cmnd. 5460–I, 1973.

White Paper, *Scotland's Parliament*, Cm. 3658, 1997.

White Paper, *A Voice for Wales: The Government's Proposals for a Welsh Assembly*, Cm. 3718, 1997.

Treasury Committee, 2nd Report, *The Barnett Formula*, HC 341, 1997.

Procedure Committee, *The Procedural Consequences of Devolution*, HC 185, 1998–9.

The Government's Response to the Report of the Procedure Committee on Devolution, HC 814, 1998–9.

Her Majesty's Treasury, *Funding the Scottish Parliament, the National Assembly for Wales, and the Northern Ireland Assembly: A Statement of Funding Policy*, HMSO, 2000.

Memorandum of Understanding Between the United Kingdom Government, the Scottish Parliament, the Welsh National Assembly and the Northern Ireland Assembly, Cm 4444, 1999.

Department of the Environment, Transport and the Regions, *Regional Government in England: A Preliminary Review of Literature and Research Findings*, HMSO, 2000.

Policy and Innovation Unit, Cabinet Office, *Reaching Out: The Role of Central Government at the Regional and Local Level*, HMSO, 2000.

Books and articles

Bates, T. StJ. N. (ed.), *Devolution to Scotland: The Legal Aspects* (T. and T. Clark, 1997).

Bogdanor, Vernon, and Field, William, 'Lessons of History: Core and Periphery in British Electoral Behaviour: 1910–1992', *Electoral Studies*, 12 (1993).

Bradbury, Jonathan, and Mawson, John (eds.), *British Regionalism and Devolution: The Challenges of State Reform and European Integration* (Jessica Kingsley Publishers, 1997).

Bulpitt, Jim, *Territory and Power in the United Kingdom: An Interpretation* (Manchester University Press, 1983).

Crick, Bernard (ed.), *National Identities: The Constitution of the United Kingdom* (Blackwell, 1991).

Dalyell, Tam, *Devolution: The End of Britain?* (Cape, 1977).

Hadfield, Brigid, 'Scotland's Parliament: A Northern Ireland Perspective on the White Paper', *Public Law* (1997).

Hazell, Robert (ed.), *The State and the Nations: The First Year of Devolution in the United Kingdom* (Imprint Academic, Thorverton, 2001).

Hazell, Robert, and Jervis, Paul, *Devolution and Health* (Nuffield Trust Series, No. 3; 1998).

Heald, David, *Financing a Scottish Parliament: Options for Debate*

(Scottish Foundation for Economic Research, Discussion Paper No. 1; July 1990).

—— *Formula-Based Territorial Public Expenditure in the United Kingdom* (Aberdeen Papers in Accountancy, Finance and Management; 1992),

Hogwood, Brian W., and Keating, Michael, *Regional Government in England* (Oxford University Press, 1982).

Hope of Craighead, Lord, *Working with the Scottish Parliament: Judicial Aspects of Devolution* (Hume Occasional Papers, No. 54; David Hume Institute, Edinburgh, 1998).

Jones, Barry, and Keating, Michael, *The European Union and the Regions* (Oxford University Press, 1995).

Jones, Timothy H., 'Scottish Devolution and Demarcation Disputes', *Public Law* (1997).

Keating, Michael, and Bleiman, David, *Labour and Scottish Nationalism* (Macmillan, 1979).

MacCormick, Neil, 'The English Constitution, the British State and the Scottish Anomaly', *Scottish Affairs* (1998).

Madgwick, Peter, and Rose, Richard (eds.), *The Territorial Dimension in United Kingdom Politics* (Macmillan, 1982).

Norton, Philip (ed.), *The Consequences of Devolution* (King-Hall Paper No. 6; Hansard Society for Parliamentary Government, 1998).

Rawlings, Richard, 'Concordats of the Constitution', *Law Quarterly Review* (2000).

Robinson, Fred *et al.*, *Who Runs the North-East Now? A Review and Assessment of Governance in North-East England* (Department of Sociology, University of Durham, 2000).

Rose, Richard, *Understanding the United Kingdom* (Longman, 1982).

Sharpe, L. J. (ed.), *The Rise of Meso Government in Europe* (Sage, 1993).

Steed, Michael, 'The Core-Periphery Dimension of British Politics', *Political Geography Quarterly*, 5 (1986).

Taylor, Bridget and Thomson, Katarina (eds.) *Scotland and Wales: Nations Again?* (University of Wales Press, Cardiff, 1999).

Tindale, Stephen (ed.), *The State and the Nations* (Institute for Public Policy Research, 1996).

Tomkins, Adam, *Devolution and the English Constitution* (Key Haven, 1998).

In addition, the Constitution Unit, University College, London produces regular reports monitoring devolution; while the Institute of Welsh Affairs, Cardiff, produces regular reports on devolution in Wales.

Index